PRACTITIONER RESEARCH

FOR EDUCATORS

A Guide
to Improving
Classrooms
and Schools

Viviane Robinson
Mei Kuin Lai

CORWIN PRESS
A SAGE Publications Company
Thousand Oaks, California

For information:

Corwin Press
A Sage Publications Company
2455 Teller Road
Thousand Oaks, California 91320
www.corwinpress.com

Sage Publications Ltd.
1 Oliver's Yard
55 City Road
London EC1Y 1SP
United Kingdom

Sage Publications India Pvt. Ltd.
B-42, Panchsheel Enclave
Post Box 4109
New Delhi 110 017 India

Printed in the United States of America.

Library of Congress Cataloging-in-Publication Data

Robinson, V. M. (Viviane M.)
Practitioner research for educators: A guide to improving classrooms
and schools / Viviane Robinson, Mei Kuin Lai.
    p. cm.
Includes bibliographical references and index.
ISBN 978-0-7619-4683-0 (cloth) — ISBN 978-0-7619-4684-7 (pbk.)
    1. Education—Research—United States. 2. Teaching—Research—United States.
3. School improvement programs—United States.
I. Lai, Mei Kuin. II. Title.
LB1028.25.R62 2006
370'.7'2—dc22   2005009584

This book is printed on acid-free paper.

09 10 9 8 7 6 5 4 3 2

Acquisitions Editor:	Rachel Livsey
Editorial Assistant:	Phyllis Cappello
Production Editor:	Laureen Shea
Copy Editor:	Pam Suwinsky
Typesetter:	C&M Digitals (P) Ltd.
Proofreader:	Sally M. Scott
Cover Designer:	Rose Storey
Graphic Designer:	Lisa Miller

Contents

Preface

We are passionate about improving students' learning and achievement. We are passionate about supporting those whose dedication to students' learning leads them to continually improve what they do to meet their students' needs. It is for all those educational practitioners—teachers, administrators, principals, professional developers, and local and central government officials—that we have written this book. Its purpose is to help them improve the practices for which they are responsible by conducting research that is of immediate relevance to their problems and questions, and is sufficiently rigorous to yield trustworthy information.

We emphasize the importance of conducting research rather than relying only on the research of others because we have learned from our experience of working with schools in New Zealand that sustainable school improvement requires teachers and school leaders to undertake context-specific inquiry into the impact of teaching on the learning and achievement of their students (Earl & Katz, 2002; Elmore, 2000). Each school and classroom is different—there are no silver bullets in education that will work regardless of context. This does not mean that each teacher must invent his or her own approach (Ball & Cohen, 1999). Indeed, the wisdom of others, including that which is found in the published research literature, is essential for good quality teacher research. It does mean, however, that teachers must learn, through their own inquiry, how to adjust their practices in ways that have the best possible impact on the attitudes, understandings, and skills of their students.

What does such teacher research involve? How can teachers research their own practices in ways that improve their own teaching and student learning? We propose problem-based methodology (PBM) as a framework for teachers and school leaders to use to investigate and improve their own practices. The methodology shows practitioners how to examine their own implicit theories—those that determine what they do—to test whether those theories are working as intended and to find out how to improve them.

Problem-based methodology was specifically designed by Viviane Robinson, the first author, for those who wanted their research to contribute directly to the improvement of practice. Her first book on the methodology, *Problem-Based Methodology: Research for the Improvement of Practice* (1993), was targeted at educational and social science researchers rather than practitioners themselves. The book explained why the work of external researchers was often perceived as irrelevant by practitioners and showed how the research/practice gap could be reduced through the use of PBM.

Because the primary audience of the 1993 book was external researchers, many of its key ideas were not readily accessible to practitioners. In the years since its publication, much work has gone into making these ideas more accessible. Viviane has been teaching experienced graduate teachers and administrators how to use PBM to investigate and improve practices in their own schools and classrooms. The second author, Mei Lai, has also been teaching PBM in her role as professional developer in government-funded school improvement initiatives in urban multicultural school districts and rural schooling communities. Using PBM, she designed and led professional development programs that showed principals, teachers, and administrators how to inquire into the effectiveness of their own practices and test whether or not they were working in the ways they assumed. Many of the practitioner voices that are included in this volume are drawn from the teachers who participated in Viviane's graduate class or in Mei's professional development programs. Every extract from these teachers' reflections has been used with their permission. Where a teacher's work has been published, the published reference is also cited. This book is a culmination of 11 years of working with these practitioner groups. Our goal is to help more educational practitioners investigate their own practices in the interests of better teaching and better outcomes for their students.

POSITIONING THE BOOK

Given the considerable current interest in the nature, status, and purpose of practitioner research, it is important to try to locate this book within this very broad and diverse landscape. The landscape is an unsettled one, the site of numerous controversies about such matters as the purpose of practitioner research, how to judge its quality, whether teachers can be "stand-alone" researchers, and whether, however desirable, teacher research is practically possible (Anderson, Herr, & Nihlen, 1994; Cochran-Smith & Lytle, 1999b; Haggarty & Postlethwaite, 2003; Labaree, 2003).

This volume will show practitioners how to improve practice by understanding its causes, evaluating it against shared standards of what is more or less desirable, and determining whether and how improvement is required. Our focus on understanding the values, reasoning, and practical constraints that account for current practice, prior to attempting to change it, is central to problem-based methodology. This is an important point of difference between PBM and many approaches to action research. While the latter is also focused on context-specific improvement of practice, it typically does not involve analysis and evaluation of practitioners' theories about the practices in question (Haggarty & Postlethwaite, 2003). When practitioners' theories are bypassed, improvement is often limited to changes that are consistent with current ways of thinking. This severely limits the scope for the improvement of practice.

A second difference between much practitioner research and PBM centers on how research quality is judged. There is disagreement about whether practitioner research should be judged differently from traditional research, which has as its primary purpose the discovery of generalizable knowledge. The way to judge the research quality of PBM research reflects its central goals of understanding and improving practice. These two goals require a concern for the accuracy of claims about current practice and how it can be improved. There is an ethical obligation for practitioner researchers to be concerned about the quality of the information they use and the validity of the inferences they draw from it. This also applies in traditional research.

The concern for relevance, however, is higher in PBM research than in traditional research because its purpose is to capture what is powerful in a particular context. PBM also recognizes the importance of the interpersonal process through which research is conducted—a process that we characterize as respect. Quality PBM research therefore requires high levels of rigor, relevance, and respect.

THE ORGANIZATION OF THE BOOK

The book is organized in three parts. The first part lays the groundwork that is needed before undertaking a specific investigation. Chapter 1 makes the case for why practitioners should conduct their own research by showing how the active involvement of teachers and school leaders in investigating their own practices has led to improvements in student achievement in a community of schools with a history of underachievement. In Chapter 2 we explain the main features of PBM and demonstrate how to use PBM to conduct a detailed investigation and evaluation of practice. This process involves understanding and evaluating the theories that shape these practices. Any attempt to improve practice impacts on the aspirations and responsibilities of others. Hence, in Chapter 3, we explain how PBM incorporates an account of the values and skills needed to involve others in the analysis and evaluation of current theories of practice. Chapter 4, the final chapter of Part I, shows how to conduct PBM research in a rigorous manner to improve the quality of information and the quality of the conclusions drawn from the research.

The five chapters of Part II describe how to do a research project. Part II begins with the 40-20-40 rule: a reminder that 40 percent of a project is in the planning, 20 percent in the fieldwork or doing, and 40 percent in the analysis and reporting. These chapters are characterized by a continual emphasis on the decision-making processes required to complete a project that answers one's research questions. There is also an emphasis throughout Part II on the process of doing research, with illustrations of interviewing, validity checks, feedback meetings, and the communication of research findings in both oral and written form. The chapters in Part II are planning the research (Chapter 5), selecting research methods (Chapters 6 and 7), analyzing information (Chapter 8), and communicating the research (Chapter 9).

In Part III, Practitioner Research and School Improvement, we return to some of the questions we asked in Chapter 1 about the reasons it might be important for practitioners to conduct research as well as consult the research of others. We discuss how the use of PBM in a large-scale school improvement project has contributed to a collaborative culture of inquiry among teachers, principals, professional developers, and university researchers, dedicated to improving teaching and learning through data-based investigation and revision of their own theories of practice. By learning how to do PBM research in their own settings, these practitioners have become investigators of their own teaching as well as critical and informed consumers of the research and ideas of others. Their schools have built some of the capacity and infrastructure needed to enable them to examine critically the links between their own teaching programs and the achievement and attitudes of their students.

The intellectual origins of this book were described in the preface to the 1993 volume, so we will not repeat those acknowledgments here. In preparing this more practitioner-oriented volume, we owe a huge debt of gratitude to the New Zealand Ministry of Education, who funded much of our work, and to Mary Sinclair and Brian Annan, in particular, who pioneered intensive university-practitioner partnerships in the interests of better approaches to school improvement. We also wish to thank the Woolf Fisher Research Centre and all those teachers and principals who allowed us to use extracts from their reports or their written or oral reflections on their experiences of PBM research. This includes our graduate students in "Research for Educational Practitioners," who kept asking when the next draft chapter would be ready and who gave us considerable encouragement and feedback. Finally, we give heartfelt thanks to Claire O'Loughlin and Janet Rivers, without whose superb editing and research skills completing this manuscript would have been a great deal more difficult.

—*Viviane Robinson*
—*Mei Kuin Lai*
Auckland, New Zealand

The contributions of the following reviewers are gratefully acknowledged:

Gary L. Anderson
Department of Administration, Leadership, and Technology
The Steinhardt School of Education
New York University
New York, NY

Rick Atkins
Massachusetts Field Center for Teaching and Learning
University of Massachusetts, Boston
Boston, MA

Arlene C. Borthwick
Associate Professor and Program Director, Technology in Education
National-Louis University
Wheeling, IL

Cathy Caro-Bruce
Staff and Organization Development Specialist
Madison (WI) Metropolitan School District
Madison, WI

Joseph W. Check
Chair, Educational Leadership Department
Graduate College
University of Massachusetts, Boston
Boston, MA

Roxana M. DellaVecchia
Professor and Assistant Dean
College of Education
Towson University
Towson, MD

Linda L. Elman
Research and Evaluation
Central Kitsap School District
Silverdale, WA

Jeffrey Glanz
Dean of Graduate Studies
Wagner College
Staten Island, NY

Jean McNiff
Professor
Independent Researcher
University of Limerick, Ireland
St. Mary's University College, London

Mildred Murray-Ward
Assistant Provost for Assessment
California Lutheran University
Thousand Oaks, CA

Tyrone Olverson
Principal
Lincoln Heights Elementary School
Princeton City School District
Cincinnati, OH

Rose Weiss
Adjunct Professor
Nova Southeastern University
Fort Lauderdale, FL

Jody M. Westbrook-Youngblood
District Facilitator for Professional Learning
San Antonio Independent Schools
San Antonio, TX

About the Authors

Viviane Robinson completed her doctorate at Harvard University and subsequently took a position in the School of Education at the University of Auckland where she is now Professor. She is passionate about doing research that makes a difference to practice, and it is this passion that motivated both this book and her previous, more theoretical volume, *Problem-Based Methodology: Research for the Improvement of Practice* (1993). She has considerable experience in the formative evaluation of school reform initiatives and in teaching teachers how to research their own schools and classrooms. She has published extensively about how to understand and close the research-practice gap, and on organizational learning and school improvement. Viviane is the Academic Leader of the induction program for New Zealand's school principals and Director of a master's program in educational management.

Mei Kuin Lai completed her doctorate at the University of Auckland and has since worked as an education consultant to support practitioners (teachers, principals, administrators) and Ministry of Education officials as they develop inquiry as part of their daily lives. Her current role at the Faculty of Education at the University of Auckland involves bringing the research and practice worlds together by supporting practitioners and education consultants in embedding inquiry into their current roles and by developing collaborative researcher-practitioner projects that improve teaching and learning. She has had extensive experience in training practitioners, particularly those involved in Ministry of Education School Improvement Initiatives, to effectively analyze and use data on student learning to improve school practices. Her work encompasses a variety of school settings across New Zealand, from multicultural urban settings to small rural communities. She is currently in charge of developing a training program for education consultants (School Support Services Facilitators) at the Faculty of Education to develop inquiry as part of their roles.

To our families and to teacher-researchers
everywhere and those who support them

PART I

The Need for Practitioner Research

1

Educators as Researchers

Michelle[1] made it. She beat the odds.

Two years ago, Michelle was a typical child in a poor urban community of primarily ethnic minorities. She was about two years behind the average New Zealand student in reading, and while she made a year's worth of progress every year, she could not catch up to the other students in her age group. Last year, Michelle made 18 months' progress in reading. This year she made sufficient progress to achieve above the national expectations for children of her age.

Michelle was not the only one. In 2002, the average student in Michelle's school was about two years behind the national average for students of a similar age. Two years later, the average student in Michelle's school was less than a year behind the average student. In addition, increasing numbers of schools in her community were helping their students to make similar gains in reading achievement (McNaughton, Lai, MacDonald, & Farry, 2004).

So, how have these improvements been achieved? A key factor has been the active involvement of teachers and school leaders in ongoing school research—that is, practitioners as researchers inquiring into their practices with the aim of making sustainable improvements in teaching and learning in their schools.

And that is the purpose of this book—to help you, as teachers and school leaders, to improve the practices for which you are responsible by

---

1. Not her real name.

conducting research that is of immediate relevance to your problems and questions, and is sufficiently rigorous to yield trustworthy information.

There are three important elements to this purpose. First, the goal is to help teachers *conduct* research rather than just consume the research of others. Teachers usually treat research as something that is done by outsiders who come into their workplace with an idea of what to study and then collect data, analyze it, and write a report. The school then decides whether or not to use the research. In this traditional model, those who produce research and those who use the research are two different groups of people, doing very different jobs.

If you think about researchers and practitioners as different groups, you reinforce the idea that teachers react to the research of others rather than generate it themselves. If you think about "researcher" and "practitioner" as different *roles*, however, then you can see how these roles overlap, and how teachers can be both.

The first goal of this book, then, is to show you how to develop your research skills so you can add the role of researcher to your repertoire. While much can be learned from the research of others, we argue that there are also considerable advantages in learning how to become producers of research rather than just consumers. Becoming a producer of research can mean working alone, such as when a teacher decides to systematically observe how a child plays with other children. It can also mean working with groups of other teachers or partnering with external researchers and professional developers when there is a need for additional resources or specialist expertise. Whether teachers work alone or with others, adding the role of researcher to their repertoires will help them become better teachers.

The second goal is to help you do research that is *relevant* to your problems and questions. Teachers are often skeptical of the relevance of others' research to their own settings because of the highly contextual nature of practice. They wonder whether a particular research study will be useful in their classrooms, where the students may be quite different from those involved in the original study. They want to know whether the research takes into account the complexities of what *they* are up against in *their* particular settings. Many teachers believe that published research makes a limited contribution to the understanding and improvement of educational practice because it bypasses rather than engages with these complexities. This book presents an approach to doing research that takes seriously the complexity and particularity of practice.

Our third goal is to help you do research that not only speaks to practice but is also sufficiently *rigorous* to provide a trustworthy basis for making decisions about how and what to teach. This is an ethical and professional matter, because the decisions of teachers and administrators affect the lives of children. These decisions need to be based on quality information rather than unchecked impressions.

In this book, then, we present a methodological framework for conducting research that is relevant to your work, is rigorous, and is respectful of those whose practice is being studied. We show how this framework can be applied to the various phases involved in carrying out research that has the power to improve practice.

TEACHERS AS RESEARCHERS

While it would be unrealistic to expect teachers to pursue substantial research in the course of their full-time work, we believe there are good reasons why a research role should become a more important part of teachers' professional lives. Perhaps the most compelling reason lies in the nature of good teaching. Good teaching is reflective, based on high-quality information, and constantly improving. It is these very qualities that provide the significant common ground between the roles of teacher and researcher. The following two scenarios illustrate what we mean by this common ground.

Story A: Low Reading Scores

Lisa, an assistant principal of an elementary school, is concerned about the low reading scores of the children in the first-grade classes. Her teachers have told her for years that when the children come to school they are not ready to begin learning because they lack the necessary prereading and social skills.

How do you think Lisa should address this issue?

Story B: A Request for Funds

A staff member asks for money to purchase an expensive resource kit for his math program. As usual, funds are tight, but the staff member insists on the importance of the resource.

How do you think the department head should decide whether to approve the expenditure?

It would be easy for Lisa, the assistant principal in Story A, to accept the views of her staff and continue to offer a program that teaches prereading skills for the first six weeks of the year. After all, her teachers have always believed strongly in the idea of "readiness to learn." But how do the teachers know that the students are not ready to learn to read? Is it good enough to delay teaching reading on the basis of the unexamined beliefs of these first-grade teachers?

Similarly, it would be easy for the department head in Story B to accept the view of her staff member and purchase the math resource. After all, she has a good relationship with the staff member and wants to support his enthusiasm. But is staff enthusiasm an adequate indication of the value of the resource? What is the staff member's enthusiasm based on? Is it good enough to base decisions that have important consequences for children on unexamined convictions?

Good teaching and good decisions are based on high-quality information, not on taken-for-granted assumptions about the causes of children's reading failure or the worth of new curriculum resources. The quality of information improves when everyone is open to the possibility that what they had previously taken for granted may not stand up to scrutiny. Teachers who are skilled in processes of inquiry can detect weaknesses in their own thinking about practice and help others to do the same.

Table 1.1 summarizes how a skilled inquirer would think about Story A. In this story, which is based on a real example, it was hard for teachers to detect the assumptions they were making, because their experience of the children and their families seemed to confirm their view that the children were not "ready to learn" (Symes, Jeffries, Timperley, & Lai, 2001; Timperley & Robinson, 2001). One teacher saw it differently, however. She believed that the children's skills on school entry were higher than her colleagues recognized—a view that was shown later to be correct when the teachers decided to assess the children formally at school entry. Table 1.1 summarizes the questions the teachers asked in order to test the accuracy of their beliefs about their new entrant children.

Table 1.1   Testing the Claims About Reading Failure

Teachers' Claims	Possible Inquiry Into the Claims
The first-grade students have low reading scores.	What evidence is this conclusion based on? How good is that evidence?
The cause of the low reading scores is lack of prereading and social skills on school entry.	What evidence is there for this claim? Has the school assessed these prereading and social skills?
	What other explanations have been considered?

The same process of inquiry applies to Story B. Table 1.2 summarizes the type of questions that the department head should ask before approving the request for funds for the math resource.

Table 1.2   Testing the Claims About the Math Resource

Teacher's Claims	Possible Inquiry Into the Claims
The math resource is important.	What does he mean by "important"?
	What evidence is available to judge the importance of the resource?
	What criteria should the school use to judge the resource's importance?

Even though the math teacher may be genuinely convinced about the usefulness of the new resource, strength of conviction is no substitute for inquiry and evidence, especially when it comes to making decisions about how to foster student learning.

In summary, good practice in situations like those described in Stories A and B involves

- Detecting the assumptions that are being made
- Recognizing that they should be checked rather than taken for granted
- Knowing what questions to ask to check the assumptions
- Knowing what additional information may be required
- Engaging others in the process of detecting and checking assumptions

These two stories make clear how good practice requires values and skills associated with inquiry. The values include openness to evidence and argument, which means being willing to uncover and check one's own and others' taken-for-granted assumptions. Another important value is a deep concern for accuracy, so that what one believes is, as far as possible, based on the best available information. A certain humility is also required, so that there is space for differing views—views that are treated as sources of learning and improvement rather than as personal challenges. These values and skills are also widely accepted as essential qualities of a good researcher. They form the common ground between research and good teaching that leads us to argue that learning to do certain sorts of research is not an extravagant extra for busy teachers, but an essential part of their professional lives.

WHY MAKE THE EFFORT TO DO RESEARCH?

In case you do not find our argument for doing research compelling enough, we continue our discussion of the case of Michelle, which we introduced at the beginning of this chapter. Both of us were involved in the case—Mei Lai primarily as a professional developer and Viviane Robinson as a university-based external researcher. Michelle's story shows how she not only caught up to the national average in reading achievement for her age group but exceeded it—one story that is becoming typical of many in a community of schools with historically underachieving students.

The achievement gains made by Michelle and her classmates were hard won. Karen Mose, the director of a combined elementary and middle school in the community (Southern Cross Campus), reflects on what the schools were like 20 years ago:

> When I first arrived at my new school, there was an obscenity written in chalk on the floor. The windows of the staffroom had bars on them to prevent vandalism and uninvited entries into the staffroom. There was a level of violence in the playground that needed to be

managed. The students didn't have the skills to sort out problems among themselves any other way and these issues flowed over into the classroom. Managing the behavior got in the way of teaching. We couldn't even test the students to find out where they were because the teachers had trouble getting them to sit down in the classroom and not call out the answers during tests. The teachers worked extremely hard, but no one thought about student achievement because their energies were spent getting through the day. There was an acceptance that this was the way it was and you got on with what you could teach within it. The community was taking the students away—the rolls were falling and the possibility that the school could close became clear. The relationship between schools in our community was poor—there was fierce competition.

The situation called for an intervention, a new way of working together. At this point, the Ministry of Education started a partnership with our school and other schools in similar situations to address the issues. They did not come in "top down" because they too did not know what to do to improve education in the area. The boss I worked for started the process of collecting student achievement data to inform a discussion with the staff and the ministry about how to improve education.

The situation that school leaders such as Karen faced was compounded by the fact that New Zealand schools do not have nationwide compulsory testing at elementary and middle school level. This is because, in New Zealand, there is a strong emphasis on supporting teachers to understand and use their own assessment information. Thus, the information needed even to understand the magnitude of the student achievement problem was missing.

The Ministry of Education appointed Brian Annan to improve education in Karen's school and many others in the community. Brian listened to people talking about how busy they were in their schools. However, when representatives of all these groups were asked what needed to happen to raise achievement, they did not know, because many had not thought about improvement in terms of raising achievement. Brian concluded, "We needed to inquire into the busy-work so that we could replace ineffective practices with ones that would impact positively on achievement."

Karen and Brian, like many leaders in the community, realized that improvements in student outcomes could not be achieved by doing what schools and the Ministry of Education had always done. All parties interested in improving student achievement needed to interrupt their routines, reflect on their current practices, and seek out more effective ones. However, at that stage in New Zealand, teachers were generally not trained in inquiry skills, which meant that external support was needed to help them inquire into their own practices.

The schools in Karen's community decided to work together to develop inquiry skills to raise student achievement, and to call on external expertise to support them. Karen, who was elected as the chairperson for these schools, put it this way:

> The original goal was to raise achievement, and unless we were able to inquire into the causes underlying the lack of achievement, we were just going to perpetuate what we'd been doing. We could say the words, but we didn't know what the problem was. We needed all the knowledge we could get to help us identify what the actual issue was. We needed someone who would challenge what we kept saying was the problem and what we were doing about the problem. We couldn't have done it on our own.
>
> In addition, we had lots of research on our community but we didn't read it. It belonged in another world, the researchers' world. The size of the research put me off for a start, how was I to read this with all the things I had to do? I didn't know how to pick out the key messages or know how to check if the methodologies were correct. It was like we were on one train track and the researchers were on another and there was no crossing over. What was crucial was how to tap into that body of knowledge to use at the operational level in the school. We needed the research interpreted. . . .
>
> So we needed a teacher, an analyst, a problem solver, a research literate individual. . . . We agreed that we needed someone to challenge our assumptions, develop our skills in using achievement information, expand our thinking and enable us to become evidence-based decision makers. (Mose & Annan, 2003, p. 5)

The schools hired Mei Lai, the second author of this volume, to help them systematically analyze data to uncover teaching and learning needs. Her brief was to challenge schools' ineffective practices and get results (namely, to raise student achievement). Mei describes how she approached the task, using problem-based methodology (PBM):

> We roughly knew that the average student was about two years behind their New Zealand peers (there was no way of measuring this reliably at that stage). The previously completed reports of external evaluators had suggested that the staff in the area did not have the capacity to inquire into their own practices to improve them (Robinson, Phillips, & Timperley, 2002). So, I was faced with developing a program to improve school capacity and student achievement. In thinking about how to solve these problems, one very important tool in my toolkit was PBM. I quickly realized that I could employ the principles of PBM to create a program to build capacity and raise achievement almost simultaneously.
>
> To begin with, I recognized that what was critical to the whole process was the relationship between the schools' leadership and myself. After all, my role was to challenge and critique their practices.

Given the sensitive nature of the task, I found that the inter-personal processes included in PBM were useful in maintaining positive relationships while being critical of school practices. Moreover PBM's emphasis on understanding practitioners' view-points was important in ensuring that the program was collabora-tive and took into account key constraints such as the need for sustainable improvements and the need to create an infrastructure to collate and aggregate achievement data.

I started the professional development program by integrating the relevant PBM concepts into a simple framework that schools could use. Groups of teachers had to identify an achievement prob-lem, diagnose the issue underlying the lack of achievement, develop a strategy to solve it, and measure the improvements. All these had to be justified by evidence. I wanted teachers to make explicit links between what they were teaching and how students were learning by evaluating the impact of their practices on student learning and by developing more effective teaching practices.

Halfway through the professional development, Mei measured the improvements in school leaders' capacity to analyze and use student achievement information to change ineffective teaching practices and develop more effective ones. Brian Annan, the school improvement coor-dinator charged with improving education in the community, was part of a team of educators checking the improvements made by schools. He describes their progress:

> The case studies on how schools were analyzing and using achievement information to improve their practices were a country mile ahead of where they had been. When we started working in the community, only a small handful of schools had the capacity to inquire into their own practices. Now, all the schools participating in the school reforms were routinely linking aims with outcomes and working out how to detect and correct errors, both of which are essential elements of organizational learning. They were in a much better position to improve achievement.

In addition to increases in teacher skill levels, schools had begun to raise student achievement. The early successes suggested that this approach was starting to bear fruit. However, the rates of gain in achievement had to be increased if the schools were to make a significant change in student achievement levels.

In the next phase, schools formed partnerships with external researchers and professional developers who could help them learn from their achievement data and build the curriculum and pedagogical knowl-edge they needed to accelerate children's progress. In the process, many assumptions about what students needed were challenged and changed. The result was statistically significant improvements in achievement on age-adjusted standardized tests of reading in all year levels and in all participating schools from the beginning to end of the school year (McNaughton, Lai, MacDonald, & Farry, 2004). (See Chapter 10 for more details.)

Despite this progress, the teachers in the community are not resting on their laurels. All parties acknowledge that their work is far from over. Karen Mose, who has been there from the beginning of the journey, reflects on what has been accomplished:

> The journey has been extremely rewarding but the frustration is that the gains are very fragile and external reasons such as staffing changes can rip it all apart. It still can feel like one step forward and two steps back. But the fact that we are doing this as a group, with the whole community of schools, gives us the strength to push forward, deal with the issues, and take opportunities when they present themselves. The journey is never over though—different students need different approaches so we are constantly growing the culture of inquiry to deal with these. I've stopped looking for the pot of gold because we need to continually challenge where we are at and what we need to do next.

This case illustrates the importance of teachers conducting research so that they can take the lead in improving their own practice. As in this case, their research will often be done in collaboration with other teachers, professional developers, and external researchers. The latter two groups have a special role in providing supervision and additional expertise, and in introducing teachers to relevant published literature. In our view, the value of teacher research is that it

- Improves outcomes for students
- Develops context-specific solutions to problems
- Provides effective professional development
- Helps to sustain improvements in teaching and learning

We discuss each of these in turn next.

Improved Outcomes for Students

The first and most important reason for teachers to conduct their own research is to improve outcomes for students. In many situations, as in the case just outlined, outcomes cannot be improved by continuing to teach in the same way. There are different ways teachers come to realize that something new is needed. Sometimes what is happening in their classrooms and schools falls short of their own standards of good practice. Sometimes it falls short of the standards and expectations of those to whom they are accountable. Whatever the trigger for change, teachers who are skilled inquirers are able to investigate what is going wrong and craft new practices that are more likely to work.

Context-Specific Solutions

The second reason for conducting research is that there are no simple solutions in teaching that are guaranteed to work regardless of the type of student, the teaching program, or the teacher's experience. Even the most well-researched approaches and programs have to be adapted to a particular situation. Teachers need research skills to be able to base these adaptations on quality information about how the program is working in *their* context. Teachers who work with students who are achieving well below expectation need inquiry skills precisely because the learning opportunities provided to their students so far have not met the students' particular needs. Doing more of the same is unlikely to make a difference. Without systematic inquiry and experimentation, supported by colleagues, principals, and appropriate resources, it is very hard for individual teachers to break the school and teaching routines that have contributed to the failure of such students. With systematic inquiry and appropriate support, teachers can make the sort of difference that was achieved by those in the case study.

Effective Professional Development

The third reason for teachers doing research is that it is a very powerful form of professional development. There is a new research-based consensus that professional development that improves teaching and learning is collegial, job-embedded, and evidence-based (Ball & Cohen, 1999). The focus of the professional development is teachers' own practice; the test of its effectiveness is its impact on teaching and learning. This represents a substantial shift from traditional forms of professional development. Rather than discuss how the ideas of experts might apply to a teacher's own classroom, this new form of professional development involves helping teachers to gather evidence about and learn from what is happening in their own contexts. This was the main focus of the professional development in the case outlined earlier. Using research skills, teachers learned how to solve their own educational problems by investigating what worked for their students and learning new ways of meeting their needs.

Sustainable Improvement

A final reason to conduct research is connected to the idea of sustainable improvements in teaching and learning. For schools such as those in our case study, sustainable improvements are critical, as we know that gains in student outcomes made through school improvement initiatives are fragile unless schools learn how to maintain and extend the gains. Recent research on sustainability shows that it requires teachers and principals who can use evidence to investigate and strengthen the links between how teachers teach and what students learn (Cochran-Smith & Lytle, 1999a; McLaughlin & Oberman, 1996). For classroom teachers, this could mean meeting together to discuss students' work and how to improve it through more effective instruction. For principals, this could mean using aggregated information about student achievement to evaluate teaching programs and resources, and to adjust them in ways that help teachers make the shifts that are needed to improve outcomes for students. This type of inquiry builds the systems, routines, and teacher culture that are essential for sustainable improvement in student learning.

CONDITIONS THAT SUPPORT TEACHER RESEARCH

While the reasons mentioned indicate why it is desirable for teachers to do research, we also need to ask whether it is realistic to expect busy teachers to do so. We think it *is* realistic if teachers have the right sort of support. An important part of that support is high-quality professional development where research skills can be learned and practiced using on-the-job problems.

Another crucial feature of support is people who can provide high-quality feedback on your research. Such people could include colleagues, professional advisors, or university-based teachers and advisors. Such groups are necessary because it is very difficult to improve your own practice by reflecting on it in isolation. The assumptions that guide your teaching practice will tend to shape your analyses and evaluations. Your study of a difficult-to-manage student, for example, will be shaped by the very beliefs and assumptions that make him or her difficult to manage in the first place. Without the feedback of others, it is very difficult to step outside your own point of reference. That is why we encourage you to involve others in your research, by either forming a research group or inviting the feedback of others at key points of self-study. If you are working on your own, there are particular research techniques, such as tape-recording and systematic observation, that help ensure that the information you collect is not unduly influenced by your own frame of reference.

The importance of involving others in your research is emphasized by John Ackroyd, an assistant principal at an Auckland high school who teamed up with other high school teachers who were studying the same graduate course on practitioner research. The focus of John's research was the teacher evaluation policy for which he was responsible. (These are called teacher appraisal policies in New Zealand.) John is disarmingly candid about how his fellow teacher-researchers helped him to question his own assumptions about how the policy was working in his school:

> I was convinced that our appraisal system at school was focused on the quality of teaching and learning. Another person in our research team had the opposite view. So in a way, the glove was thrown down and I said, "Okay, let's find out."

One of the first things the group had to do was decide what they meant by "a focus on teaching and learning." John learned that his definition was much wider than his colleagues', which explained why he thought that nearly everything that was discussed in an appraisal interview was about teaching and learning. He explains it this way:

> My initial definition of teaching and learning (and that's where my thinking was faulty) was that, for example, if a teacher did their playground duty, that would inevitably impact on their teaching and learning, because in my view, seeing what students were interested in and getting to know them in the playground would have a huge impact on how they were taught. But that view was challenged by the other research team members, who believed that there are teachers who do their duty but don't actually use it to learn about their teaching or their students' learning at all.
>
> We discovered in our research that my assumptions were wrong. The teacher appraisal procedures were not focused on teaching and learning. If I hadn't conducted the research, I would still be of the opinion that the teacher appraisal system was focused on teaching and learning—when it clearly wasn't.

Finally, there is no doubt that teacher research flourishes in schools and school districts where there is a culture of inquiry. Part of that culture includes making decisions on the basis of good information, and using regular meetings and professional development time to support systematic investigation into selected school and teacher practices. We say a lot more about a culture of inquiry in Chapter 10.

SUMMING UP

In this chapter, we have discussed and illustrated the benefits of integrating a research role into a teacher's repertoire. We have shown how many of the skills required to do research, such as how to detect and test taken-for-granted assumptions, are also central to good teaching practice. The case study illustrated how teacher research can improve outcomes for students, ensure relevance by developing solutions specific to the context the teachers are working in, be a powerful form of professional development, and provide a strong foundation for improvements in teaching and learning to be sustainable. We also briefly discussed the conditions that support teacher research, including professional development that focuses on developing the skills of inquiry, and the need for colleagues, professional advisors, or university-based teachers who can provide high-quality advice and feedback.

The overriding objective of this book is to help teachers to conduct research that is relevant and rigorous and that improves practice in the interest of better education of students. In the chapters that follow, we present and defend a methodological framework that shows you how to do just that.

2

Tailoring Research to Solve Problems

As we outlined in Chapter 1, the goal of this book is to show you how to conduct research that will improve the quality of teaching and learning in situations that you care about and have some control over.

We presented a case in which teachers worked together within and across local schools to evaluate and improve their teaching programs so that students could learn more. These improvements were sustainable because the teachers had not learned simply to implement new instructional strategies—they had learned how to describe, explain, evaluate, and improve the teaching programs for which they were collectively responsible. Mei Lai, the second author of this book, helped the teachers to learn these research skills by introducing them to problem-based methodology (PBM)—a research framework that was developed by Viviane Robinson, the first author, to help teachers improve their practice through inquiry (Robinson, 1993).

INTRODUCING PROBLEM-BASED METHODOLOGY

Problem-based methodology is a methodological framework rather than a prescription. It can accommodate many different research methods, such as questionnaires, interviews, observations, and diaries, and both qualitative and quantitative information. The central purpose of PBM is to explain, evaluate, and improve teaching practices in ways that are rigorous as well as relevant to the particular context in which a teacher is working.

The PBM framework is outlined in Table 2.1. On the left-hand side of the table are four key questions about practical endeavors, and on the right are the answers to those questions that are provided by PBM.

Table 2.1   The Framework of Problem-Based Methodology

Key Questions	Answers Provided by PBM
What is a practical problem?	A situation that requires a solution
How is the problem solved?	By formulating a theory of action comprising: • A set of constraints • Actions • Consequences (A theory of action may be an espoused theory or a theory-in-use)
How is adequacy of the solution judged?	By evaluating the theory of action against four criteria: • Accuracy • Effectiveness • Coherence • Improvability
What type of research relationship fosters improved solutions to problems?	A relationship based on "learning conversations" Key values: • Valid information • Respect Key strategies: • Advocacy • Inquiry • Use of the "ladder of inference"

SOURCE: Adapted from Robinson (1993, p. 24).

In the first part of this chapter we discuss the first question raised in Table 2.1—the nature of practical problems, including those that arise in teaching. We then address the second question by showing how problems are solved by employing a "theory of action." Theories of action solve problems because they include an account of the nature of the problem (a set of constraints) and of the action that will solve it. How a teacher consciously or unconsciously solves a practical problem will therefore be determined by the content of his or her particular theory of action. Once you know a teacher's theory of action for a particular teaching practice, you know exactly what influences have shaped that practice. In other words, the theory of action shows you how the teacher solved the problem he or she was facing.

If PBM is going to help improve practice, it also needs an explicit process for evaluating the adequacy of the existing solution. There is no point talking about improvement if there is no fair and transparent way of deciding what is more or less desirable in particular circumstances. The third section of the chapter introduces the criteria used in PBM to judge the adequacy of teachers' current solutions to problems—the third question in Table 2.1.

The fourth question in Table 2.1 is an unusual one for a book about research, for it asks about the type of social relationship that fosters the improvement of solutions to practical problems. We believe that if the teacher research movement is to fulfill its potential, then explicit attention needs to be given to the type of relationship that is required between teacher-researchers and those they seek to influence. We address this issue in Chapter 3 by discussing the values and skills that are needed to do research that is simultaneously respectful of others and rigorous in its pursuit of improvement. We illustrate this relationship with examples of what we call "learning conversations" between teacher-researchers and research participants.

TREATING TEACHING PRACTICES AS SOLUTIONS TO PRACTICAL PROBLEMS

One way to think about teaching is as a complex network of practices. In any one teaching day, a teacher will engage in thousands of different practices, with each practice solving a problem about what to do in a particular situation. For example, if a teacher decides to ask a rude student to leave her class, that is her solution to her practical problem of how to manage his behavior. If a math teacher decides to increase the time he spends teaching decimal fractions, that is his solution to the problem of how to improve the students' understanding of decimals.

Note that the teacher in each of these examples could have solved the problem in a different way. The teacher of the rude student could, for example, have thought of the student as needy rather than rude, and talked to him about how he experienced the lesson. The math teacher could have solved his problem by changing his explanation of decimals rather than by using more time to teach the same way.

The fact that we describe teaching practices in PBM as "solutions" to problems does not mean that they are the only possibilities or that the solutions are good ones. Once we realize there are numerous possible solutions to practical problems such as those outlined, we can ask questions such as "Why has this particular solution rather than another alternative been used?" Answering this involves providing an explanation for the teacher's response to the student's behavior or for the math teacher's decision to spend more time teaching decimals. Such explanations involve discovering the relevant theories of action of these teachers. Another important question to ask is "How good is the solution?" Answering this question involves the evaluation aspect of PBM.

Before we discuss the explanation and evaluation aspects of PBM, however, we should spend more time on the idea that teachers' practices are solutions to problems. To many readers this may seem counterintuitive. When you think about the hundreds of on-the-run decisions teachers make every day, it may not seem sensible to describe their work as problem solving. After all, the traditional understanding of the term "problem solving" implies a deliberate process of thinking things through. It usually involves gathering information about the problem, evaluating alternative actions, and choosing a preferred option. This type of problem solving is associated with meetings, committees, task forces, or individual reflection—times when people are not making on-the-run decisions.

We agree that teachers often have neither the time nor the information required to problem solve in this highly deliberate way. Many practical problems are solved very quickly, without taking time out for reflection or for meetings. Furthermore, teachers are frequently unable to describe how they have arrived at the solutions they employ.

However, these arguments do not mean that practices are not solutions to problems. Rather, they mean that practical problem solving involves much more than planning and deliberation. Recent research on problem solving, much of which has its origins in cognitive science, recognizes that most practical problems are solved by simply doing what is routine (Sternberg & Horvath, 1995). Rather than solve every problem afresh, teachers adopt and adapt the solutions that are already available in their community of practice. For example, teachers have a repertoire of classroom routines for gaining students' interest and attention. The problem of how to motivate students is solved by automatic recognition of which routine is appropriate in a particular classroom situation rather than by information gathering, analysis, and deliberate choice. The teachers save time and effort by using a routine that is the result of their own or others' prior problem solving. This means that practical problem solving is a cumulative process with much of the relevant knowledge being located in the routines of the whole community of teachers rather than in the head of an individual teacher (Spillane, Halverson, & Diamond, 2001).

Since much of the knowledge involved in practical problem solving is tacit, research-based inquiry can help teachers become aware of the assumptions they are making about the nature of the problems they encounter, and of the relationship between those assumptions and their preferred solutions. In the language of Table 2.1, this means revealing the theories of action that teachers are using. Such inquiry provides opportunities for interrupting automatic routines, questioning the status quo, and debating the adequacy of solutions to problems. When someone challenges the adequacy of these solutions, then a phase of more deliberate problem solving can begin, in which information is gathered and a new solution is found. Over time, this new solution will itself become routine and automatic, until someone—perhaps a teacher-researcher—questions the status quo and the problem-solving cycle starts over again.

THEORIES OF ACTION
PROVIDE SOLUTIONS TO PROBLEMS

We turn now to the second question outlined in Table 2.1: "How is the problem solved?"

We have already emphasized that there are numerous possible solutions to any particular practical problem. This is because one person's account of a problem and how to solve it will frequently differ from that of a second person. The teacher in the first example solved the problem of the misbehaving student by expelling him from her class, because she saw it as the student's responsibility to adapt to her classroom program. Given this account of the problem, one can see why the teacher solved it by expelling the student. It is possible that a colleague who teaches the same student might understand the problem quite differently. The colleague might see the problem as lying not with the student's failure to take responsibility, but with a teaching program that is too difficult. For this colleague, the solution lies in a program that engages the student's interest and makes it possible for him to succeed.

In this example, the teacher and her colleague hold different theories of action—that is, different theories about the nature of the problem and what to do to solve it. All teachers are theorists in the sense that they have systematic, though frequently tacit, understandings of how to act in given situations.

The concept of a theory of action was first put forward by Chris Argyris and Donald A. Schön in 1974 (Argyris & Schön, 1974). It conveys the idea that people's behavior is embedded in a set of beliefs, values, and understandings about how to achieve their goals under a given set of conditions. Theories of action are both guides to action and sources of explanation. They are guides to action because they specify how to achieve particular purposes under given conditions. They tell these two teachers how to interpret and deal with the student's misbehavior. In other words, they tell teachers how to understand the problem and, therefore, how to solve it. Theories of action are also powerful sources of explanation. If you can discover what people's theories of action are, you can go beyond seeing what they do to understanding why they did it (Argyris & Schön, 1974).

PBM, then, is an approach to teacher research that investigates teachers' thinking as well as their actions. Teacher-researchers who are investigating others' behavior will be seen as more helpful and more understanding if they find out how those they are studying have understood the situation they are up against. Teacher-researchers who are investigating their own or others' practice gain far greater insight into and control over what they do if they ask themselves powerful questions about the assumptions and beliefs that lie behind the particular practice they are investigating.

The following example makes this point. It is based on work done by Lisa, the assistant principal whom we introduced in Chapter 1, who was studying the teaching of reading in her elementary school. She knew that many of her colleagues shared a theory of action that included the concept of reading readiness. This concept told them that students needed to display certain prereading skills before they could benefit from reading instruction. The teachers further believed that they were good judges of the level of a child's readiness. These beliefs had a powerful influence on how the teachers solved the problem of organizing their reading program. Part of their solution was to delay the introduction of reading instruction for up to six weeks after school entry for those children whom they judged not ready to read.

Having discovered the reasons for this practice, Lisa was then in a position to involve her colleagues in an evaluation of the adequacy of their solution. She could challenge powerful taken-for-granted assumptions by asking her colleagues to explain what they meant by "not ready," by helping them to check the accuracy of their judgments of "readiness," and, most important of all, by questioning their assumption that children who did not display sufficient readiness could not benefit from reading instruction. In short, she did something much more powerful than challenge the reading program—she investigated and challenged the theory of action that sustained it. The result, as we indicated in Story A in Chapter 1, was that the teachers discovered that the children had more skills on school entry than they had assumed. They realized that the low reading achievement was due more to delayed instruction than to the students' lack of readiness.

Inquiry that makes a theory of action explicit truly empowers because it provides an account of the links between what teachers do, why they do it, and the consequences of their practice, as our next example shows. We introduced Karen Mose, the director of a combined elementary and middle school (Southern Cross Campus), in the case study in Chapter 1. Here, Karen reflects on what she learned about her own theory of action from teacher-researchers that she had invited into her school to study how her staff were responding to her introduction of standardized achievement testing. The research made her realize that her solution to the problem of how to introduce the testing was not having the impact she had anticipated, as some of her teachers felt little ownership of the process. More important than this insight, however, was the connection that she could now make between this consequence for staff and the assumptions she herself had made about how to introduce the changes:

> The research made me realize that my perceptions and the teachers' perceptions weren't the same. I had brought in the testing in a certain way—I drove the whole process of testing students and analyzing the data. The school context at that time required a top-down approach. However, the context after three years [when the research was done] had changed, and the research made me realize that I didn't need that top-down approach on an ongoing basis. So

I needed to change with the context of the school, and it was time for me to start empowering the teachers to do the testing and analyze the data. I couldn't see this before the research because I was locked into my own perception [that I needed to do it myself].

COMPONENTS OF A THEORY OF ACTION

So far we have emphasized how it is important to scrutinize theories of action in order to understand and improve practice. We have introduced the idea that when people formulate a theory of action, they are formulating the solution to the practical problems they face. This means that the solution to the problem consists of actions, the sets of constraints that led to those actions being chosen, and the consequences of these actions. In this next section we explain more about theories of action by describing and illustrating their three components (as outlined in Table 2.1).

The Power of Constraints

We start with the idea of a set of constraints and their relationship to problem solving. We have explained that teaching practices are solutions to problems and have already argued that the key to understanding practice is to discover the problem for which the practice is the solution. This involves asking such questions as "What factors led the teacher to use this strategy or action rather than one of the many possible alternatives?" In the language of PBM, this means discovering what we call the *constraints* on the problem. A constraint is usually understood as something that stops you doing what you would otherwise do and is therefore typically viewed as a bad thing. However, the next example shows you why constraints, although they stop us doing lots of things, are actually our friends— without them we could not solve any problems at all.

Imagine an elementary school teacher who wants to prepare his classroom for a new school year. Imagine too that he will be starting a new school and is keen to try out a new approach to teaching—one in which he gives his students far more control over their own learning than he has done in the past. He knows very little, however, about his class and what he is expected to teach. He wants to know what his room looks like but has been unable to visit; he does not know the ages of the children he will be teaching, nor how many there are or what curriculum he is expected to follow. Nor is he able to obtain information on the school's assessment policies. In the end, he decides not to do any advance preparation—he will sort it all out when he gets there on the first day. The teacher has, in effect, decided that the problem cannot be solved until he has more information. Without information about the children's ages, prior learning, the curriculum, the physical layout of the classroom, and so on, he has no rational way of deciding among an infinite number of possible solutions to his problem of how to implement a new approach to teaching. In the language of PBM, the problem cannot be solved until there are more constraints on the solution.

Constraints describe conditions that must, as far as possible, be met by the solution. These conditions help to define the shape of the problem, and therefore to limit or constrain what would count as a solution. By narrowing the range of possible solutions, constraints make it clearer what an adequate solution would look like. Imagine that the teacher in the example just presented did know the ages of the children in his class. That immediately restricts or constrains his decisions about the type of lesson planning he needs to do. If he also had information about their prior achievement, his planning options would be even further constrained, thus making it easier for him to decide how to prepare for the new teaching year.

In summary, teachers, like any problem solvers, solve their myriad of practical problems by setting or accepting constraints on their solution. As we emphasized earlier, this does not mean that they sit down and think about every problem they face. In most cases they use the problem solutions that have become routine in the setting they are working in. The power of teacher research lies in its capacity to make these tacit problem-solving processes explicit, and thus open up the possibility of improving practice by finding a better solution to the problem.

There are many different types of constraint. The most obvious type involves the goals, beliefs, attitudes, and values of the people doing the problem solving. The teacher in the example was committed to using a more student-directed approach in his new class. That value constrains his preparation by ruling out, for example, lessons in which students have very little choice about what and how they are going to learn. Conversely, it rules in the preparation of numerous different group and individual activities and assessment procedures in which students are aware of their learning goals and gain rich feedback about their progress toward them.

Another type of constraint includes teachers' perceptions of institutional constraints such as legal, regulatory, and resource issues. The teacher knew he was not entirely free to determine his own curriculum, which was why he wanted information about what he was expected to teach. A further type of constraint includes problem solvers' perceptions of other people who are involved in the situation. The teacher wanted information about the ages and prior achievement of his students so he could take the information into account in his lesson preparation. Strictly speaking, it is not the ages and prior achievement of the students that are the constraints, but the teacher's perceptions of their implications for his teaching. Features of the physical environment also constrain how practical problems are solved, which is why the teacher wanted information about the layout of his new classroom. Finally, other practices provide important constraints on how a particular problem can be solved. This is why the teacher wanted information about the school's assessment policies and procedures—he wanted to determine whether the school's assessment practices would be compatible with the type of student-centered assessment he was hoping to implement.

Typically, considerable tension exists between the various constraints that a practice must satisfy in order to provide a workable solution to a problem. For example, if the school's assessment policy is tightly specified, it may be very difficult for the teacher in the example to both comply with the policy and satisfy his own commitments to student-centered assessment practices. What the teacher ends up doing will reflect trade-offs between these two constraints. This example shows why it is important not to treat constraints simply as a list of conditions to be satisfied. Lists do not tell us anything about the relationships among the various constraints. When constraints are in tension with one another, a solution that would satisfy one constraint to a high level may make it impossible to satisfy others to a similar level. It is this tension between constraints that makes the work of teachers so challenging—much of their work requires them to satisfy multiple conflicting constraints. Teacher-researchers make a valuable contribution when they are able to make these tensions explicit and help those involved to discuss them in non-blaming and nonjudgmental ways. (For more on the nature of such discussions, see Chapter 3.)

Since there are multiple, varied, and interrelated constraints that must be met in order to adequately solve an educational problem, we speak in this book about *sets* of constraints. The word *set* signals the need to look at all the constraints in a particular situation, and to recognize that the extent to which one constraint can be satisfied depends on its relationship with all the other constraints in the set.

The following example illustrates the contribution that researchers can make to the improvement of practice by understanding the tensions among the constraints that explain the practice they are investigating. When Viviane, the first author, was working with the schools we described in the case study in Chapter 1, she realized that many of the parents had little idea how far behind their children were in school. The parents relied for their information on the school's twice-yearly written reports. Viviane analyzed a sample of these reports and discovered that in many cases the teachers described students as "excellent" even though their achievement levels were well below what would be expected for their age.

It would have been easy for Viviane to criticize the teachers' reporting practice from the standpoint of her own understanding. For her, the main constraint on the problem of how to report was the need for accuracy. Clearly, this constraint had not been given sufficient importance by the teachers. But such criticism assumed that the problem the teachers were trying to solve was how to report accurately. Further investigation of their constraint sets showed that the problem they were solving was a much more complicated one than that. They were determined to implement a "positive" reporting policy because they were concerned about the self-esteem of the students and their families. The emphasis on being positive meant that, over time, reporting routines had evolved that, in effect, gave far more weight to self-esteem than to accuracy (Robinson & Timperley, 2000). The unintended consequence of the teachers' solution to the problem was inaccurate reporting.

Viviane's research triggered a new round of discussion about reporting practices in the district. There was frank discussion about the dilemma that many teachers experienced between the two constraints of accurate reporting and protecting self-esteem. Solutions were sought and found that did not sacrifice one for the other. By critically examining their assumptions about what counted as being positive, about parental reactions to inaccurate and accurate reporting, and about the harm that truth telling might engender, teachers revised their understanding of the problem and hence of how it could be resolved. Their new reporting practices, and the parent communication strategies that accompanied them, better met the accuracy constraint without harming self-esteem. In the language of PBM, teachers had revised their understanding of the problem and as a result had formulated a new solution. The result was a new theory of action for reporting.

Actions Integrate Constraints

The second component of a theory of action is the action undertaken to satisfy the various constraints. This is the obvious, easily seen part of a theory of action. Teacher-researchers can observe how they or their colleagues give students feedback, relate to students in the schoolyard, or implement a new teaching program. This information tells them what is being done—but teacher-researchers usually also want to know *why* something is being done, and this requires investigating the relevant constraints. Teachers do not just act; they have reasons for doing things, and knowledge of those reasons provides insight and opportunity to evaluate and revise a theory of action. This is why PBM is so concerned with the thinking that lies behind the action as well as with the action itself.

As indicated previously, practical problems are solved through actions that attempt to integrate all the constraints in a satisfactory manner. The degree of integration that is achieved will vary from very high (the actions satisfy all constraints to a considerable degree) to quite low (the actions satisfy the constraints to a low degree). In the reporting example discussed, the initial actions (reporting practices) satisfied the accuracy constraint to a low degree and the self-esteem constraint to a higher degree. The subsequent actions (new reporting practices) satisfied both these constraints to a high degree.

Although we have been emphasizing problems and problem solving, that does not mean that all problems can be solved in a satisfactory way. Some problems may not be solved satisfactorily because the various constraints on the solution are too hard to integrate. In such cases, existing practices are continued. The status quo is especially likely to continue when people disagree about how to describe the problem; that is, when they cannot agree on its constraints and/or their relative importance. A curriculum leader, for example, may believe that there is too much duplication of content across the school's various courses in language arts. The problem does not get addressed, however, because he knows from past discussions that several language arts teachers think that the duplication is acceptable. In other words, while the curriculum leader treats avoidance of duplication as an important constraint on the solution, some of his staff see it as of little importance. Until the impasse is addressed, perhaps by making it explicit through a PBM research process, the status quo will remain.

Actions Have Consequences

The third component of a theory of action describes the consequences of the action that has been employed. Information on consequences contributes to the evaluation of solutions and of the theories of action in which they are embedded. One way of breaking the impasse among the language arts teachers in the earlier example would be to investigate the consequences of offering courses that duplicated one another. If the teachers researched the extent of the duplication, its resource implications, and how students experienced the courses, they could use that information to reconsider the importance that they each gave to duplication.

All practices have both intended and unintended consequences. *Intended consequences* are often expressed as goals or objectives. For example, the intended consequence of a school's policy on sexual harassment is to eliminate any such behavior in the school. *Unintended consequences* are those that have not been anticipated, and can be either positive or negative. A school might discover, for example, that after involving its parents for several years in an afterschool reading program, not only has the program improved children's reading (intended consequence), but several parents have decided to go back to school (unintended positive consequence).

Prakash Naidoo, a senior teacher in a New Zealand urban high school, reflects on what he learned from his research about the unintended negative consequences of his school's policy on teacher aides. The school provides aides to support teachers who have learning disabled and non-learning disabled students in the same class:

> My school has a mainstreaming policy, where students with learning difficulties are taught alongside students without learning difficulties. To help our teachers cope with mainstreamed students, my school put a teacher aide in every classroom. However, a lot of the teachers started relying on teacher aides to teach these mainstreamed students instead of viewing them as additional support. Consequently, teachers started interacting less with the mainstreamed students.

In short, the teacher aide policy had the unintended consequence of reducing the interaction between students with learning disabilities and their teachers.

It is important when evaluating a particular practice that teacher-researchers consider not only the extent to which goals have been achieved but also the extent to which any costs have been incurred in the process. This requires inquiry into both intended and unintended consequences. Published research on the practices in question is a good source of information about possible unintended consequences. For example, there is now evidence that high-stakes assessment policies and practices can produce a series of unintended negative consequences, such as narrowing of the curriculum, exclusion of students from testing, and blatant cheating (Amrein & Berliner, 2002; Mehrens, 1998). Teacher-researchers studying assessment in a high-stakes environment should probably check for evidence of such unintended consequences.

Types of Theories of Action

Finally, it is important to recognize that there are two kinds of theories of action, which are distinguished on the basis of the evidence from which they are derived (Argyris, Putnam, & McLain Smith, 1985). Theories of action that are derived from people's descriptions of how they act, or have acted in the past, and from the explanations they give for such actions are called *espoused theories*. Theories of action that are derived from firsthand observations are called *theories-in-use*. Because people are not always aware of what causes their actions, the theories that people claim to be using and the theories that are actually determining their behavior may not be the same. This means that when you are investigating a particular practice, you need to be aware that the reasons teachers give for their current practice do not necessarily provide an accurate explanation of that practice. Such explanations must always be carefully checked. We describe and illustrate how this is done in the subsequent chapters on planning, information gathering, and analysis (Chapters 5–8).

INVESTIGATING THEORIES OF ACTION: AN EXAMPLE

In this section we bring together our discussion of the components of a theory of action by showing how a group of teacher-researchers with support from Viviane, the first author, were able to use this approach to challenge their colleagues to reexamine the theory of action that perpetuated their school's practice of tracking.[1] The case illustrates the power of research that reveals the connections between how people think about practical problems and the routines they develop to solve them. It also shows how critical evaluation of current theories of action can trigger theory revision and the possibility of an improved solution.

This example differs from those we have used so far in that it concerns an administrative rather than a classroom-based problem. In our experience, many teacher-researchers want to investigate such problems because

---

1. "Tracking" is known as "streaming" outside of the United States.

administrative practices constrain their classroom practices and because they themselves have administrative responsibilities.

The teachers in this project came together initially as part of a larger school review, initiated by the principal, that was intended to promote organizational learning.

Revealing the Constraint Set

Working within a PBM framework, the first goal of the project was to explain the practice of tracking. The problem of how to allocate students to classes and programs could have been solved in other ways. So what factors explained why the chosen solution was to track, rather than to use, for example, mixed-ability groupings? The teacher-researchers discovered that the practice of tracking could be explained by three main constraints.

The first constraint related to parental preferences. The teacher-researchers discovered through interviews and attendance at meetings that the school leadership gave considerable weight to the preferences of a group of parents of high-achieving children. These parents wanted their children in an accelerated class where they could have a challenging curriculum and work with teachers who did not have to pitch their lessons at a level more suited to the less able students. The school leadership believed that the academic reputation of this urban multicultural high school was very dependent on being able to attract and retain the enrollment of the children of these families. The leadership was concerned that this group of parents were "mobile"; that is, they would enroll their children elsewhere if their preferences were not met. Hence the leadership's commitment to the retention of an accelerated class for high achievers.

The second constraint was that the allocation process had to be workable for teachers, many of whom were not comfortable teaching mixed-ability classes. They were not experienced in preparing units of work at different levels of ability and in organizing their classrooms so that students were working on different activities.

The third constraint on the solution was the belief that tracking was a more efficient form of pedagogy than mixed-ability teaching. Staffroom debates about the allocation problem revealed that many staff and administrators believed that mixed-ability teaching required more teacher preparation than a tracked class where only one set of resources was usually required. The greater teacher effort was not rewarded, in their view, by greater benefit to the students.

The requirement to satisfy the preferences of the "mobile" parents, the need to take account of the lack of confidence of some staff in mixed-ability teaching, and the belief of many staff that mixed-ability teaching is simply inefficient had led the school's leadership to track students. Together, these three constraints explain why a tracked rather than a non-tracked alternative was used to solve the allocation problem.

The teacher-researchers were also able to trace the intended and unintended consequences of this arrangement. While, as intended, the "mobile" parents and many staff were satisfied, the teacher-researchers also revealed two important unintended consequences of tracking. One was resource inequity, as the most qualified teachers were assigned to the high-track classes. The second unintended consequence was the widening achievement gap between high-track and low-track students as each cohort moved through the school.

By revealing the theory of action for tracking, the teacher-researchers had brought to the surface the taken-for-granted beliefs and assumptions that explained why it persisted in the school. Making this theory of action explicit enables everyone to debate its adequacy. We turn to this aspect of PBM in the next section.

EVALUATING THEORIES OF ACTION

Since the purpose of PBM is to improve practice, teacher-researchers need the tools to enable them to ask and answer questions about the quality of theories of action. They cannot sit on the "evaluative fence." They must be prepared to engage in discussion about the desirability of particular practices and to defend their judgments.

Given the complexity of most educational problems, it is perhaps not surprising that there is often disagreement about the nature of a problem and how to solve it. Often such disagreements are resolved through political persuasion. In PBM, by contrast, they are resolved through a process that we call *theory competition*, where the theories in question are rival theories of action. Competing theories of action are different views about how to understand and resolve a practical problem. Competing theories of action are evaluated against the set of four standards outlined in Table 2.1—accuracy, effectiveness, coherence, and improvability—which are applicable to any theory of action. (The interpersonal processes that are required to make theory evaluation and revision a collaborative process are discussed and illustrated in Chapter 3.)

Accuracy

A theory of action includes an account of the problem and how to solve it. Embedded in those accounts are many factual claims. Given that people make important decisions on the assumption that the claims are accurate, it is essential to check that this is the case. For example, the theory of action outlined in Figure 2.1 includes several claims about others' beliefs or states of mind. The school leadership believes that "mobile" parents want an accelerated class and that some staff do not feel confident teaching in a mixed-ability class. Since people make many mistakes about the state of mind of others, it is important to question such claims in order to verify their accuracy. (We discuss how to do this in Chapter 4 under validity and in Chapters 6 and 7 on information gathering.)

Figure 2.1 also includes another type of factual claim—this time about the qualities of particular practices. For example, Figure 2.1 implies that

Figure 2.1   A Theory of Action for the Allocation Problem

Practical Problem	How to Allocate Students to Teachers
Constraint Set	Satisfy "mobile" parents who are believed to want an accelerated class & Recognize limited teacher skill in mixed-ability teaching & Strive for pedagogical efficiency ↓
Action	Tracking ↓
Consequences	• "Mobile" parents and many staff are satisfied • Resource inequity between high and low tracks • Achievement gap widens

tracking is a more efficient type of teaching than mixed-ability grouping. Again this is an important claim because, as it stands, it rules out any mixed-ability teaching. It is important to question the claim by determining what is meant by "efficiency" and what the view based is on.

Sometimes accuracy checks reveal clear mistakes in people's thinking. More often, the result of such checking is the discovery that what seemed like a black and white issue now looks to have more shades of grey. For example, sympathetic probing of the views of the "mobile" parents might reveal that what the parents really want is that their children encounter a challenging curriculum, and that they believe the only way this can be achieved is in an accelerated class. To portray them as insisting on an accelerated class may not be accurate—the constraint that parents really care about might be the provision of a challenging curriculum. If the evaluation of accuracy showed this to be true, it would open up more possibilities about how the problem may be resolved, because there are many ways of providing for a challenging curriculum besides offering an accelerated class.

Effectiveness

The second standard for evaluating the adequacy of a theory of action is effectiveness. This standard evaluates whether the theory delivers what was intended. Since what was intended is described by the constraints that have been set on the problem, the question to ask here is "Has the solution satisfied the constraints?" In the tracking example, this involves asking whether (1) the "mobile" parents are in fact satisfied with the current arrangements, (2) whether the tracking arrangements meet the needs of staff in terms of their confidence and skill levels, and (3) whether tracking is an efficient way of teaching students.

Information from mobile parents might suggest that they were indeed satisfied with tracking. Since staff themselves wanted the tracking solution, it might be assumed that it satisfied their needs, but it would be worth checking this assumption to see if their experience confirmed their original preference. As for the efficiency constraint, some work would need to be done to establish what was meant by "efficiency" and how it could be assessed. If it meant that students learned better in groups of similar ability, then monitoring the progress of each group could help the teachers to make a judgment in this area. It may turn out, as is suggested by some of the published research on tracking in U.S. high schools (Oakes, 1985, 1987, 1992), that tracking is an efficient strategy for the high track students and an inefficient strategy for students allocated to low tracks.

Coherence

Teachers are very aware that it is possible to solve one problem in ways that make it harder for them to solve others for which they are responsible. That is why taking a "big picture" approach, rather than a piecemeal problem-by-problem approach, is so important for the improvement of practice. The coherence criterion for evaluating theories of action considers the big picture, for it asks whether the theory that teachers have used to solve a particular problem is compatible with high-quality solutions to all the other problems for which they are responsible (Thagard, 2000; Walker, 1987). This means that the constraints that have been set for a particular problem can be challenged, even if they are effectively met, if those constraints are too narrow or produce significant negative unintended consequences.

The coherence criterion provides a very tough test of a theory of action, but its practical importance becomes obvious when we apply it to Figure 2.1.

It would be quite reasonable to criticize the theory of action portrayed in Figure 2.1 on coherence grounds even if it were demonstrated to be effective. Effectiveness simply means that the solution works in terms of what the problem solvers themselves take to be important. As we have discussed earlier, this means evaluating whether tracking has satisfied the mobile parents, proved workable for staff with limited skill in mixed-ability teaching, and is efficient.

The theory of action in Figure 2.1 fails the coherence test because tracking has produced unintended negative consequences, namely resource inequity and a widening achievement gap. In short, the school has solved one problem (how to allocate students) in ways that create others (inequity). On the basis of this evidence, the teacher-researchers wanted the constraint set revised to include an additional equity constraint.

In summary, the coherence criterion for theory evaluation allows researchers to go beyond what problem solvers themselves have taken as important and to ask whether there are other values that should influence the choice of solution for the problem.

Improvability

The final standard against which to assess the relative adequacy of theories of action is that of improvability. This standard suggests that, given the complexity of educational problems and the uncertainty of our knowledge about how to solve them, it is important to develop theories that are testable and able to be revised to meet changing situations. Such theories also need to be developed to make it easy to detect and correct mistaken assumptions and faulty reasoning. They incorporate feedback loops that provide information about both intended and unintended consequences of action so that beliefs about what works and why can be made explicit and checked. They also incorporate feedback loops about whether the theory needs to be revised to better meet changing situations. This may involve monitoring the effectiveness of the theory or the changing situation so that the effectiveness of theory can be continually checked and improved.

Figure 2.1 is too sketchy to be able to judge whether or not the school's theory of action incorporated the type of feedback loops that would enable errors and unintended negative consequences to be detected. Nor is the figure able to demonstrate whether the theory is open to be revised by the school. It does suggest, however, what would need to be investigated in order to evaluate the improvability of the theory. The teacher-researchers could determine whether teachers and administrators were interested in feedback about the consequences of tracking, especially those consequences such as resource inequity and the widening achievement gap that they themselves had not anticipated. Detecting the latter would require teachers and administrators to step outside their own frame of reference, and to give weight to goals and values that they had previously not taken into account. These are some of the qualities that are relevant to evaluating the improvability of a theory of action.

Developing Alternative Theories of Action

Implicit in the evaluation of a theory of action is the possibility of an improved alternative. Teacher-researchers who critique the inequity of tracking, for example, imply that a more equitable alternative is possible. From the school leadership's point of view, however, the equity value is difficult to embrace if it means sacrificing other important constraints such as satisfying the preferences of "mobile" parents. If criticisms of the existing theory of action are to be influential, they must suggest how an alternative theory is more likely to satisfy *all* the agreed constraints and not just those that are preferred by the teacher-researchers or the colleagues they are trying to influence.

Figure 2.2 shows a possible alternative theory of the allocation problem that could better satisfy both the school leadership's original constraints and the new equity constraint raised by the teacher research. The difficult process of how to negotiate such a revision is discussed and illustrated in the next chapter. Here we explain how to move beyond the evaluation of the original theory of action to the alternative portrayed on the right-hand side of Figure 2.2.

Figure 2.2   An Alternative Theory of Action for the Allocation Problem

Practical Problem	How to Allocate Students to Teachers	
	Original Theory of Action	**Improved Theory of Action**
Constraints		Equal or better resources for the lowest achieving students
	"Mobile" parents prefer accelerated class	Parental preference for accelerated class in selected subjects (math, language)
	Limited teacher skill in mixed-ability teaching $\rightarrow$	Increased level of teacher skill allows mixed-ability teaching in some subjects (English, health, biology)
	Pedagogical efficiency	Theory of pedagogical efficiency differentiated by subject
	↓	↓
Action	Tracking	Untracked form classes with a few tracked subject classes
	↓	↓
Consequences	• "Mobile" parents are satisfied • Resource inequity • Achievement gap widens	Evaluation under way

The alternative theory of action portrayed in Figure 2.2 was reached by reformulating and resolving the problem as follows:

1. An equity requirement is included in the set of constraints to meet the concerns of the teacher-researchers. This additional constraint is expressed as "equal or better resources are provided for the lowest achieving students." If this constraint can be better satisfied, the new theory of action will be more coherent than the original.

2. The preferences of the "mobile" parents for an accelerated class are explored and negotiated to test whether there are ways of satisfying their concerns that do not lock students into permanently tracked classes. Is the parents' concern the extent to which their children are being academically challenged? If so, what subjects does this apply to? This knowledge increases the number of possible solutions that can satisfy the school leadership's desire to please the mobile parents. For example, if mobile parents' real concern is for a more challenging curriculum, then accelerated classes could be offered in those areas where staff and parents agreed they were needed, and the remaining subjects could be taught in mixed-ability groups.

3. Rather than treating teachers' limited confidence and ability in mixed-ability teaching as a given, the restriction imposed by this constraint could be loosened if the level of teachers' skill and confidence is lifted, so that some mixed-ability teaching becomes a more practical possibility. This would mean that teachers' current skill levels would be less likely to rule out more equitable allocation strategies. Priority for upskilling teachers could be in those subject areas where parents and staff agreed to have mixed-ability grouping.

4. The teachers could be challenged to learn more about the adequacy of their views on the "efficiency" of tracked and untracked classes by engaging with the research literature and with the range of views held by teachers of different subjects. Engaging in research may loosen the restriction imposed by this constraint and widen the number of possible solutions that can satisfy the teachers who are concerned about pedagogical efficiency. For example, if research shows that tracked classes are pedagogically efficient in some subjects but not in others, then more possibilities open up about how to be efficient without sacrificing equity.

These reformulated constraints open up new possibilities for solving the allocation problem in ways that overcome the criticism of the original theory of action. The possibility we outlined in Figure 2.2 involves allocating students to an untracked "home room" class where they are taught most subjects, and, for those subjects that require confident mastery of prior skills and knowledge, tracking students according to prior achievement in the subject. The improvability criterion can be met by ongoing staff debate of the relative adequacy of the two theories of action informed by information about parental, staff, and student reactions to and experience of the new arrangements.

SUMMING UP

In this chapter we have presented problem-based methodology and have shown how this approach to doing research helps teachers to both understand and improve their practice. First, this approach provides compelling explanations of practice by revealing its underlying theory of action. Such inquiry enables teacher-researchers to make explicit the links among what teachers do, why they do it, and the consequences of their practice. Second, PBM offers four standards for judging the adequacy of teachers' solutions to their problems. These standards are used to judge the *accuracy* of any factual claims, the *effectiveness* of the solution, whether the solution creates other problems (its *coherence),* and the openness of the theory to feedback and revision (its *improvability*). Third, we have shown how the process of theory evaluation opens up possibilities for developing an alternative theory of action that will further improve practice.

3

Collaborating to Improve Practice

It usually takes more than high-quality research to improve practice. In addition to their inquiry skills, teacher-researchers need the communication and interpersonal skills to recognize and manage the relationship challenges that arise when inquiry, evaluation, and change are contemplated. When teacher-researchers have the right relationship skills, they can help people work together to build a research culture in their schools.

The importance of relationships in problem-based methodology (PBM) is signaled by the fourth question in Table 2.1, which asks, "What type of research relationship fosters improved solutions to problems?" By the end of this chapter, we will have answered this question, and you will have completed your introduction to the methodological framework that underpins our approach to teacher research.

THE IMPORTANCE OF
RELATIONSHIPS IN TEACHER RESEARCH

The following list presents typical questions that teacher-researchers ask about the relationship dimension of their work:

- Will our research be experienced as criticism?
- We have very different views of how to teach reading—won't doing some research on the effectiveness of our programs just make matters worse?
- We want to get feedback from students, but the department head seems very threatened by that idea. Should we do something else instead?

- We are just classroom teachers—will the management team listen to us anyway?
- I don't want this project to damage my relationship with colleagues. Yet we have found some things that could really upset them. Should I tone down our findings?

In all of these challenges, people feel caught between doing what they think is best for their professional relationships and doing what they think would benefit the quality of teaching and learning in their school. They experience a tension between these two goals.

We have become convinced that these tensions are important enough to warrant explicit discussion in this book. We have seen practices that many people believe to be ineffective continue unchallenged because people are concerned that questioning them will damage collegial relationships. We have also seen the opposite—where people do challenge what they believe to be ineffective, and the result is damaged relationships and no change to the practices they criticized.

The teachers and administrators whom we introduced in the case in Chapter 1 recognized that learning how to overcome this type of challenge was essential to the success of their school improvement work. Here is how David Valgre from Southern Cross Middle School explains the decision to include work on communication and interpersonal skills in the professional development curriculum of the teachers involved in that school improvement initiative:

> In order for teachers to engage in meaningful discussions about student achievement data, we need to build relationships among teachers so that these discussions will focus on how to examine the data to improve teaching, rather than on blaming someone or excusing the poor results. Having strong relationships will mean that hard questions about teaching practices can be asked without causing defensive reactions.

Those readers who intend to work mostly on their own might question the relevance of this chapter to their research efforts. We would suggest, however, that even the efforts of solitary teacher-researchers have an important social dimension. They may need to gain the cooperation of others before they can make successful changes in their own practice. In addition, it is very difficult for them to identify and evaluate their own theory of action. They need a second pair of eyes—someone who does not share their assumptions about their students and how to teach them. As soon as a second person is involved, the same issues arise—how can they work together positively while addressing difficult issues openly and honestly?

As noted earlier, one of the common features of all the questions listed is a perceived tension between building and maintaining positive working relationships and doing research that rigorously investigates, evaluates, and improves practice. For many people, the tension between these two goals is so strong that they experience it as a dilemma. They cannot see how they can maintain good relationships and be true to their research goals. We have found the work of Chris Argyris the most useful resource in finding a practical way through this type of dilemma. Argyris is a social and organizational psychologist who for the past 20 years has been working with practitioners to create organizations that learn and improve through robust internal inquiry (Argyris, 1982; Argyris, Putnam, & McLain Smith, 1985; Argyris & Schön, 1974).

Argyris writes about two types of conversation. The first type, which we call a *controlling* conversation, occurs when one party tries to impose his or her view on the other party. In this type of conversation, the attempt to exercise control creates a strong tension between robust inquiry and maintaining a positive relationship. We argue that this controlling style creates or at least exacerbates the tension between these two goals.

We call the second type of conversation a *learning* conversation because it is focused on learning about the meaning and quality of each other's views. There is far less tension in this type of conversation between the relationship and the research task, because points of actual or possible difference between people are treated as opportunities to learn rather than as obstacles to be overcome.

The skills and values of a learning conversation are applicable whenever disagreement or discomfort is anticipated. This can happen at any stage of the research process. The conversations we present in the next two sections illustrate how learning conversations apply to the communication and checking of a draft research report. The application of learning conversations to other stages of the research process is discussed further in the final section of this chapter.

The background to the two conversations is the high school we discussed in Chapter 2, which tracks its students into a more academic "high" track and a more vocational "low" track. A group of teachers in the school decided to examine the fairness of the school's tracking policies. They were motivated by their professional reading on tracking, particularly the work of Jeannie Oakes, whose 20-year program of research has demonstrated the deleterious effects of tracking on the educational outcomes and life choices of students in low-track classes and programs (Oakes, 1985, 1987, 1992). In the hypothetical conversations presented, one of the teacher-researchers is discussing the preliminary research findings with the school principal. The principal was aware of the research and had given it his blessing.

CONTROLLING CONVERSATIONS

In the first conversation, the teacher-researcher adopts a controlling style in an attempt to persuade the principal to adopt the team's recommendations.

A Controlling Conversation

Teacher: So here is a summary [showing a table] of the ethnic and social backgrounds of students in our lower tracks, compared to those in higher tracks. We've also summarized the experience and qualifications of those who teach in each track. You'll notice that the lower track students typically have teachers who are less qualified than those who teach the upper-track students.

Principal: Yes, well, I think I knew that, but it is helpful to have all that detail in a table.

Teacher: According to our reading, especially the work of Professor Oakes, the probability of the lower-track students gaining college admission is much lower than students in the academic tracks. These consequences are likely to greatly reduce their future earning power.

Principal: Yes, well, those students just don't survive in the upper tracks. We've been down that road. . . .

Teacher: We would recommend introduction of more mixed-ability classes.

Principal: You think we haven't already considered that? [getting angry] You will recall we have had discussions with staff on several occasions about this. While the English teachers want it, math and science teachers are opposed. And the parents of students in accelerated classes are adamant they want that program retained. . . .

Teacher: Yes, that came through in our interviews too. Parents of upper-track students work hard to protect their privilege. We think that should be balanced by greater advocacy for the needs of students who are currently in the low tracks. Otherwise the school is unwittingly reinforcing the privilege of high-track students and families.

Principal: Well, that's easier said than done. You must realize that the financial viability of the school is at stake here. If any more middle-class families enroll their children elsewhere, we will have to reduce our teaching staff. I'm sure you wouldn't want that.

Teacher: Well, those are our recommendations. . . .

We call this a controlling conversation because the teacher-researcher's agenda seems to be to persuade the principal that tracking is wrong and should be replaced by more mixed-ability classes. There is little evidence that the teacher-researcher is open to the principal's point of view. (The same point could be made about the principal, because the conversation deteriorates into a futile attempt at mutual persuasion.) The teacher-researcher employs three main communication strategies, the second two of which are controlling.

1. The first strategy is the use of a high level of advocacy of his own point of view. The teacher-researcher explains how he sees the

situation (low-track students get less qualified teachers) and why he thinks it is unacceptable (the students are unable to win college entry; they have limited life chances). High advocacy is not necessarily controlling, especially when, as in this case, the speaker is able to say what his point of view is based on. This makes it easier for others to understand what is meant and to make up their own minds about whether they agree with the other person's thinking.

2. The second strategy is the low level of inquiry into the views of the principal. This is controlling because it suggests that the only relevant point of view is the teacher-researcher's. He does not ask why the school tracks its students and so learns little about the theory of action that explains the practice he is trying to change. The principal, out of frustration, eventually offers some reasons (teachers are divided about mixed-ability teaching; the school needs to retain enrollments), but the teacher-researcher does not acknowledge or probe these views. He acts as if he does not want to know in case the new information distracts from his goal of having the school introduce more mixed-ability classes.

3. The teacher-researcher's third communication strategy is his unilateral evaluation of tracking. This means that he is using his own values to judge the school's solution to the problem of how to organize its students, without negotiating the acceptability and relevance of those values to the principal. Such negotiation is needed because, as we saw in Chapter 2, people will set different constraints, including values, on the problem. While the teacher-researcher evaluates tracking in terms of equity (Do students in high and low tracks get comparable access to high-quality teachers and to college admission?), the principal evaluates tracking in terms of the satisfaction of staff and some parents, and in terms of the impact on the size of the school roll. Each party pursues what is important to them without taking into account what is important to the other party.

In Chapter 2 we discussed four standards (accuracy, effectiveness, coherence, and improvability) that are used in PBM to evaluate theories of action. These standards prevent the type of unilateral evaluation that occurs in this conversation because they require the important constraints, including values, of all parties to be taken into account. We use two of these standards to illustrate what we mean.

The effectiveness standard asks whether the theory satisfies the constraints that are important to the problem solvers themselves. If that standard had been used by the teacher-researcher, he would have investigated whether tracking was working, as the principal intended, in terms of staff and parent satisfaction and meeting enrollment targets. If the research team, for various practical reasons, had not been able to expand their study in this manner, a unilateral evaluation could still have been avoided by acknowledging that the evaluation was partial and did not take other important values into account, such as those that concerned the principal.

In discussing the effectiveness standard, we explained why an evaluation must not be limited to the constraints that are important to those being evaluated. Even if a theory of action works as intended, what works may not be desirable. That is why a theory of action should also be evaluated against the coherence standard—so that questions can be raised about the adequacy of what counts as effective. This is what the teacher-researcher attempted to do by asking questions about the equity of tracking. He wanted the principal to give this value much more importance than he had so far. He was unsuccessful, in our view, because he asked the principal to take what he valued more seriously, while demonstrating little interest in the values that were of importance to the principal. Without acknowledgment of the legitimacy of each other's values, the two parties could not begin to explore whether a new solution could better satisfy what they both considered important.

In this section, we consider the likely consequences of controlling a conversation in the manner illustrated. Consequences for both improving teaching and learning and for professional relationships are considered.

The first point is that the teacher-researcher learns little about the factors that explain why the school tracks its students, and hence little about how to change the practice. This is a direct consequence of advocating his own perspective without also inquiring into the perspective of those he is trying to influence. In the language of PBM, the teacher-researcher has bypassed the theory of action that explains the situation he is trying to change. This means he is likely to misunderstand or have limited understanding of what is involved in making the change he is advocating.

Second, the principal is likely to feel that the teacher-researcher has failed to fully understand his situation and is "pushing his own agenda." He may also feel prejudged and unfairly evaluated. The result could be defensiveness on the part of the principal, attack of the teacher-researcher, or some combination of the two. The teacher-researcher could then see the principal as overly sensitive and experience a dilemma between pursuit of his improvement objective and maintaining a good relationship with his principal. He may not realize that his own behavior has exacerbated the dilemma—it is the controlling way that he is pursuing improvement rather than the pursuit of improvement itself that is causing the threat and defensiveness.

Finally, the outcome of the conversation is likely to be an impasse—the research will not change school practice, and the principal will not persuade the teacher-researchers that tracking is the best possible solution to the problem of how to organize students. Rather than see the teacher-researchers as a resource for school improvement, who are committed to understanding and resolving the whole problem, the principal may see them as advocates for only that part of the problem that they care about. In the following box we have characterized this controlling approach to the improvement of practice as the "D-C-R" approach: Describe, Criticize, and Recommend. You may have been on the receiving end of it yourself from well-meaning advocates of change.

How Not to Be Influential

D   **Describe** the situation from your point of view and ignore the point of view of those you are trying to influence.

C   **Criticize** the situation without negotiating the evaluative framework you are using. Ignore what the recipients of the evaluation believe to be important.

R   **Recommend** improvements based on your theory of the problem and how to solve it. Ignore the implications of your recommendations for what others believe to be important.

The D-C-R pattern applies, of course, to external researchers as well as teacher-researchers. One of the reasons why many of the former are not as influential as they would like is that they move from description to criticism without discovering the theory of action that explains the practices that they want to change. (Readers who are interested in reading more generally about how research influences practice could refer to Hammersley, 2000; Robinson, 1993, 1998; Weiss, 1979.)

LEARNING CONVERSATIONS

In learning conversations people recognize the importance of treating differing accounts of a problem as a resource for learning better ways of thinking about and resolving the problem. This means they are open to learning from others about the accuracy and adequacy of their own assumptions, beliefs, and values. The drive in a learning conversation—for better quality thinking and reasoning—contrasts with the drive in a controlling conversation—to protect one's own views from challenge.

Next, we present a second version of the previous conversation. This time the teacher-researcher's interpersonal values and skills are more consistent with what we call a learning conversation.

A Learning Conversation

Teacher: [Has just completed a brief presentation on the ethnic and social backgrounds of the students in the academic and vocational tracks and on the characteristics of the teachers assigned to each track.] Is there anything that you think I have missed?

Principal: No, I think we knew all that but not in the detail that you are showing us in those tables.

Teacher: So how do you feel about the picture it presents?

Principal: Well, it is not a matter of feelings—we don't have much choice about it really, given what we are up against. I think it is very important you fully understand our situation. Our parents are very vocal about what they want for their children.

Teacher: I agree. We picked that up in our interviews. This diagram shows our understanding of why the school continues to track students. [Teacher then explains an earlier version of Figure 2.1 to the principal, including the evidence it is based on. This early version includes the two constraints of satisfying mobile parents and the limited teacher skills in mixed-ability teaching, but it does not include the constraint of pedagogical efficiency.] How accurately have we understood the reasons why you track?

Principal: Quite well. Those are the dilemmas we face. If we don't meet the demands of some parents for an accelerated class we lose many of our most able students. That is likely to start a downward spiral of falling enrollments, further middle-class flight, and difficulty retaining and attracting the best teachers. And many of the staff here are reluctant to teach mixed-ability groups anyway. . . . But there is one really important thing I think you have missed. There is no evidence that mixed-ability groups work for low academic students. That's a third reason why we have gone for tracking.

Teacher: As I understand the published research, the evidence is very mixed, depending on the teaching subject and the quality of teaching. What you are saying, though, is that impact on student learning is another important consideration in deciding how to allocate students?

Principal: Yes, I am. We have always thought that mixed-ability grouping was both more efficient and better for the students.

Teacher: It is very complex to measure, but our analysis of the achievement data for this school suggests that the low-track students are getting further behind the standard expected of their age group. It is possible that being grouped together in low-track classes is not helping them learn as you would wish.

Principal: So you are saying that these low-track students are not getting a fair deal?

Teacher: Yes, that may be an unintended consequence of the school's current strategy. I think there may be other grouping strategies that can better meet equity values while still meeting the other constraints you have talked about. For example, a combination of tracked and mixed-ability classes, depending on the subject, may reduce the achievement gap while still being acceptable to staff and parents. [Introduces and discusses the ideas in Figure 2.2, the alternative theory of action.]

This is a learning conversation because the principal is treated not as someone to be won over, but as a contributor to the process of describing, explaining, and evaluating how the school tracks its students. The conversation illustrates three strategies that are typical of a learning conversation:

1. As in the first conversation, the teacher-researcher advocates his own point of view. He describes, using supporting evidence, what he has learned about tracking in the school and why he is critical of the practice. By putting his views on the table, he makes it easier for the principal to identify where he agrees and disagrees. It is important to note that advocacy can be associated with both controlling and learning conversations. Advocacy becomes controlling when views are expressed without supporting argument and evidence and without inquiry into the reactions and views of others. It is very hard to question someone's views if they are expressed as bald conclusions and the speaker makes no space for a reaction. We discuss more about the difference between controlling and learning forms of advocacy in the subsequent section on the "ladder of inference."

2. Unlike the first conversation, the teacher-researcher inquires into the principal's point of view. The research itself was designed to investigate rather than bypass the reasons the school tracks its students. This communicates interest in and respect for others' viewpoints. In addition, the teacher-researcher makes a direct request for feedback about his analysis. He asks, "How do you feel about the picture it [the research summary] presents?" and later asks further, "How accurately have we understood the reasons why you track?" These direct questions invite the principal to critically evaluate the teacher-researcher's analysis rather than to give it his uncritical acceptance or rejection.

3. The teacher-researcher's evaluation is a negotiated evaluation. In learning conversations, differing accounts of a problem and how to solve it are treated as competing theories. Decisions about which is the preferable theory are made on the basis of a negotiated rather than a unilateral evaluation. In the learning conversation described, tracking is evaluated against values that are important to the principal, and, in addition, against values that are important to the teacher-researcher (equity of access to quality teaching and college admission). Having acknowledged the legitimacy of each other's values, the principal and teacher-researcher then work together to find a solution that better satisfies all the values that they now consider important.

The consequences of a learning conversation are likely to be the following. First, the participants move from an implicit, taken-for-granted account of a problem and its solution to an explicit understanding that can then be evaluated and revised. Since they understand more about what maintains tracking, they will be in a better position to decide whether and how to change it. For example, the teacher-researcher in the conversation knows, from his inquiry into the causes of tracking, that successful change will involve addressing the concerns of some teachers about their ability to teach mixed-ability classes and the concerns of some parents about whether their children will experience a sufficiently challenging curriculum.

Second, teacher-researchers who are skilled in learning conversations will be able to establish relationships with those they seek to influence that are characterized by empathy and trust rather than by defensiveness and frustration. The influence will be two-way rather than one-way, as each party learns from the other. In the conversation the teacher-researcher learned that his initial analysis was incomplete (it omitted the importance of efficient pedagogy), and the principal learned from the teacher-researcher that the low-track students were not progressing as he intended.

Finally, over time the values of a learning conversation begin to establish a culture in which constructive critique of colleagues' practice and shared responsibility for improvement becomes the norm. Building positive relationships and improving practice become mutually reinforcing rather than competing goals.

In the following box we have characterized the learning conversation approach to improvement as the D-E-E-R approach: Describe, Explain, Evaluate, and Recommend. Compared to the controlling D-C-R approach, discussed earlier in this chapter, it greatly increases the chance that the teacher-researcher will be influential.

How to Be Influential

D   **Describe** the situation and check that others accept the accuracy of your description.

E   **Explain** the situation by revealing the constraints, including values, that have produced the situation you are studying. Check the accuracy of your explanation with those involved.

E   **Evaluate** the situation using an agreed evaluative framework.

R   **Recommend** improvements, based on the agreed evaluation, that will better satisfy all the agreed constraints on the problem.

In concluding this section, we return to the views of John Ackroyd, whom we introduced in Chapter 1. John was the high school assistant principal who was responsible for reviewing the teacher evaluation system in his school and who learned from his research that the system was not working as he had intended. In an interview with author Mei, John explained how his group of teacher-researchers had been able to use learning conversations to benefit from the very different views they each brought to the project.

I think because of our work—our reading of Argyris and Schön and [learning about] learning conversations—we were trained in that way of thinking—of open discussion. So that was one thing that helped us—that process of putting things on the table to be challenged.

John went on to describe how learning about learning conversations had also changed how he dealt with colleagues who held different views from his own.

Mei: So, if you had differences in the past, you wouldn't have tested them out?

John: Well, I had a colleague from a different department and we would often theorize about why kids were learning or not learning, and we had completely different viewpoints on things. He was a science teacher and I was an arts teacher, so we were in a different faculty, and we used to argue a lot. But I don't think we ever resolved anything. We theorized and theorized and probably were convinced of our own arguments.

Mei: So the difference now is actually getting things resolved, whereas in the past you put forward the ideas and then just walked away?

John: Yes.

THE LADDER OF INFERENCE: A LEARNING TOOL

In the introduction to this chapter we listed some of the dilemmas that arise for teacher-researchers between maintaining positive collegial relationships and investigating and improving practice. These dilemmas are not unique to the context of teacher research. They arise, as well, in everyday professional conversations with colleagues. This point was made by John Ackroyd in the previous section when he talked about how learning conversations not only helped him learn from his teacher research team but also changed the way he talked through disagreements with colleagues.

In this section, we introduce you to one of the tools that helped John integrate his new skills into his everyday practice. This tool, which is called the "ladder of inference," was first developed by Chris Argyris (1990) and was later adapted by other writers on organizational and interpersonal inquiry (Boyett & Boyett, 1998; Stone, Patton, & Heen, 1999).

The ladder of inference is a powerful tool for helping people to recognize their tendency to make claims about the world that they assume to be true, and, therefore, expect others to accept without question. By using the ladder, people can become more aware of what led them to make those claims and of the possible ways in which they could be wrong. When people realize their claims are not self-evident, and that other interpretations of the same behavior or events are possible, they become much more open to learning from others.

The steps of the ladder are shown in Figure 3.1, which you should read from the bottom step upward. We explain how the ladder works with a story below about two teachers, Selina and Charles, who both teach the lower grades in an elementary school. They are part of a professional development group that has commited itself to improving the achievement of their students in reading by gathering information about and discussing how they are teaching their students.

Figure 3.1 The Ladder of Inference

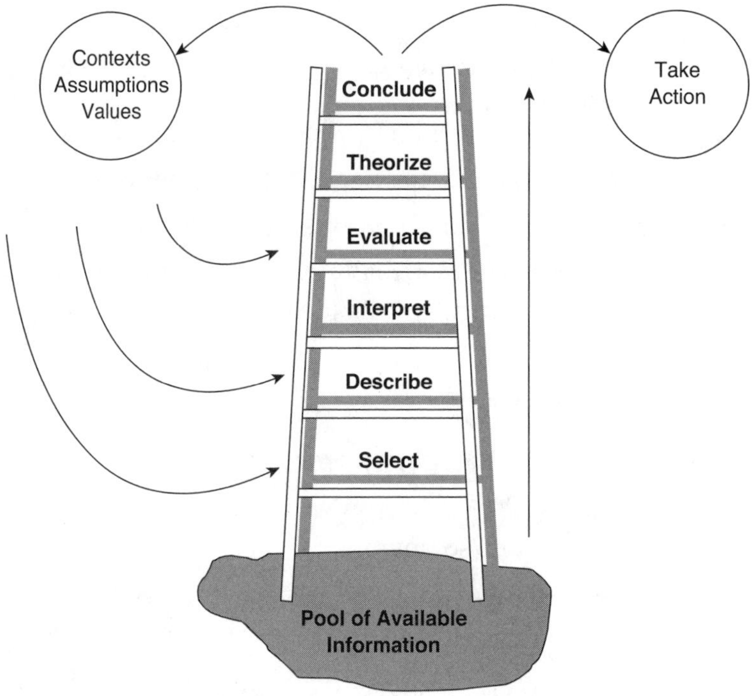

NOTE: Explanations of the Ladder of Inference are available in Argyris (2000).

Story: A Disagreement With a Colleague

Selina has been worried about how Charles, who teaches next door, runs his class. Now that they are both part of the same professional development group, committed to helping each other improve, she feels obligated to talk to him about her concerns about the behavior of his students. Yesterday, when she walked past his door, she noticed that the children were running about in his cluttered, open-plan classroom. She tried to speak to Charles about her concern that the children were noisy and were wasting time, but was surprised to learn that he believed strongly that time was not being wasted, and that the noise level was acceptable because young children need time for energy release after every period of formal instruction. This made her even more concerned. Would Charles have sufficient time to devote to formal reading instruction if he continued allocating large blocks of time to "energy release"? Selina felt that Charles's approach would result in his students falling behind in their reading achievement. Charles disagreed. He thought his students were doing fine and that his approach was working. Selina felt stuck—it seemed like she and Charles just had completely different views on what was good for these children. Yet they were supposed to work together!

The ladder of inference works like this:

1. The pool of information at the bottom of the ladder represents all the information that could be relevant to this situation.

2. The rungs of the ladder represent the various types of claims that can be made about information. The further the rung is up the ladder, the more it involves an interpretation or inference about the meaning of the information at the bottom. Thus, the further up the ladder one goes, the more likely it is that people will disagree about the correctness of the claim. That is why they need to be careful about how they climb the ladder of inference.

3. The first rung of the ladder represents the way we select from this pool. This is not a bad thing—it is simply impossible to notice everything. What is important is to recognize that you have been selective and that other people will take different information from the pool.

4. The second rung represents the process of naming or describing what is happening. Selina names what the children are doing as "running around" and "noisy." Charles might or might not agree with those two descriptors. It is important for Selina to recognize that these are descriptive claims and to be open to the possibility that they might not be so obvious to Charles.

5. The third and fourth rungs represent the way people interpret and evaluate what they have noticed and described. As indicated on the left-hand side of Figure 3.1, the context of the conversation and people's prior assumptions are powerful influences on how people interpret and evaluate what they notice. Selina has a history of listening to the noise because she teaches next door to Charles and is convinced that a more structured classroom would bring better results. Those experiences and convictions shape how she interprets and evaluates Charles's teaching—all that running around and noise is a "waste of time."

6. The fifth rung recognizes how people seek consistency between individual interpretations and experiences by weaving them together into a coherent theory of action. Charles believes that young children need certain conditions to learn (for example, opportunities to release energy), so he provides those conditions in anticipation that they will be good for their learning. Selina also has a theory about how to teach such children, but it is very different from that held by Charles. Neither teacher recognizes that, like any theory, theirs might not be true.

7. The sixth rung shows how theories provide conclusions about the situation and what to do about it. Selina concludes that Charles runs a sloppy classroom and that the children are not learning. It was this conclusion that prompted her to speak to Charles. Charles concludes that his clasroom is fine and that he does not need to change his teaching.

USING THE LADDER OF INFERENCE IN A LEARNING CONVERSATION

How do Selina and Charles resolve their differences? Do they give up, so as not to damage their relationship? Do they use power and control to try to push each other off the top of their ladders, as the figures are doing in Figure 3.2?

Figure 3.2 Arguing at the Top of Different Ladders of Inference

Pool of Available Information

Here are some simple guidelines for getting onto the same strong ladder and climbing it together.

1. As soon as you recognize you are on a different ladder from your colleague, do not climb any more rungs.

2. Slow down and stop advocating your own position.

3. Use your inquiry skills to identify the lowest point on your ladder at which the other person sees the situation differently.

4. Inquire into the disagreement until the other person confirms that you have correctly understood their point of view.

5. Check that the other person correctly understands your point of view.

6. If the difference remains, work out a way of checking out your differing claims that is acceptable to each of you.

7. When you have checked out and revised your claims, build the next rung of the ladder together.

8. Continue the process and see what you now conclude!

The most difficult parts of building a shared strong ladder are checking and resolving disagreements (Steps 6 and 7). Below we provide examples of how Charles and Selina could inquire into their disagreements and test out the quality of the thinking that lies behind them. Notice how the checks that we suggest in the right-hand column of Table 3.1 are carefully crafted to match the content and logic of the disputed claims. The skill of inquiry is not just to ask questions but to craft questions that test the reasoning that has led to the claim (Phillips, 1987b). General questions like "What do you think?" do not draw attention to what it is that has been taken for granted, and therefore, what it is that needs to be tested.

Table 3.1   Selina and Charles Check the Quality of Their Thinking

Inferences and Claims	*How to Check the Claim*
1. Selina believes time spent on energy release is wasted time.	• What leads her to believe that?
2. Charles believes time spent on energy release is beneficial.	• How does he know it is beneficial? What happens if he doesn't give children this time?
3. Selina believes too much time is spent on energy release and not enough on formal reading instruction.	• How much time is spent on these sorts of activities? • How much time is spent on reading instruction and practice? • How does it compare to the instructional time spent by other teachers in the group?
4. Selina believes children in Charles's class are behind in their reading.	• What is Selina's view based on? What evidence does she have about the children's reading achievement?
5. Charles believes the children are doing fine.	• What is Charles's view based on? What evidence does he have about the children's reading achievement? • What expectations have been set by the group about the expected level of achievement?

Much of the material we have presented in this chapter about learning conversations and the ladder of inference are applicable to day-to-day professional conversation as well as to more formal teacher research activities. It is crucial for the improvement of practice that the values and skills that underpin these two tools are not confined to research activities. There is not enough time to research everything, yet there is a need for teachers to be able to identify and check assumptions about what does and does not work in their own and other's classrooms. The ladder of inference and learning conversations are powerful tools for achieving this goal.

THE PLACE OF LEARNING CONVERSATIONS

We explained earlier that learning conversations are applicable throughout the research process. When you anticipate or experience a tension between the requirements of your research and your relationships with colleagues, learning conversations help you to resolve it by checking your beliefs about where the tensions lie and by inviting the other affected parties to help you resolve the problem.

We illustrate some more situations in which you may experience this tension in Table 3.2. In the first two columns we describe examples of this tension at different stages of the research process. In the third column we give the outline for a learning conversation about how to resolve the tension.

Table 3.2 Using Learning Conversations Throughout the Research Process

Key Decision	Example of Tough Challenge	How to Address Through a Learning Conversation
1. Establish the research question. (Chapter 5)	Teachers want to know how effective the school anti-bullying program is, but perceive the school management as not keen to evaluate it, as so much money has already been invested.	1. Check whether teachers' perceptions of management are correct. 2. If correct, ask management the reason for their concern. 3. Give reasons why teachers believe the program should be evaluated. 4. Discuss with management whether the risks of doing the research could be minimized. 5. Discuss with management what benefits they believe could come from the research. 6. Invite management to participate in the oversight of the research to maximize the benefits to the school while reducing the risks.
2. Select research methods for collecting information. (Chapters 5, 6, and 7)	A teacher-researcher believes that classroom observations are essential to answering a question about implementation of a new language program. His colleagues, however, do not want to be observed.	1. Find out the basis of colleagues' concerns. 2. Explain why you think observations are essential. 3. Invite feedback about your reasons. 4. Give feedback about colleagues' reasons. 5. Check that each party believes they have been understood by the other. 6. Work together to see if the remaining agreed legitimate concerns can be met, with or without classroom observations.

Table 3.2   Using Learning Conversations Throughout the Research Process

Key Decision	Example of Tough Challenge	How to Address Through a Learning Conversation
3. How much information is needed? (Chapter 5)	The principal wants a report on the impact of formative assessment on students' attitudes toward their learning. She wants it done for all year levels. Teachers believe that the project is too ambitious and that a study of selected year levels would be more practical.	1. Ask the principal why she wants all year levels, and how much work she thinks is involved. 2. Use the research planning process discussed in Chapter 5 to show the principal what would be required to meet her request. 3. Ask the principal which groups of students are her priority. 4. Work together to design a study that meets the practical constraints and the priority information needs.
4. Analyze information. (Chapter 8)	A group of teacher-researchers wants to monitor how much teacher feedback to students is about their academic work and how much is about their behavior. The teacher-researchers disagree among themselves about how to categorize some of the feedback.	1. Accept and acknowledge the difference, rather than blame or assume who is right and wrong. 2. Treat the difference as a group problem. 3. Invite each member to explain why they have categorized the feedback as "academic" or as "behavioral." 4. Agree on exactly what is causing the difference; for example, an ambiguous definition of "academic" feedback. 5. Fix the problem by, for example, clarifying the definition.
5. Communicate research findings. (Chapter 9, and Chapter 4 for ethics)	Teacher-researchers have completed a study of student absence from class. It seems that student absence from some teachers' classes is much greater than from others. How can the results be presented in a way that is respectful of colleagues yet makes the issues clear?	1. Raise the general problem of potential embarrassment with all the staff who are interested in the findings. 2. Do not identify individuals at this stage. 3. Make a group decision about the process needed to make the information available to responsible staff and at the same time avoid unnecessary embarrassment to individual teachers.

SUMMING UP

In this chapter, we have discussed the fourth question in the PBM framework outlined in Table 2.1—that of the type of relationship skills you need if your research is to foster improved solutions to problems. Relationship skills are important for overcoming tensions that may result from a need to maintain positive working relationships while also doing rigorous research.

We introduced the concepts of controlling and learning conversations, and showed how controlling conversations, which are characteristic of the D-C-R (Describe, Criticize, and Recommend) approach to research, can be counterproductive. We also showed the positive outcomes that result from learning conversations, which typically use a D-E-E-R (Describe, Explain, Evaluate, and Recommend) approach.

We then discussed the concept of the ladder of inference and its value as a tool for increasing your awareness of how you reach conclusions. Finally, we emphasized that learning conversations are applicable at every stage of the research process.

4

Combining Rigor and Respect

In Chapter 3, we explained that one of the unique features of research using problem-based methodology (PBM) is its emphasis on the relationship between the person conducting the research and the research participants. We characterized that relationship as a "learning conversation" in which different points of view are respected and treated as a resource for reciprocal critique and learning. PBM is also concerned, however, with the discovery of knowledge—knowledge about theories of action and how to improve them. This requires an equal emphasis on rigor—hence our chapter title, "Combining Rigor and Respect."

Knowledge is different from beliefs. When a teacher states, "I believe that Johnny has made progress," we treat the statement as an expression of her point of view, which may or may not be true. However, when she says, "Johnny has made progress," she is making a very different type of claim—one in which she is asking her audience to accept, as a matter of fact, that Johnny has made progress. When teacher-researchers claim to know something about students, or about what works or does not work in classrooms, questions should arise about the basis of their claims. These are questions about validity—about whether or not claims to know something are justified. Valid claims are those that are justified by argument or evidence (Fay, 1996).

The concept of validity is crucial to PBM's goal of improving practice through research that is both respectful and rigorous. The aspect of respect is achieved through the type of relationship described in Chapter 3. The aspect of rigor is achieved through the pursuit of validity.

In this chapter, we explain what we mean by "validity" in PBM research and then describe the main procedures involved in achieving it. Throughout, we show the overlap between these procedures and the values and skills that underpin learning conversations and the ladder of inference. We argue that validity must be pursued through a relationship of respect—neither rigor nor respect should be sacrificed for the other.

The final section of this chapter is devoted to ethical decision making and the requirements of institutional ethics committees. We also discuss how teacher-researchers can address the tensions that sometimes arise between ethical requirements and the requirements of rigorous and valid research.

THE CONCEPT OF VALIDITY

There are many types of claim to know something, and questions of validity are relevant to all of them. In Chapter 3 we discussed some of these different types of claim as we went up the ladder of inference (Figure 3.1). The bottom rungs have the more straightforward claims, such as *descriptions* of what is happening in a classroom. The validity of such claims depends on their accuracy. For example, if a teacher claims that he talks to male students as much as his female students, the validity of the claim depends on whether relevant evidence, such as observations of his classroom, shows this to be true.

Further up the ladder we have *interpretations* of what is happening. The validity of an interpretation is established by showing how it is more plausible than other possible interpretations. For example, a teacher might interpret a student's refusal to participate in a group activity as rebelliousness. The validity of the teacher's interpretation (rebelliousness) is established by showing that this particular interpretation is more plausible than other possible interpretations (for example, student objection to the peer culture in this particular group).

Near the top of the ladder are *theories of action*. In professional discussion, people seldom express all the claims that make up their theories of action. They may talk, for example, about what works in their classroom or make a claim about the fact that one curriculum is preferable to another. The validity of these claims depends on the validity of the implicit theory from which they are derived. This becomes clear if you think about how you would debate a colleague's claim that one curriculum was better than another. You would probably ask your colleague for the basis of his comparison. If he said he thought one curriculum was more up to date, or more interesting for students, or provided better explanations of key concepts, you would probably want to ask further questions about what led your colleague to make these particular claims. If the validity of these supporting claims proves to be doubtful, then the validity of the conclusion about which curriculum is better is also in doubt. In summary, the validity of the claim that one curriculum is preferable to another depends on the validity of a network of interrelated claims. That is why checking the validity of such claims involves uncovering and evaluating the whole theory.

Busy practitioners can be impatient with abstract theoretical discussion about concepts such as validity. Yet, in our experience, even though teachers may not use the term "validity," they often have strong and divergent views about the idea. In addition, teachers' views have powerful consequences for the way they react to research findings and professional opinions. It is essential, therefore, that we tackle the issue of validity in PBM. In order to avoid abstract discussion, we begin with the story of a hypothetical high school science department, whose members have decided to work together to improve their teaching of science.

Story: Debating How to Evaluate Science Teaching

The science department staff were disappointed in last year's results in scientific problem solving. It seems that the students score well in knowledge of scientific ideas and concepts, but have difficulty using those ideas to understand and solve applied problems. At their first meeting to discuss the matter, the teachers became aware that they had very different approaches to teaching scientific problem solving. They decided they should pair up and observe each other's lessons so they had some concrete information about how they each taught this topic.

Disagreement quickly emerged, however, about what and how to observe. One group, whom we shall call the "technicians," thought the department should first consult the published research on scientific problem solving to find a definition of good teaching, and then construct a standardized observation checklist based on that definition. They argued that in order to get valid information, the group had to agree on one objective way of defining and measuring good science teaching. Without a standardized approach, the observations would not be comparable as they would be too easily influenced by the subjective preferences of both the observer and the teacher being observed.

Some of their colleagues, whom we shall call the "professionals," argued that these observation procedures were unacceptable and would not produce valid information. In their view, there was no one definition of good science teaching that could be applied across the group, because each teacher had developed their own style and so each observation had to be sensitive to what each teacher was trying to achieve. The checklist approach only would capture what could be easily measured and, far from being neutral, it would bias the observations toward science teaching that was teacher rather than student directed. Instead of using a one-size-fits-all approach, the "professionals" wanted each teacher-observer pair to decide what and how to observe. What counted as valid information would vary for each teacher.

By the third meeting, the department could see they were at an impasse. If they went the way of the "professionals," they would have a variety of definitions of good science teaching, observations tailored to each definition, and no way of comparing across teachers. If they went the way of the "technicians," they would have comparable observational data whose validity and relevance would be rejected by many in the group.

It is clear that the members of the science department in the example have different theories of science teaching, at least with respect to the teaching of scientific problem solving. Far from being a problem, that is a potential resource for the group. What is a problem, however, is that they cannot agree on how to evaluate the validity of their theories. In the remainder of this discussion, we identify the strengths and weaknesses of the approaches to validity taken by the "professionals" and the "technicians" and conclude with an account of validity that integrates the strengths of each. Many of the concepts we use to do this have already been introduced in Chapter 2 in the section on the evaluation of theories of action.

The insistence of the "professionals" that the evaluation is tailored to the goals and values of each teacher's theory of science teaching reflects a view of validity that is broadly known as "relativism" or "subjectivism." In this view, people not only have different theories, but those differences are associated with different approaches to their evaluation (Fay, 1996). This means that the members of the science department can help one another reflect on their theories but cannot help each other judge whether one theory is better than the other because there is no common standard against which the theories can be judged. This approach to validity presents difficulties for teachers trying to improve practice. If there is no common way of evaluating whether, for example, one theory of teaching is better than another, then how can teachers decide between differing views?

Paradoxically, extreme relativist positions, which are intended to be respectful of difference, end up promoting an indifferent tolerance of each other's theories rather than a rich dialogue about how to teach. As Fay (1996) concludes, "Instead of joining us to others in ways that are respectful and appreciative, relativism separates us into enclaves of mutual incomprehension" (p. 82). If the science department staff accept this view, they cannot adopt a common view of good teaching and a collective approach to research-informed improvement.

There is, however, some wisdom in the "professionals'" view. You may have recognized its similarity to the effectiveness standard of theory evaluation discussed in Chapter 2. This standard assesses the degree to which a theory meets the constraints, including values and goals, that are important to those who use it. The "professionals" understand that if those values and goals are ignored, the classroom observation data are likely to be both misinterpreted and rejected by those who are observed. Where the "professionals" go wrong, however, is in insisting that effectiveness is all that is involved in the evaluation of theories of action. Theory evaluation, whether the theories are held by teachers or by external researchers, must incorporate an outside perspective so that what the theorists take for granted can be challenged. This is the purpose of including the coherence criterion in the four criteria discussed in Chapter 2 for the evaluation of theories of action.

The "technicians'" view of validity displays the opposite strengths and weaknesses. In the interest of objectivity, they end up rejecting the standard of effectiveness altogether, judging it to be value-laden and subjective. But this is too narrow a view of objectivity—there is no way of ever removing all the value-laden and subjective interpretations involved in judging the validity of a theory (Fay, 1996). Turning to the published literature, as the "technicians" want to do, is a good strategy for gaining a broader perspective, but it affords no certainty of being more objective, because the group members' interpretation of the literature will be filtered through their own theories and the literature may also be conflicting and flawed in some way.

The way forward for the science department staff is to treat their differences as competing theories and evaluate them by using the criteria for theory evaluation we outlined in Chapter 2. This would require them to make all their various theories explicit and examine whether there is sufficient evidence to support them (accuracy). They then need to evaluate each theory that has met the standard of accuracy against its particular constraints (effectiveness) and against any additional criteria that are suggested by the literature and/or by colleagues (coherence). If the teachers adopt an approach of continuous improvement of their theories, they do not have to agree on everything, nor reach a perfect solution. They can work together to improve their teaching in a manner that respects each teacher's approach while bringing a fair and rigorous critique to all of them (improvability). In practical terms, this means that each teacher could specify how to judge the effectiveness of his or her own teaching, collect relevant data, and reflect with colleagues on what it suggests about his or her effectiveness. Each teacher should also collect data on one or two aspects of their teaching that colleagues believe to be important but that they would not have otherwise evaluated. This latter information challenges them to think about other possible solutions to the problem of how to teach scientific problem solving.

PROCEDURES FOR INCREASING VALIDITY

As a teacher-researcher, your primary job is to make theories of action explicit and to involve others in their evaluation and revision. We turn now to the approaches that you can use throughout your study to increase the validity of your account of the theory of action you are investigating. The better your research design, methods, and analysis, the stronger the argument you can make for the validity of your description of the relevant theory of action.

The key to improving validity is being skilled in noticing when you are wrong—when assumptions, hunches, and initial understandings turn out to be mistakes. Therefore, it is important to design your study in ways that increase the chances that you will avoid error and detect those that you may have made. This does not mean that your work will be error free. Research findings should always be expressed with tentativeness and open-mindedness, since there is always the possibility of error. The best you can do in the face of inevitable fallibility is to describe the steps you took to increase the validity of your research.

In Chapter 3, we introduced the ladder of inference—a tool for representing how people make claims about the world. We discussed how people can leap to conclusions that may not be warranted by the information at the bottom of the ladder. The adequacy of such conclusions is established by examining how people reasoned their way up the ladder, from the information at the bottom to the conclusions at the top. Exactly the same principle applies to demonstrating the validity of your own research. The four key strategies for increasing validity are portrayed diagrammatically in Figure 4.1. Procedures are needed to (1) reduce bias in how you select information, (2) increase the accuracy of your description of what you have selected, (3) increase the plausibility of your interpretations through audit trials and triangulation, and (4) establish the reasonableness of your conclusions through seeking participant feedback. The validity of your research findings will depend on how well you complete each of these procedures.

Figure 4.1   Using the Ladder of Inference to Increase Validity

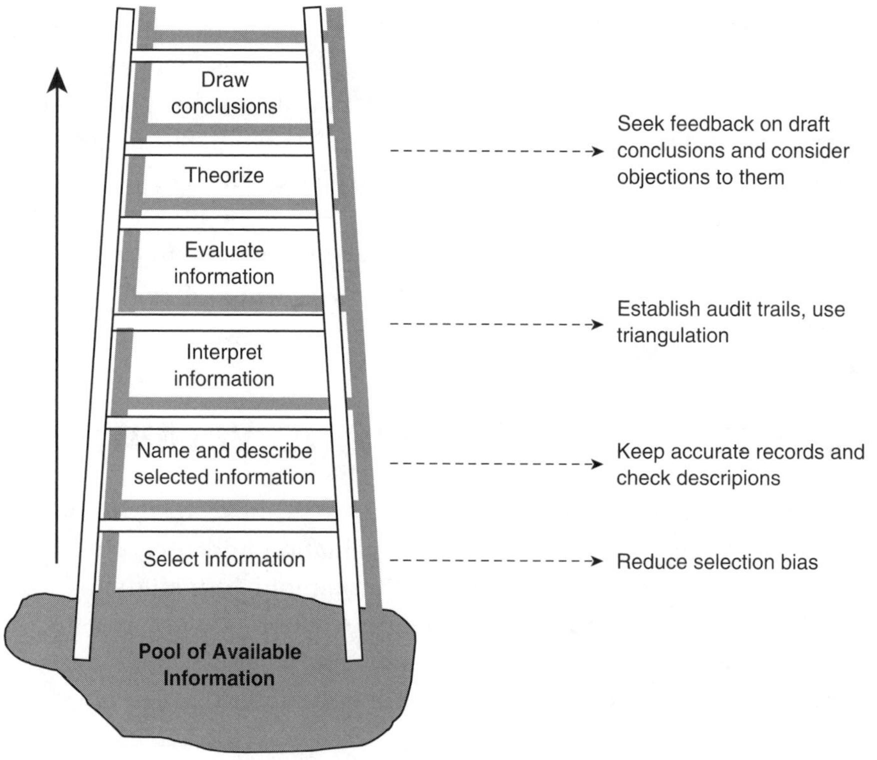

Reducing Selection Bias

At every stage of your research, you select from the available pool of information—you select who to talk to or observe, and what questions to ask or observations to make. Selection is an inevitable part of doing research and does not, in itself, threaten its validity. After all, you must select what is relevant to your research question and set aside what is not. It is wrong to believe that the mere selection of a question, research approach, and theoretical framework produces bias. Bias is produced when the manner in which you select favors answers to your research questions that fit your existing political or practical commitments (Hammersley, 2000). This means that you pay insufficient attention to evidence that challenges or questions your existing views. We now consider how to reduce two types of selection bias: sampling bias and confirmation bias.

Sampling Bias

Selection biases can threaten validity at every stage of the study. In selecting whom to talk to or observe, you can introduce bias by selecting those who are atypical of the whole group. This is called *sampling bias.* For example, a study of how teachers implemented an innovation would be biased if those who were less positive about the innovation were intentionally or unintentionally underrepresented in the sample.

Confirmation Bias

The tendency to give more weight to data and data sources that confirm rather than disconfirm your prior assumptions and hypotheses is known as *confirmation bias.* A teacher-researcher who was favorably inclined toward the innovation might, quite unconsciously, probe colleagues' positive comments and gloss over the negative ones, and do the same when analyzing the data. The way to counteract this bias is to build procedures into your study that force you to search for and take notice of disconfirming information. The three strategies listed here describe some of these procedures:

1. Make emerging conclusions very explicit by writing them down or communicating them to others.

2. Describe what you would expect to see or hear if your tentative interpretation was incorrect or oversimplified. For example, after observing the way a colleague gave feedback to his students, you may be thinking that he gives them a lot of feedback about their behavior but very little about how they are understanding and completing their academic work. The information that would disconfirm this tentative conclusion would be examples of the teacher giving academic feedback. If you describe what would count as disconfirming information, you will be more likely to double check that you have not overlooked these examples.

3. Review the information obtained to make sure appropriate weight has been given to both confirming and disconfirming evidence. This may involve reviewing documents, interview records, or observation notes to ensure that information that both supports and challenges emerging conclusions has been taken into account.

The conscientious use of these three strategies will enable teacher-researchers to develop more valid conclusions and demonstrate their validity to others.

The following example shows how a deliberate search for disconfirming evidence helped a group of teacher-researchers develop a more valid understanding of the practice they were studying (Millward, Neal, Kofoed, Parr, Lai, & Robinson, 2001). The teacher-researchers were interested in the impact of a literacy intervention on children's achievement in reading and writing. They collected and analyzed student writing samples, and then compared achievement in writing with the reading achievement of the same students. Data on reading had already been recorded by class teachers as part of their regular assessment cycle. Much to their surprise, the writing achievement was higher than the reading achievement. Would it be valid to conclude that the students were performing better in writing than reading? They tested the validity of this conclusion by deliberately trying to prove it wrong (trying to disconfirm it). They considered the following alternative explanations:

1. The teaching of writing in the children's classes was better than the teaching of reading. This possibility was discounted after informal observations of the teachers' reading program showed that it was of a high quality.

2. Insufficient time was devoted to reading instruction. This possible explanation was ruled out after examination of the school timetable.

3. The reading assessments were affected by poor oral language skills in English. This explanation was ruled out on logical grounds, as it would have affected both writing and reading.

4. The reading data were less valid than the writing data. This explanation was checked by:
   • Noting the writing data had been collected and analyzed by the teacher-researchers using standardized procedures, including the moderation of their assessments. No such procedures had been used by the teachers who supplied the reading data.
   • Retesting of two classes by a literacy consultant, which showed the students were reading above the level indicated by their class teachers.

The teacher-researchers concluded, therefore, that the reading data were less valid than the writing data, and that there was probably not a significant difference between the students' achievement in reading and writing. There was therefore no need to further investigate the teaching of reading, since there was no evidence it was any less successful than the teaching of writing!

Improving Accuracy of Description

The validity of research findings can be compromised by inaccurate description. Accuracy requires careful record keeping and attention to detail. For example, if you are interviewing, you will increase accuracy if you use a tape recorder as you will not have to rely on notes or your memory.

If you are not able to make audio or video recordings, you can ensure your field or interview notes are accurate by checking them with the colleagues you observed or interviewed. The purpose of the check is to establish that you are working with data that are reliable; that is, all the relevant parties agree the records accurately capture what occurred or was said. An additional strategy for increasing accuracy of description is through use of a second observer or interviewer.

Establishing Audit Trails and Triangulation

You can also increase the validity of your research by using audit trails and triangulation to establish the plausibility of your interpretations and inferences. As we have already argued, there is more than one way to interpret any piece of information. What is important with respect to validity is to show that the inferences drawn from the data are relevant and reasonable.

Audit Trail

When you can show others the original field notes, checklists, observation notes, or sections of an interview from which you drew a particular inference, you have established an audit trail. By organizing and retrieving the original information in this manner, you can check, and invite others to check, the validity of your interpretations.

The idea of the audit trail applies throughout the study—it is not just something you worry about at the end. It applies every time you move up a rung on the ladder of inference. For example, in an interview, you will naturally make inferences about what people mean. Since there are a myriad of ways in which people can misunderstand one another, it is crucial that inferences about other people's meanings are carefully checked. In a face-to-face interview, this can be done by paraphrasing or summarizing what you think was meant, and asking whether the paraphrase or summary is accurate.

Many inferences refer not to a specific piece of information, but to a pattern of evidence. The question, then, is how you can demonstrate that the pattern of evidence supports the conclusion that has been drawn. Imagine that a group of teacher-researchers who have been studying school culture describe their principal's leadership as "democratic." This inference cannot be defended by pointing to one or two comments in an interview or to how the principal ran a particular staff meeting. It must be defended by showing that, in the context of all the relevant information, the principal used a predominantly democratic approach. In this case, the relevant information includes all the information about the principal's leadership—including the times when he behaved in an autocratic rather than democratic fashion. The conclusion that he has a democratic style is defended by showing that the occasions on which he behaved democratically (confirming evidence) far outweigh the occasions on which he behaved autocratically (disconfirming evidence). If you have established an audit trail, you will be able to retrieve both types of evidence and thus respond easily to questions about how the conclusions were reached.

Triangulation

An important procedure for the validation of interpretations is that of *triangulation*. This refers to a navigational and survey technique where the precise location of a point is established by the convergence of observations taken from different angles. When applied to educational research, it means that a conclusion reached on the basis of one set of methods or sources of evidence is confirmed by the use of at least one additional method or source of evidence. In the example given, triangulation could be used to check the interpretation that the principal is "democratic" by interviewing teachers about how they experience his staff meetings as well as by observing the meetings. If they experience him as leading the meetings in a democratic fashion, then the conclusion that the principal has a democratic style is strengthened. Triangulation has increased the validity of this conclusion by showing how two different methods (observation of staff meetings and teacher interviews) have independently produced the same conclusion. The point of triangulation is not simply to employ different methods, but to check whether each of these diverse methods leads to a similar conclusion (Hammersley & Atkinson, 1995).

Seeking Participant Feedback

Finally, an important way of increasing the validity of your research is to check whether the participants recognize the validity of your accounts. This type of validity check is called "member checks" (Lincoln & Guba, 1985) or "respondent validation" (Hammersley & Atkinson, 1995). These latter authors describe the purpose of respondent validation as follows:

> The value of respondent validation lies in the fact that the participants involved in the events documented in the data may have access to additional knowledge of the context—of other relevant events, of temporal framework, of others' ulterior motives for example—that is not available to the [researcher]. . . . In addition, they have access to their own experience of events, which may be of considerable importance. Such additional evidence may

materially alter the plausibility of different possible interpretations of the data. (Hammersley & Atkinson, 1995, p. 228)

It is important to note that the purpose of such checking is to increase validity and not simply to gain agreement. As Denis Phillips, the philosopher of social science, has noted, it is possible to find people who agree with a claim regardless of its validity (Phillips, 1987a). For example, a principal may claim that bullying in the playground is decreasing, and his teachers may agree with him. However, both principal and teachers may be wrong. Gaining agreement will only increase validity if it is the result of careful consideration of the grounds on which the claims are made.

In gaining participant feedback, you must be clear about what is being checked, because different procedures are required for different types of evidence and analysis. A draft research report in PBM will often include both a description and an evaluation of teachers' theories of action. Teachers are unlikely to find an evaluation of a theory of action credible if they believe your account of the theory is wrong. The first step, therefore, is to check the accuracy of the description of the relevant theory or theories of action. This involves checking that you have accurately understood the constraints and how they explain the actions you are studying. The links you are claiming between actions and intended and unintended consequences should also be checked.

There are particular challenges involved in establishing the validity of constraints that represent participants' motives and purposes. It is very easy to misread others' intentions. Such misreading arises because motives and beliefs cannot be directly inferred from behavior, and self-reports are often unreliable. If you disagree with such self-reports, you should try to resolve the issue in a learning conversation in which the basis of each party's views is checked. Once research participants agree that they have been correctly understood, you should then disclose and check your critique of the participants' theory of action. This step is not, however, a one-way process, for the participants' theory is also a source of critique of your own theory. There should be a genuine debate about the relative adequacy of your and the participants' theories of action.

There may be good reasons for you to disclose your theory well before the feedback of a draft research report. Early disclosure is important when you use your particular perspective as a lens through which to observe colleagues or question them about their practice. Without such disclosure, colleagues may feel manipulated as they attempt to second-guess "where you are coming from" and why they are being asked particular questions.

The following example shows how Claire, a senior elementary school teacher, reaped the rewards of disclosing her theoretical perspective on teacher evaluation. She had a particular interest in whether teacher evaluators spent time talking with teachers about the links between their teaching and their students' achievement. Since Claire believed that student achievement was unlikely to be a strong focus of the evaluations, she decided to find out what was discussed and why.

She designed an interview that began by asking teachers to recall what was discussed and why (exploring the teachers' theory). Toward the end of the interview she disclosed her own views and asked for feedback. Her account of what happened shows how disclosure can enrich understanding of the other person and increase trust:

> I was initially reluctant to disclose my theory because the teachers hadn't really focused on the link between their teaching and student achievement in the interviews. I didn't want to impose my theory on them. Rather I wanted to use it to generate dialogue about the relationship between teaching and student achievement.
>
> So I asked the teachers, "How do you feel about teacher evaluations focusing on student learning?" I also gave them concrete examples of what I meant by this and connected my ideas to what they had already told me about teacher evaluations. I also expressed my own uncertainties about my ideas (so that I didn't sound as though I was going to impose these on them) and checked my own understanding of what they had already said.
>
> Teachers reacted to this disclosure in two ways. First, they were positive and enthusiastic about the theory I disclosed. One teacher said, "I think this is a great idea. You're using hard data about learning to get a teacher to focus on teaching practices." Second, they were enthusiastic about the disclosure itself. The tone of the interview changed. There was renewed enthusiasm and energy in the interview and greater dialogue on the issue. Teachers gave me more insight into their thinking and asked me for my ideas on how this theory could be put into practice. One teacher, who had previously described her evaluation practice as positive, now reevaluated it as needing improvement, and suggested how she could have used her students' portfolios as part of her evaluation. So, disclosing my theory to teachers has been very useful. Teachers were genuinely interested in the ideas, and many seemed to have been enlightened by the process.

While participant feedback provides an important validity check, it also serves ethical purposes. Researchers who base attributions about others on the basis of unchecked assumptions are guilty of a form of imposition. Such unchecked attributions are likely to engender resistance to researchers' findings and recommendations.

It is also important to remember that if a participant disagrees with your findings, you are not necessarily wrong. Objections signal the possibility rather than the certainty of invalidity. While participants may on some occasions know their own minds, they may on other occasions be blind to the real determinants of their actions. Argyris's (1982) research on the frequent incongruence between people's espoused theories and theories-in-use (see Chapter 2) provides ample warning against uncritical acceptance of participants' objections. It is your openness to their objections and your consideration of their likely merit that will help increase the validity of your research conclusions.

DIFFERENT APPROACHES TO VALIDITY

We have presented and defended an approach to validity that defines it as the extent to which research findings are justified by evidence and argument. This definition implies that validity cannot be determined by examining the findings alone—the findings must be judged in terms of the adequacy of the research processes that produced them. The key issue in determining validity is whether those processes involved rigorous attempts to examine and eliminate alternative interpretations of the evidence.

Some contemporary writers on qualitative and practitioner research, however, reject this notion of validity because they mistakenly associate it with a search for "objective truth" (Lincoln & Guba, 1985). In its place, they propose a range of alternative conceptions of validity that emphasize the empowerment of practitioners and the improvement of practice.

Bradbury and Reason (2001), for example, in their *Handbook of Action Research,* discuss criteria of validity that include the quality of relationships between researchers and practitioners. Are the participants, they ask, energized and empowered by the research experience? Similarly, Lather (1986) proposes the importance of *catalytic validity*—that is, the extent to which the research triggers transformative change. A second alternative criterion proposed by these writers concerns the practical outcomes of the research. Does it improve the situation or solve the problem, and does it do so in a sustainable manner (Bradbury & Reason, 2001)?

While we agree with the importance of both these qualities, we do not see them as alternative conceptions of validity. PBM research is, at its best, valid, empowering of participants, and generative of practical improvement. The latter two criteria are not about validity. Rather they express additional goals that are characteristic of several approaches to practitioner and action research. Research is primarily about the discovery of new knowledge, and validity is central to the achievement of that goal (Pring, 2000). PBM research, like action research, embraces additional goals concerned with improving practice through analysis, evaluation, and theory revision. Valid research findings facilitate the achievement of these additional goals, but the concept of validity should not be stretched to include any purpose other than the production of well-founded research conclusions.

PBM AND GENERALIZATION

One of the common criticisms of teacher and action research is that it is so small scale that the findings apply only to the situation in which it was conducted (Robinson, 1993). In other words, the findings may be valid for that setting, but do they have external validity—that is, will the knowledge that teacher-researchers generate about one setting be applicable to other similar settings? The answer depends on the extent to which teachers employ similar theories of action. To the extent that teachers understand and solve common problems in similar ways—that is, employ similar theories of action—the findings of PBM research will be highly generalizable. To the extent that their theories are unique to a particular context, the findings from one PBM study will not be generalizable to other contexts.

In principle, there is a trade-off between relevance to a particular setting and generalization to other settings. The better a piece of research captures the richness of a particular theory of action, the less likely, one would predict, that it will be applicable to other contexts where different theories operate. In practice, however, there is a lot of overlap between how teachers in different settings tackle their common problems. For example, we have completed a series of small-scale studies on reporting to parents that describe how and why teachers report as they do (Marino, Nicholl, Paki-Slater, Timperley, Lai, & Hampton, 2001; Robinson & Timperley, 2000; Timperley & Robinson, 2004). Even though the initial studies were conducted in a few elementary schools in poor urban areas, some teachers across New Zealand recognized that those same factors led them to write positively biased reports to parents. They judged the research to be highly relevant to their own situations, because the theory of action that produces positive reporting applies across many different types of schools.

ETHICAL DECISION MAKING

We have covered the concept of validity, procedures for increasing validity, and briefly discussed the factors that determine whether or not the findings of PBM research will be generalizable. We now turn to ethical decision making. In discussing research ethics, we show the strong links between this topic and the skills and values of a learning conversation (discussed in Chapter 3).

Teacher research, like any professional activity, involves obligations to treat others in an ethical manner. While the obligation itself is readily accepted, it is not always easy to determine how to act ethically in any particular research situation. The difficulty is not in understanding ethical principles, but in knowing how to apply them when other things are at stake, like the quality of the research itself (Hammersley & Atkinson, 1995; Pring, 2000).

Some teacher-researchers will be able to turn for guidance on these matters to the research ethics committee associated with their district or local authority, with their funding agency, or with a collaborating university. Research ethics committees have been established in many of these organizations to regulate the research activities of their own staff and of outsiders seeking permission to conduct research in their organization.

As a first step, therefore, you should check whether you need to seek permission from any such committee in order to conduct your research. The procedural guidelines issued by many such committees provide helpful information on relevant ethical principles and on how to prepare an application for permission to conduct your study.

For many of you, however, there is no relevant committee to turn to. Even if you do have access to one, it is important to understand some of the relevant ethical principles so you can apply them to your unique context and situation. Much of the guidance you need to do this was provided in Chapters 2 and 3. Chapter 2 discussed the role of constraints in problem solving, and these ideas apply directly to ethical problem solving. The skills and values of a learning conversation, discussed in Chapter 3, are also very relevant to the respectful and ethical treatment of those you are working with. Our purpose in having this additional separate section on ethics is to show you how an understanding of learning conversations can help you address common ethical challenges that arise in teacher research. As we point out throughout our discussion, there are no rules to follow in the making of ethical decisions. We treat ethical decision making as a problem-solving process that involves, like all problem solving, the satisfaction of multiple constraints, many of which may be in tension with one another.

We begin by presenting a short case and discuss how the ethical challenges it raises could be met by teacher-researchers. Finally, we present five procedural suggestions intended to help you make wise ethical decisions about the conduct of your research.

Reviewing a High School Teacher Evaluation Policy

In Chapter 1, we introduced John Ackroyd, an assistant principal in an Auckland high school who was responsible for the teacher evaluation program in his school. The program was developed after considerable consultation with staff and was designed to promote teacher development rather than to satisfy strong accountability purposes. The principal had asked John to review the program and present a report by the end of the year. Since John was doing graduate study at the same time, he took the opportunity to invite three other high school teachers enrolled in one of his classes to use the review for their group research project. John was the "insider" in the team—he was studying his own school and a program for which he had direct responsibility. The other three team members were either current or past high school teachers who had experienced similar programs in their own schools.

The situation described raised several ethical issues for John and his team. We discuss them next.

Free and Informed Consent

One of the most widely accepted principles for the ethical conduct of research is that of free and informed consent. As Hammersley and

Atkinson (1995) describe it, this means "that the people studied by social researchers should be informed about the research in a comprehensive and accurate way, and should give their unconstrained consent" (p. 264). There is a variety of ways in which people can be informed and express their consent. Institutional ethics committees will usually specify how this should be done and will provide appropriate forms on which information about the study is provided to participants, and on which they give their written consent.

John's group decided to obtain written consent from all participating teachers. Why did the group make this decision? This is a reasonable question, given that John had been asked by his principal to complete the review and write a report. Was his report a research project or was it part of his job responsibilities? If it was the latter, then was formal consent from participating staff needed? As we have emphasized throughout this book, one of the goals of PBM is the integration of practitioner research into the everyday work of teachers. The more successful that integration, the more blurred the boundaries become between these two activities. Schools that are learning organizations—organizations dedicated to the continuous improvement of their theories of action—will review their activities by the collection and analysis of systematic data. It is hard to imagine that they would require formal written consent on every such occasion.

John's group obtained written consent from participants because the review was serving a dual purpose: that of John's research and the review of school policy and procedure on teacher evaluation. The written consent ensured that staff were aware of the research purpose and of the additional information gathering and reporting requirements that would be needed to fulfill it.

We turn next to the decision the group made that John would explain the project to his colleagues at a staff meeting, seek their feedback, and invite them to indicate their willingness to be interviewed by putting a slip into his staff mailbox. The question to be considered is whether this procedure, given John's senior role in the school, gave colleagues, especially those who were more junior, sufficient freedom to decline to participate.

The assumption is made by some institutional ethics committees that teachers will find it difficult to decline to participate in research activities when the request comes from people who hold positions of power in their own organization. In other words, the consent they give will be inevitably coerced rather than freely given. This issue has important implications for teacher research, since it is usually conducted in the school in which at least one member of the research group is employed, and there will typically be a power imbalance between that member and some of the research participants.

The implications of these power differentials for gaining free and informed consent need to be carefully considered. For example, if principals or school board members request some teacher research, as happened in John's case, it is important that the principle of free and informed consent for individual participants is protected by allowing staff to volunteer their participation. In other words, a distinction must be maintained between institutional consent and individual consent. Both may need to be obtained. In addition, teacher-researchers need to consider whether colleagues who decline to participate will be "singled out" in any way. If that is a likely possibility, then a more anonymous process for gaining consent is required.

However, while issues of power and consent need to be considered, we do not think it is helpful to assume that junior staff will feel coerced by requests to participate from senior colleagues. Such an assumption may be valid where school cultures are hierarchical and status conscious and where feedback and information flow in a predominantly top-down rather than bottom-up direction. But not all schools are like that—indeed, some junior staff may feel patronized by the assumption that they are not capable of saying "No" to a senior colleague.

The best guide we can give you is to use your knowledge of the existing power relations in the school to decide how to inform staff of your project and provide them with a real choice about participating. Check your decision process against the ladder of inference—for example, ask yourself what evidence leads you to conclude that your process will provide for free and informed consent. Discuss your plans with your team, or if you are working on your own, test out your plans with a colleague. Do they perceive an element of coercion? If so, how might it be mitigated?

Prevent Harm

A second common principle of research ethics is the prevention of harm. Harm may result from the process of doing the research or from its publication. In the context of teacher research, harm that occurs during the research process itself is usually associated with the public exposure of previously sensitive issues, with embarrassment, or with the stress that results from additional effort and time commitments.

Teacher-researchers have an ethical obligation to reduce possible harm by anticipating it and discussing the possible risks of their research with those who are likely to be involved. Institutional ethics committees will usually require explicit discussion of harm in an application for permission to conduct research.

Some research methods pose more risks to participants than others. Classroom observations of teachers, for example, are much more likely to cause threat and embarrassment than are interviews of those same teachers about their teaching. It would seem, therefore, that harm reduction would be served by using interviews rather than observations. Every ethical decision, however, is constrained not only by ethical principles but by the requirements of the research question itself. In the previous example, consideration must be given to both the harm that might be caused by classroom observations and to the validity of a project on teaching that relies on teachers' reports of what happens in their own classrooms. In short, there are multiple conflicting constraints on this particular decision. Use of interviews reduces harm and increases the likelihood of gaining consent. On the other hand, it may also reduce the validity of the research and, therefore, its potential for improving practice. Since the improvement of practice is an important goal of PBM, the goal of harm reduction and the goal of improvement must be considered together.

Our advice is that, as far as possible, you involve those whose participation you are seeking in the resolution of these dilemmas. The trade-offs then become clearer, people feel more responsible for the decision, and more people learn about what doing research involves. (See Table 3.2 for suggestions on how to resolve such issues.)

Harm can also arise from dissemination and publication of research. We have encouraged many teacher-researchers to publish their work in professional journals and to speak about it at professional gatherings (see Chapter 9). In each case, careful procedures are followed to ensure that participating teachers and school communities consent to such publication and benefit from the publicity it brings. The result has usually been considerable pride in the resulting publication and publicity. In some cases, we have decided, in conjunction with participating schools and teachers, not to publish because the possible damage outweighs the possible benefit. We describe next some questions that might help you to decide how to weigh the costs and benefits of the dissemination and publication of your research.

Question 1. How do we protect the school and ourselves from being damaged by the dissemination of this research?

Answer 1. Involve relevant participants in discussion and revision of the report to identify and eliminate any information that may be harmful. Discuss the implications of the revision for the integrity of the report. If agreement cannot be reached about how to prevent harm while preserving research integrity, do not disseminate the research.

Question 2. How do we ensure that individuals and schools cannot be identified?

Answer 2. This question assumes that individuals and schools do not want to be identified. This assumption should be checked, as anonymity prevents schools and teachers from being recognized for their commitment to research and improvement. If anonymity is still desired, use pseudonyms and seek consent of relevant participants for use of quotations that might enable them to be identified despite such anonymity. Discuss the possibility that despite these precautions, individuals might still be identified by readers from within and outside the school.

Question 3. How do we ensure that readers will not unfairly prejudge or misunderstand our school?

Answer 3. We can never guarantee the reactions of others. An account of, for example, ineffective teaching or poor achievement always holds the potential to damage a school's reputation and to embarrass its teachers. Such accounts can do particular harm in areas where schools are already subject to negative publicity. Such harm is far less likely to occur if any negative findings are fully explained. PBM provides such explanations by identifying the constraints that caused those negative findings. When readers know the circumstances that gave rise to ineffective practice, then any criticism is likely to be less personal, the harm is reduced, and the reader is better informed. In sum, this means that you should make sure that before you release a report, that any writing of the D-C-R (Describe, Criticize, Recommend) variety (see Chapter 3) has been replaced by writing of the D-E-E-R (Describe, Explain, Evaluate, Recommend) variety (see Chapter 3). Examples of both types of writing are provided in Chapter 9.

Harm is also reduced, and benefit to others increased, if the report describes the steps that have or will be taken to address the negative findings. It is important to remember, though, that in some circumstances it may be necessary to withhold from public release those portions of the research findings that are most subject to misinterpretation, or that are so potentially damaging that the benefits of public release are outweighed by the costs to the research participants.

General Guidance on Ethical Decision Making

In conclusion, we offer the following as general guidance in making ethical decisions about the conduct and reporting of your research:

1. There are no rules to follow—only awareness of ethical principles and wise application to your particular context.

2. Ethical decision making is a form of problem solving. There are both ethical and research constraints to be satisfied, and there are frequently tensions between the two. For example, it is possible to reduce the risk of harm in ways that make your research not worth doing.

3. Where you can, involve others in making ethical decisions that affect them. This provides you with support and increases everyone's learning about how to do research.

4. Use learning conversations and the ladder of inference to test your own and others' assumptions about the impact of your research on others. For example, do not assume that everyone wants to be anonymous, or that they will not feel free to decline an invitation from a senior colleague to participate in a school-based research project.

5. Work on increasing benefit to participants as well as minimizing harm. The more potential benefit that teachers see in a research project, the more risks they will be prepared to take. For example, if colleagues understand how much more benefit will be gained from the research if it includes observations of their teaching, they may be more prepared to be observed.

SUMMING UP

In this chapter, we have discussed how validity is central to achieving the goals of PBM research. Those approaches to validity that either ignore teachers' own values and reasoning, or that treat them as unchallengeable, are not helpful to conducting research that is both respectful and rigorous. The concept of validity that we advocated integrates respect and rigor by using the standards of theoretical adequacy discussed in Chapter 2. We also outlined a range of steps that researchers can take to increase the validity of their own research: reducing selection bias, maintaining accurate records, establishing audit trails, using triangulation, and seeking feedback from research participants.

Finally, we discussed how ethical decision making is a problem-solving process that frequently involves resolving the tension between respectful treatment of participants and the conduct of rigorous research. We provided a case of how to resolve these tensions using the skills and values that are central to learning conversations. The chapter concludes with practical guidelines for ethical decision making.

PART II

Doing Practitioner Research

5

Planning
Your Research

Having decided to do research, busy teachers are often inclined to launch straight into data collection. Their first questions are often about who to interview, or whether or not to use a questionnaire. These questions cannot be answered, however, until numerous prior decisions have been made about the exact nature of the research questions and the approach that will be taken to answer them. This planning stage, which may also include a review of relevant literature, takes about 40 percent of the time and effort needed to complete a whole project. Data collection itself takes only about 20 percent of the total time, while making sense of and writing about the data, once it has been collected, takes up the remaining 40 percent. The "40-20-40 rule" indicates the relative importance of these three research phases. If you want to complete your research in one year, this rule tells you that you should spend approximately 20 weeks on each of the first and third phases, and only 12 weeks or so on the second phase. If you want to finish it in 10 weeks, then about four weeks should be spent on the first planning phase.

The 40–20–40 Rule

- 40 percent of your project is planning to collect the information.
- 20 percent of your project is collecting the information.
- 40 percent of your project is making sense of and writing about the information you have collected.

In this chapter we guide you through the seven key decisions involved in planning your research. We also provide a template that can be used to submit a project proposal to research supervisors, funding agencies, and governing bodies.

LEARNING FROM THE RESEARCH OF OTHERS

Many of you will not have the time to write a formal literature review as part of your research planning.[1] You should try, however, to read on the topic that interests you so that you can move beyond your own frame of reference and learn from the experience of others. Relevant professional and academic reading will help with all aspects of planning, including settling on a research question and the approach to take in answering it.

Practitioners who are unfamiliar with the published literature on a topic might prefer to access the experience of others by talking to relevant colleagues rather than by reading research. A school that has decided to tackle the problem of playground bullying, for example, might approach staff from similar schools who have tried a well-known anti-bullying program. The experienced staff can explain how they implemented the program and offer their opinions about its effectiveness.

It is important, however, to check such opinions against the published research literature. First, the experience of those spoken to may not be typical of all those who have used the anti-bullying program. Second, the information gained through published research is usually more reliable than that obtained through personal accounts because published reports have been subject to a process of quality control.

Research reports are not accepted for publication in most scholarly or professional journals unless experts in the relevant field have attested to their quality. One of the main jobs of such independent reviewers is to check that claims about such matters as the success of a particular program are based on sound reasoning and evidence. In contrast, teachers' claims about the success of a program are often based on their impressions of its impact.

In summary, reading relevant literature is worthwhile, because it provides you with a platform from which to plan your own study.

KEY PLANNING DECISIONS

There are seven key decisions to consider when planning your investigation. Since there are numerous dependencies between these decisions, they do not constitute a step-by-step sequence. Some will need to be considered

---

1. A number of excellent texts provide guidance on how to locate and read research, and how to complete a formal literature review; see for example Hart (1998, 2001) and Locke, Silverman, & Spirduso (2004).

simultaneously, while others will be revisited as the implications of earlier decisions become apparent.

Seven Key Planning Decisions

1. Establish the research question.

2. Design the study.

3. Select research methods for collecting information.

4. Decide how much information is needed.

5. Decide how to analyze the information.

6. Consider practicalities.

7. Incorporate collaborative processes.

Establishing the Research Question

In our experience, most teachers can nominate topics that they want to research. Teachers' daily experience presents them with a range of challenging practical problems, and a research project provides them with an opportunity to investigate them further. They may find it more difficult, however, to move from the practical problem or challenge to a workable research question.[2]

For example, a group of teachers may be interested in investigating students' learning styles. It is impossible for the teachers to plan their inquiry, however, until they have narrowed its focus. Do they want to know whether there is any merit in the claim that students have different learning styles? Do they want to learn how to assess students' learning styles? Perhaps their real interest is in how to teach in ways that suit the learning styles of their students. Settling on a research question, therefore, involves deciding exactly what it is that you want to know. What practical challenge or problem prompted your interest in this topic? What will you use the information for? Serious attempts to answer these questions, often in discussion with interested colleagues, will help you settle on the question that you really want to ask (see also Walliman, 2001, pp. 20–23).

Your research question is the anchor for all your planning because it provides important clues about how to make all the subsequent research decisions. For example, decisions about how to collect information cannot be made until it is clear just what information is needed. This latter decision is dependent on the wording of your research question. Since the research question is at the heart of any project, it is important to determine

---

2. Although we refer to a research "question," in many cases a research project will involve several research questions, depending on the nature and extent of the project.

whether you have a good research question. The following five criteria provide a way of checking:

1. Does your question capture exactly what you want to know?

2. Is the question specific enough to be manageable with the resources available?

3. Is the project likely to gain the necessary approval and cooperation of relevant others?

4. What is the practical importance of this question?

5. What is the theoretical importance of this question?

This checking can be done on your own, although in our experience, such checking is almost always better done in learning conversations with research participants because everyone needs to be confident that the research question captures what they really want to know. (The importance of learning conversations is discussed in Chapter 3, and Table 3.2 in that chapter provides an example of how to negotiate a research question with the people being researched.)

To check your research question against the first criterion, imagine some possible answers to the question you are posing, and then decide whether those answers provide the sort of information that you really want.

Developing a good research question usually involves making it more specific by clarifying what you mean by the key terms in your question. This second criterion also has implications for the manageability of your project. The chances of completing your inquiry in the time you have available are significantly enhanced if you can be specific about, for example, which teachers, what aspects of learning, or what aspects of student experience you are interested in. The third criterion is a reminder that it is important to check out at an early stage whether you are likely to gain the necessary approval and cooperation of key people in the school to successfully complete the project.

Table 5.1 provides an example of how to use these first three criteria to test the adequacy of a preliminary question about teachers' satisfaction with the procedures used for suspending students in their school.

Do not be dismayed if your question changes several times before you settle on one that meets these criteria. Since the research question shapes subsequent decisions about research design and methods, it is important to take the time needed to get it right.

The fourth criterion about "practical importance" is crucial in problem-based methodology (PBM) since the primary purpose of this approach is to do research in ways that contribute to the improvement of practice. Practical importance can be tested by asking such questions as "What practical difference is likely to be made by having an answer to the question?" "What decisions will be made differently as a result of answering this question?" "Does my question really address the problem I want to understand and try to resolve?"

Table 5.1 Testing a Research Question

Proposed research question: "How satisfied are teachers with the student suspension procedures used in this school?"	
Criterion	*Comments*
1. Does this question capture what I want to know?	• My answer could be in the form of x percent of teachers are satisfied, and y percent are not. Will such percentages tell me what I really want to know? Should I also find out teachers' reasons for their level of satisfaction? • Am I assuming that if teachers are *satisfied*, the student suspension system must be a good one? • Can I justify this assumption? • Maybe I am more interested in the *effectiveness* of the student suspension procedures than in teacher satisfaction. Maybe I am interested in both, but pursuing both may be too big a project.
2. Is the question specific enough to be manageable?	• What do I mean by student suspension *procedures?* Do I want to confine myself to procedures or do I want to study the overall policy and purpose as well as procedures? • What are all the procedures that are used in this school? Do I have the time and resources to study all of them? Which are likely to be the important ones in determining teacher satisfaction? Which of them am I really interested in? • Who do I include as *teachers?* Only classroom teachers and not those with administrative positions? Just full-time teachers?
3. Is the question likely to gain the necessary approval and cooperation?	• This is a sensitive area in my school. What do I know about the chances of getting cooperation of key stakeholders (for example, the principal) in the school?

Finally, practitioners who are keen to make a practical contribution through their research might wonder about the value of spending time trying to determine the "theoretical significance" of their research question. This fifth criterion is crucial, however, because published theory is a source of information for challenging and revising current theories of action. Without these resources, your theoretical horizon is limited to those ideas that are implicit or explicit in current practice. Additional theoretical resources enable you to challenge the "common sense" of practice and to envision new ways of doing things. For example, a teacher may be frustrated at the teacher evaluation system in her school. She may think about the problem from a purely technical point of view (the evaluation procedures are not clearly specified; the teachers need more training in understanding the evaluation system). If the teacher was familiar with the theoretical concept of organizational learning, however, she would have the option of thinking about the problem quite differently. She could ask questions such as "What is the purpose of the teacher evaluation system?" "How appropriate is the evaluation system for these purposes?" "How does the school learn and change on the basis of the feedback that teachers give to their evaluators?" Her knowledge of organizational learning raises new questions (about evaluation purposes), and provides her with an additional framework for evaluating what the school currently does.

When a research question is linked to a wider theoretical perspective, it is no longer just about a particular problem in a particular context. It is also about a set of ideas that are relevant to many different types of practical situations.

Designing the Study

The next step is to design your research by making decisions about the logic and organization of its various elements. A research design is a strategy for ensuring that the elements of your research—namely, its purpose, questions, and methods for information gathering and analysis—are aligned and coherent, so that you end up with valid answers to your questions (Maxwell, 1996). Rather than delve into the technical details of standardized research designs, most of which are not appropriate to PBM research, our purpose here is to help you understand how to develop coherent interrelationships between the various elements of your study.[3]

Linking Research Questions to a Research Design

The design of research in PBM is guided by its practical purposes—that is, the explanation, evaluation, and improvement of practice. In Chapter 2 we argued that in any particular instance this requires teacher-researchers to inquire into the theories of action of relevant practitioners. Such inquiry serves to open practice up to scrutiny and possible improvement by identifying the links between what teachers do (actions), why they do it (constraints on action), and the consequences (both intended and unintended) of their practice.

The key to research design in PBM, therefore, is knowing how to link particular types of research questions to one or more of these three components of a theory of action. There are three main decisions to be made:

1. Does your research question require you to investigate past, current, or future practice?

2. Which component or components of a theory of action does your research question require you to investigate?

---

3. There are excellent texts available on research design that are suitable for novice researchers. These include Leedy & Ormrod (2001) and Maxwell (1996).

3. Does your research question require you to both describe and evaluate theories of action?

Table 5.2 provides a guide to making these decisions. The first column classifies research questions according to the three components of a theory of action (for a detailed discussion on a theory of action, refer to Chapter 2), while the second and third columns show how each of these types of question are investigated.

Table 5.2   Linking Types of Research Questions to the Three Components of a Theory of Action

	Questions About Past or Current Practice	*Questions About Future Practice*
Questions About Constraints on Action	**A:** Questions that seek an explanation of past or current actions • *Describe relevant actions* and • *Identify constraints on these actions*	**D:** Questions about the requirements for future policy or practice • *Propose a new set of constraints*
Questions About Action	**B:** Questions about what is happening now or in the past • *Describe the relevant actions*	**E:** Questions about the nature of future policy or practice • *Identify the constraints to be satisfied* and • *Describe one or more policies or practices that would satisfy those constraints*
Questions About Consequences	**C:** Questions about the consequences of action • *Describe actions and identify the consequences of these particular actions* or • *Describe consequences and identify the action that explains these consequences*	**F:** Questions about the consequences of future actions • *Describe the future action* and • *Predict the likely consequences*

First, ask yourself whether your research question requires you to investigate past, current, or future practice. PBM is suitable for all such questions. Questions about current or past practice fall in the second column (Cell A, B, or C). For example, the question "How do teachers give feedback to their students?" is a question that requires a description of teachers' current practice (Cell B). The question "Why have teachers rejected the new school timetable?" requires an explanation of current practice (or past practice depending on your time frame), and requires investigation of the relevant constraints (Cell A). The question "Are staff satisfied with the leadership style of the new principal?" is a question that requires investigation of the consequences of the principal's current practice (Cell C).

You may wonder why we have included historical questions. Occasionally teacher-researchers want to investigate an action or policy that no longer exists but that may have current relevance. For example, a school may be considering developing student leadership by reviving a student council that has not met for several years. Before making the decision, the school may want to investigate why the council was established (Cell A), how it functioned, including why it stopped meeting (Cell B), and whether it fostered student leadership (Cell C).

If your research question is about future practice, it falls in one or more of the cells in the third column (Cells D, E, F). In PBM, questions about future practice are answered by designing a new or revised theory of action. For example, answering the question "How should we teach in order to improve student understanding of math problems?" requires specifying a new theory of action for math teaching that is likely to deliver the required improvement.

Second, decide which component or components of a theory of action your research question requires you to investigate. This decision rests on whether your research question requires you to *explain* what is or will be happening (questions about constraints on actions), to *describe* what is or will be happening (questions about actions), or to *describe* the consequences of current or future practice (questions about consequences).

Questions About Constraints on Actions. In order to answer explanatory questions about current practice, you must design a study that both describes the relevant actions and comes up with a plausible explanation of them by identifying the constraints that have ruled in those particular actions and ruled out the alternatives (Cell A). For example, a research question "Why do teachers interact more with boys than girls in the classroom?" requires you to design a study that describes how often teachers interact with boys as compared to girls and identifies the constraints that explain their pattern of interaction. Constraints are identified by interviewing people about their reasons for doing things and by observing the conditions under which the actions do and do not occur. Inferences are then made from this information about the constraint structures that explain the actions employed. In order to explain actions, therefore, you must investigate and show the relationship between constraints and actions.

Questions About Actions. Descriptive questions about current practice (Cell B) such as "How do teachers report to parents?" or "What are the main ways teachers give feedback to colleagues?" are answered by careful description of the relevant actions. Questions about future practice such as "How can teachers set up a professional learning community in their schools?" are answered by predicting or designing future actions that satisfy the proposed constraint sets (Cells E and D).

Teachers are frequently involved in the development of new policy and practice. Table 5.2 shows how this task can be completed as a research project. It may involve using published research and surveys of students, parents, and colleagues to identify the constraints that the new policy or practice should satisfy (Cell D). It could also involve proposing alternative ways of satisfying those constraints (Cell E). For example, the question "How can our school start a book club for students?" requires proposing constraints that the book club should meet (for example, led by students not staff, involves all year levels in the school) and developing a book club that meets those constraints. Research that addresses these types of questions should be designed as a collaborative exercise so that all affected parties can contribute to the identification of the relevant set of constraints and develop new actions, policies, or procedures that satisfy them.

Questions About Consequences. These types of research question are about the intended and unintended consequences of particular actions. Sometimes questions about consequences require you to work backward from particular outcomes (for example, student achievement) to discover the actions (for example, instructional practices or policies) that explain those consequences. Other questions require the reverse design, where current actions are carefully described and then the consequences are traced (Cell C). If, for example, you are interested in the consequences of a new curriculum, you could use the curriculum goals and your knowledge of teacher and student reaction to the curriculum to collect a range of information about its impact.

Still other questions involve predicting the consequences of future or proposed actions (Cell F). Predictions can be made on the basis of relevant experience and published research. The test of such predictions comes with trying out the new ideas and seeing if the consequences (Cell C) match what was predicted (Cell F). To continue the book club example, if the predicted consequence was that more students are encouraged to read, you would check whether students were actually more motivated to read. In all cases, investigation of consequences requires a research design that establishes the links between actions and consequences.

The third decision to be made about your research question is whether it includes an evaluative component. In other words, does your question require you to move beyond a relatively neutral account of others' theories of action to evaluate the adequacy of those theories and suggest alternatives?

When evaluation is contemplated, there is always an issue about whose values are the basis for the evaluation. Part of our criticism of what we called "Describe, Criticize, Recommend" (D-C-R) research (Chapter 3) was that the values of the people conducting the research were assumed to be preferable to those of the practitioners whose work was being critiqued. PBM avoids such assumptions by using values that are important to both the research participants and the teacher-researchers themselves. The values of research participants form the basis of the evaluation of the effectiveness of a theory of action. Any additional values that the teacher-researchers believe to be important form the basis of the evaluation of the coherence of the theory of action (see Chapter 2 for discussion of evaluation of theories of action).

Studies that address evaluative questions must be designed to meet the following two conditions. First, the study must investigate and evaluate the entire theory of action (cells A, B, and C in Column 2 in Table 5.2 for past or current practice, and cells D, E, and F in Column 3 in Table 5.2 for future practice), rather than just one or two components of it. This ensures appreciation of practitioners' values and understanding of the problem and thereby avoids the D-C-R approach. For example, you should not evaluate the consequences of someone's teaching without linking those consequences to their actual teaching practice and to the constraints that produced them. The constraints tell you what the teacher herself values, and this should form the basis of your evaluation of the effectiveness of her theory of action.

Second, if the teacher-researcher is going to bring additional evaluative criteria to bear (coherence), then these criteria should be made explicit in advance. The teacher-researcher can then use both sets of values to judge the current and alternative theories of action. For example, in evaluating the high school's policy on tracking (an example we introduced in Chapter 2), the teachers' intention to evaluate the extent to which lower-track students had equal access to resources should have been discussed in advance. The consequence of not disclosing and negotiating this additional value (equal access to resources) was that the principal could have felt ambushed by the teacher-researchers.

In summary, the initial stage of planning a research design involves identifying whether your research question involves investigation of past, present, or future practice. It also requires clarity about which parts of a theory of action need to be investigated. Finally, decisions are needed about whether the research questions incorporate an evaluative component, and if so, what values will form the basis of the evaluation. In Table 5.3 we reinforce the points we have made in this section and in Table 5.2 by showing how specific research questions address the three components of a theory of action and by identifying the resulting implications for research design.

Deciding What Information Is Required

Having linked your research question to a research design (as demonstrated in Tables 5.2 and 5.3), the next step is deciding exactly what information you require. This depends on whether your question is of the "exploratory" or the "checking" variety, whether it concerns aspects of

Table 5.3   From Research Question to Research Design

Research Question	Relevance to Theories of Action (Table 5.2)	Implications for Research Design
1. *What explains the amount of academic teaching teachers give their learning disabled students?*	Cell A: Reveal the constraints that explain teachers' actions	Requires • Identification of actions that indicate teachers' distribution of attention across the two groups • Discovery of the factors that explain teachers' distribution of attention across the two groups
2. *How much academic teaching is directed toward learning disabled students compared with non-learning disabled students in the same class?*	Cell B: Describe teachers' current actions	Requires • A definition of academic teaching • A description and comparison of academic teaching across two groups of students
3. *What impact has the new professional development program had on teachers' use of assessment data?*	Cell C: Describe consequences of the PD program	Requires • Identification of actions that indicate teachers' use of data • Collection of information about these actions, both before and after the program
4. *How well do I prepare my students for their science project?*	Cells A, B, and C: An evaluative question—requires description and evaluation of the teacher's theory of action for preparing the students to do their project	Requires • Description of how teacher currently prepares her students • Explanation of why the teacher does it this way • Identification of consequences of the preparation in terms of such things as student understanding of project objectives, quality of project, student satisfaction • Development of an evaluative framework for judging the adequacy of the theory of action for project preparation
5. *What is the best way to involve students in school governance?*	Cells D, E, and F: An evaluative question—requires design of a theory of action	Requires • Proposing relevant constraints (principles, practical conditions) • Designing policies and procedures for involving students that satisfy those constraints • Anticipating the consequences of the proposed policy and procedures
6. *How much responsibility do my teachers take for the achievement of their students?*		Question is not yet explicitly connected to practice. If teacher strategies and procedures indicative of taking responsibility are identified, then the question fits under Cell B.

teachers' espoused theories or theories in-use, and on the meaning of the key terms in your question.

Distinction Between Exploratory and Checking Questions. Exploratory questions ask what is happening, why, and with what consequences. Such questions involve an open-ended search for information. Examples of such exploratory questions are "How do you teach reading?" "What led you to teach it in this way?" and "What are the results of this way of teaching reading?"

Checking questions, by contrast, ask whether something in particular is happening. For example, checking questions that are parallel to the exploratory questions listed would be "Do you teach reading through a phonics approach?" "How important was district policy in your decision to teach reading this way?" and "What impact has phonics teaching had on reading comprehension?"

Exploratory research questions require a less structured research design than checking questions, because exploration requires the ability to pursue unanticipated lines of inquiry. With checking questions, the research can be designed quite precisely to yield only that information that enables researchers to make a judgment about the extent to which *particular* constraints, actions, or consequences are evident.

It is important not to set up an opposition between these two types of questions, as exploratory and checking questions can provide complementary perspectives. The former provide valuable insight into the values and understandings that shape the practices under investigation, while the latter provide an alternative theoretical perspective. Together, the two perspectives are a source of reciprocal critique and theory revision (see Chapter 6 for an extended discussion).

Information Needed for Espoused Theories and Theories-in-Use. Research questions that address theories-in-use require different sorts of information from those that address espoused theories. In Chapter 2, we explained that these are two types of theory of action. Theories-in-use describe and explain how people act (usually based on firsthand observations). By contrast, espoused theories are based on people's reports of what they do and why. Those self-reports may or may not provide accurate accounts of what people actually do or what they actually think. That is why the distinction between theory-in-use and espoused theory is needed.

The distinction has important implications for how you collect information and report your findings. If you want to investigate theories-in-use, you require information about actual practices and their consequences. Ideally, theories-in-use are inferred from observations of practice, or at least from corroborated reports of practice. Teachers' accounts of what they do in classrooms, for example, must be reported as teachers' perceptions, and not as what actually happens, unless their perceptions have been carefully checked. Questions that address theories-in-use require, on the whole, more firsthand information, gathered through observations, fieldwork, or recordings of events and activities, than do questions that address people's espoused theories (Argyris, Putnam, & McLain Smith, 1985). Espoused theories are investigated by asking people what they want or intend, or what they think is happening.

Specifying Key Terms. Decisions about what information is required cannot be made until key phrases in your research question have been clarified. For example, a question about "teacher interactions" could refer to verbal or nonverbal, academic or nonacademic, positive or negative, or any combination of these different types of interactions. If the phrase is intended to include all such interactions, then much more information will need to be collected than if it refers only to verbal, academic interactions. Sometimes published literature provides guidance in specifying key terms, by indicating important distinctions or providing useful definitions. When there is no relevant published literature, you will have to develop a definition using your own and colleagues' experience and wisdom.

In summary, deciding what information is required involves determining whether the questions are of the exploratory or checking variety, and whether they require investigation of teachers' espoused theories, theories-in-use, or both. The specification of key terms in the research question is also important in determining the type of information that is required. Once those preliminary decisions are made, consideration can be given to the methods that will be used to collect the required information.

Selecting Research Methods for Collecting Information

There are many different research methods you can use to collect the information you require. Interviews, questionnaires, surveys, and observations are some of the most common methods used in teacher research. Research methods should not be confused with research methodology. Research methodology is "the study—the description, the explanation, and the justification—of methods, and not the methods themselves" (Kaplan, 1964, p. 18). As discussed in Chapter 2, PBM is a methodology that is compatible with the use of many different research methods.

PBM also embraces both qualitative and quantitative methods. *Quantitative methods* produce information in numeric form, such as student achievement results and the number of people who voted for a student dress code. *Qualitative methods* produce information in textual form, such as interview transcripts, diaries, and student essays. The distinction between quantitative and qualitative is a fluid one, because, as we shall see in Chapter 8, qualitative data can be categorized, coded, and counted. Once counted it becomes quantitative data. One simple rule of thumb is that qualitative data is narrative and quantitative data is numeric.

The research methods section of textbooks often describes and illustrates the major methods of data collection, lists the advantages and disadvantages of their use, and then advises readers to pick the ones that are most appropriate to their needs. However, from our experience, teacher-researchers want more specific support than that. They want guidance in *how* to decide the most appropriate methods for their purposes.

Decisions about methods are based on a number of factors. First, knowledge of the variety of educational research methods is important. This knowledge is readily available from texts on educational and social research, and there are many such texts that are written for educational practitioners (Anderson, Herr, & Nihlen, 1994; Bell, 1999; Walliman, 2001). The purpose of such reading is to learn about the general advantages and disadvantages of particular research methods. For example, questionnaires are useful for obtaining standardized information from relatively large numbers of people. Questionnaires are structured in advance and solicit the same information from everyone involved, and the answers can be readily collated and counted. This approach is less suitable if in-depth investigation of people's attitudes and experience is required. In such cases, face-to-face individual or group interviews are the preferred choice, because they provide better opportunities for respondents to communicate what is important to them. Interviews have the disadvantage, however, of being time consuming and difficult to conduct and analyze.

Second, published research on your topic describes the methods that other investigators have used. These descriptions are usually found in the methods or methodology sections of the publication, and, in some cases, the actual questionnaire, interview schedule, or observation form is reproduced in the article. With adaptation, these instruments may be suitable for your investigation.

Third, the choice of method depends on whether you are investigating or evaluating constraints, actions, consequences, or any combination of them. The methods that are suitable for each are discussed under the three subsequent headings that follow.

Methods for Collecting Information About Constraints

Individual and group interviews are a good way to learn about the possible constraints that explain particular educational policies, procedures, or practices. Research questions that explore possible constraints require a relatively unstructured research method. For example, an interview that incorporates the following sorts of open-ended questions might be appropriate:

"What led you to do *X*?"

"What did you notice about the class?"

"Under what circumstances, if any, would you do *X*?"

"What are the factors that produced this policy or practice?"

"What are the reasons why you/the organization do not use [an alternative policy or practice]?"

More structured interviews are appropriate when the research question probes the importance of particular constraints. Some useful interview questions might include:

"To what extent is X a factor in how you teach this subject?"

"Did you notice [the particular factor]?"

"Was [money] important to you?"

"To what extent did [accountability pressures] shape this policy?"

Similarly, if likely constraints are known in advance, participants could be asked to indicate the relative importance of a list of possibilities.

It is important to recognize that interviews provide information about *perceived* constraints. You cannot claim that reported constraints actually caused the relevant practices unless you have used other methods to cross-check and supplement the interview data. For example, in her study on reporting to parents that we introduced in Chapter 2, Viviane, the first author of this book, asked teachers to explain the way they had written their school reports. The teachers' explanations included the concern of the school administration to be positive and protect self-esteem. They also talked about how the limited assessment information available in some subjects constrained what they could reprot (Robinson & Timperley, 2000). They did not talk about the importance of the grading categories printed on the report and the spaces provided for teachers' comments, yet those factors were also powerful determinants of their patterns of reporting. Features of the daily environment are often overlooked when people are asked to explain what they did. That is one reason why there is often a difference between reported and actual constraints. Teacher-researchers' firsthand observations can provide clues about the constraints that are important but are not readily reported by their interviewees.

Methods for Describing Actions

Decisions about how to collect information about actions are made in a similar manner to those for constraints. If the research question requires information about what happened, it is preferable to obtain a firsthand record through observation or recording. If this is not possible, reports of what happened that are corroborated by asking others or by checking documentary records could be adequate. Uncorroborated reports of what happened contribute to an espoused theory of action. This may be sufficient if the research question can be answered with information about what people recall or believe to have happened. Decisions are also required about whether interviews or observations should be structured to focus on particular actions or activities. These decisions turn on whether the research question is of the exploratory or checking variety.

Methods for Gaining Information About Possible Consequences

We earlier indicated that research questions about consequences can involve you working backward from known outcomes to discover the actions that explain those consequences. Alternatively, the reverse design can be employed, where actions are documented and the consequences are subsequently investigated. In the latter case, one never knows what constitutes a consequence of a particular policy or practice until one has completed the investigation and made a case for the relationship. Nevertheless, some decisions need to be made about where to look for possibilities. With exploratory questions a wide net should be cast, possibly through interviewing people about their perceptions of the intended and unintended consequences of particular practices. If a theory-in-use analysis is required, then these perceptions will also need to be cross-checked against other relevant information, such as that gained through observation, analysis of relevant records, or administration of various types of tests and assessments. Since checking questions propose specific consequences to be investigated, they can be addressed by a more structured and focused approach to data collection. For example, if "teaching to the test" is believed to be an unintended consequence of an accountability policy, then information about particular types of teaching and assessment is required to answer the question.

Deciding the Sequence

After you have chosen your research methods, you need to decide the sequence in which you will use the different methods you have chosen. For example, if you want to explain particular actions, you first need to document these actions before asking teachers about their perceptions of the relevant constraints. This enables both interviewer and teacher to see whether or not the proposed explanations make sense. Alternatively, if you want to discover the actions that produced a particular consequence, you would first document the consequence and then work backward to try to identify the actions that caused it. In designing a new practice, you can either determine the consequences you want and then design a practice that will achieve them, or you can determine the important constraints and then design a way of satisfying them.

Selecting Research Methods: An Example

The following example shows how a principal integrates her general knowledge of research methods with the requirements of her particular research question to reach a decision about how to collect information that might explain the trash being dropped in the school playground. Despite several schoolwide initiatives, she is puzzled about why the problem persists. She wants to know why students drop trash rather than put it in one of the numerous trash cans.

Her desire to explain why students were dropping trash indicates that she should select a research method that will enable her to discover the constraints on students' actions. The principal knows that the common methods for obtaining information about possible constraints include interviews and questionnaires. An interview would reveal in-depth information about why students drop trash, but the principal worries about whether students are likely to be honest with her. Questionnaires have the advantage of anonymity, but previous experience tells her that students tend to write short and superficial comments, which will tell her little about why they continue to drop trash. How can she obtain in-depth information about the possible constraints involved while protecting the privacy of students? She could still use interviews, but ask an external researcher to conduct them. Alternatively, she could involve students themselves in the project and have them interview each other.

A limitation of interviewing is the number of students that can be included in the time available. She could survey the whole student population, but then she would face the problem of superficial information. Since rich information about students' attitudes and beliefs is a priority, she decides to start her data collection with students interviewing their peers using a variety of open-ended questions. Once she has a better sense of the relevant constraints, a subsequent, more structured questionnaire that investigates the importance of particular constraints on students' actions could be distributed to the whole student population.

Deciding How Much Information Is Needed

There is always more relevant information available than can be collected and analyzed in the course of one investigation. Selection, or sampling of information is, therefore, another important step in research planning.

Practitioners typically think of sampling in conjunction with people. "How many teachers should I interview?" "Should I ask every parent to complete the survey or just some of them?" "If the latter, then how should I decide which ones to select?" Sampling, however, involves more than just deciding who to talk to. It applies to all sources of information where a portion, rather than the total available information, is used. For example, imagine a senior teacher who wants to study how teachers who have been trained in a particular language arts program are implementing it in their classrooms. She will need to decide not only which teachers she should observe and interview, but also which lessons to observe and how many. All of these are sampling decisions because she is selecting rather than using all the available relevant information.

There are three key principles that you can apply to sampling decisions:

1. What is the group (for example, students, teachers, lessons, meetings) that you want your sample to represent? (generalizability)

2. What size of sample is practically possible? (practicality)

3. What is credible in the eyes of relevant decision makers? (credibility)

Sampling decisions are required when you "wish to make a generalization about a whole class of cases and have observed only some of them . . . " (Kaplan, 1964, p. 239). The "class of cases" may be all teachers in your school, or all the students in your class, or all meetings held by the board this year. The "class of cases" (technically known as *the population*) to which you want to generalize should be decided as you confirm your research question. In the case of the senior teacher just mentioned, she wanted to generalize to all teachers who had completed the training in the new language arts program. This meant that the relevant population was the 16 teachers who completed the program. Since it was impractical for her to talk to all 16 teachers, the senior teacher had to decide how to select the ones to interview.

The real challenge here is how to select the teachers in a way that those interviewed and observed are, as far as possible, representative of all 16 (the relevant population). In order to meet this requirement, you need to know something about the characteristics of the relevant population. In this case, the senior teacher is likely to know that implementation differs widely across teachers, depending on their attitude to the program. It makes sense, then, to recruit a sample of teachers who represent positive, neutral, and negative attitudes toward the program.

A good test of whether a proposed sample is adequate for the purpose of understanding and improving a particular practice is to check whether the sampling decision will be viewed as credible by the people whose practice you wish to influence. If they believe too few people or events have been selected, or that those chosen are biased in some relevant way, then a different approach to sampling may be required. For instance, in the example just mentioned, if the principal of the school believes that the research is only credible if three-quarters of the teachers (that is, 12 teachers) are interviewed, but the senior teacher only has time to sample half the teachers, she will need to enter into a learning conversation with the principal about how to select the teachers. The new sample might be negotiated after discussion of such questions as "What makes a sample of 12 teachers more credible than eight teachers?" "Is there another way credibility can be established with fewer teachers?" and, if so, "How might this be done?"

On the whole, the more variety evident in the population of interest, the larger the sample should be, especially if the variations are likely to affect your research findings. The more diverse the 16 teachers, the bigger the sample will need to be. This is particularly true if the diversity is in areas that may affect the implementation of the new language arts program, such as their support of the program, and their years of experience as a teacher.

Remember, however, that sampling is only one means to establishing credibility in the eyes of relevant decision makers. In Chapter 4, we discussed other means of increasing the credibility of your research that should be used in addition to the sampling decisions. It is also useful to remember that there are no hard and fast rules about how many people or events should be studied. Where possible, sampling decisions should be made in learning conversations with the people whose practice you seek to influence, such as in the example we described previously (see also Table 3.2 for similar examples). In such conversations, the aim is to make a decision that is practical, yet will produce credible and generalizable findings.

In introducing this section on sampling, we observed that sampling applies to every aspect of information gathering, and not just to the selection of people. In the previous example, the senior teacher, having decided how to select the teachers for inclusion in the study, must still address the question of which (and how many) of her colleagues' lessons to observe. You would use the same three principles of generalizability, practicality, and credibility to make such decisions. In our example, the senior teacher would look at the type of lessons she wishes to generalize to. Does she want to generalize to all lessons that were part of the language arts program? If she does, she needs to select the number and type of lessons that will be representative of all lessons in the program. If this is not practically possible, she may choose to focus on one type of lesson only. If the decision makers feel that this is too little, they may need to have a learning conversation about how to resolve the matter.

These three principles of generalizability, practicality, and credibility provide a rationale for the numerous decisions needed when planning research about how to select the required information. If they are kept in mind, you will be better placed to make selection decisions that recognize practical limitations while gaining credibility with relevant audiences.

Deciding How to Analyze the Information

Having established what information you require, a further aspect of research planning involves deciding how you will analyze the information once it has been collected. (Data analysis is discussed in Chapter 8.) In fact, decisions about data collection and data analysis go hand in hand, since the type of data you gather will, to a large extent, determine the type of analysis that is appropriate. For example, an exploratory approach to information gathering that uses open-ended questions places different demands on analysis than a structured approach that uses predetermined categories. In an exploratory approach, considerable work will be needed after the information has been collected to organize and summarize the variety of responses. To illustrate, an open-ended question such as "Why do teachers support the new principal?" will yield a large variety of answers such as "He's nice," "He has a democratic style," and "He listens to me," which will need to summarized in some way before you can answer your research question.

In the structured approach, analysis is often easier because the hard decisions about how to interpret the information have been made in advance of collecting it. To continue with the previous example, rather than ask teachers why they support the new principal, you might create some reasons for this support (for example, "He values teachers' opinions," and "He supports innovative teaching approaches") and get teachers to select which of these reasons apply to them. The challenge with this approach is to make sure that you have written all (or close to all) the reasons teachers will have for supporting the new principal, so it is best used when you are already familiar with the types of issues and information that are likely to be raised. You would use research and/or prior experience to judge whether you have sufficient information to take a structured approach.

Considering Practicalities

Any investigation is governed by the practicalities of the situation—for example, how much time do you have? How much money can you spend? Will you have access to all the necessary documents? Sometimes this results in a tension between your "ideal" research design and the reality of your situation. When faced with resolving this tension, the basic principle is to choose a design closest to your ideal that will get you the information you are looking for.

This could mean scaling down the size of your research by investigating fewer people or events, using less time-consuming methods, or focusing on a few cases. For example, you might want to conduct observations of teachers teaching reading before and after a professional development program, but find that the professional development has already begun. You can still make the comparison by asking teachers to recall what they did before the professional development and comparing their self-reports to observations of their teaching during and after the professional development. However, because you are aware of the limitations of self-reports, you should also seek corroborating evidence. This solution enables you to investigate the effects of professional development, despite the fact that you could not observe what happened before the program began.

Other creative solutions include dividing your investigation into two parts, where you conduct one part of your research in one year and the second part in the subsequent year. You could also increase your resources and your learning by working in a team and by involving an outside expert or adviser.

Incorporating Collaborative Processes

Planning for collaboration will increase the chances that your research will be valued and acted upon. This involves identifying the people that need to be given the opportunity to influence and become committed to your study. Normally those people are the participants and anyone else who has control over the practices you are investigating. At what points will you seek their involvement? Whose help and feedback do you need? Who can give you honest and constructive criticism? Who will not take for granted the things that you take for granted? Who should be given the opportunity to critique your draft report?

Table 5.4 provides a useful guide to help you answer these questions. This negotiation checklist outlines the conditions that PBM researchers negotiate at the outset of a research project. The checklist acts like a prompt

Table 5.4   The Negotiation Checklist for a PBM Research Project

Identify those in your research setting(s) who control access to the information and the decisions relevant to your project.

1. Seek shared ownership of the research question or problem:
   - Which practitioners or groups seek answers to the research question?
   - Why is the question of interest to them?
   - Why is it of interest to you?
   - How does each party explain and evaluate the relevant practices?
   - What limits do practitioners anticipate on their ability to improve the practice?
   - Explain how both your own and practitioners' theories about the relevant practices will be checked and challenged in the course of the project.

2. Discuss what you can offer:
   - An accurate description of the existing practice
   - An analysis of the current practice
   - A negotiated framework for its evaluation
   - Feedback at key stages of the project
   - A rigorous and respectful process

3. Explain your requirements:
   - The conditions that need to be in place so that you can do the project
   - The need for a question that is manageable
   - Information on who else should collaborate
   - Information on who else needs to be informed
   - Information you need access to
     - Documents
     - Interviews
     - Access to settings for observation
   - The opportunity to spend time with others
     - When
     - Where
     - Who
   - The opportunity to discuss draft findings as part of their validation
   - The opportunity to publish or disseminate findings

4. Identify practitioners' requirements:
   - Need to be kept informed
   - Confidentiality of data
   - Anonymity: use of real names or pseudonyms
   - Time availability
     - When
     - Where
     - Who
   - Limits to time and commitment
   - Type of feedback/reporting desired
   - Perceptions of the possible risks of becoming involved; for example, no-go boundaries, reaction to possible critique of current theories, adverse publicity
   - Desired end point: What counts as success for the participants?
   - Opportunity to discuss draft findings as part of their validation
   - Opportunity to be involved in the publication of findings (for example, review reports before publication, be a coauthor)

for the teacher-researcher who is first negotiating the project with colleagues. The negotiation process may occur in stages and be revisited as the project progresses. We recommend the use of this checklist, even by those teacher-researchers who are studying aspects of their own setting or working with close colleagues. Discussion of the negotiation checklist identifies the expectations of each party and highlights any points of difference at an early stage. It also clearly communicates the values of respect for those being researched, the rigor of the research process, and the relevance of the research to those being researched. These are the "bottom lines" of the negotiation process.

In the conversation in Table 5.5, we illustrate how an aspect of a proposed study is negotiated in a learning conversation. The conversation is about a teacher-researcher, Joseph, trying to research what children do in a particular type of lesson. He wants to observe in several classrooms, but a young teacher, Aimee, has real concerns about letting him observe her teaching. Joseph respects and explores those concerns without giving up his need for a rigorous research process.

The conversation exemplifies a learning conversation (see Chapter 3 for discussion of learning conversations) because the concerns of both parties have been explored without privileging those of either party, and they will work together openly to test whether or not to go ahead with the research.

WRITING A RESEARCH PROPOSAL

For those involved in formal projects, the culmination of all these planning decisions is the writing of the research proposal. Even if a formal proposal is not required, writing a research proposal offers practitioners a useful way of clarifying their ideas and communicating them effectively to colleagues. The format for such a proposal varies depending on its purpose and audience. The example we present in this chapter has been developed specifically to help practitioners who are undertaking a PBM project.

The written proposal signals completion of the planning phase of your project. It means you are 40 percent of the way toward completing your project!

The Proposal Template

The template consists of nine sections covering the main decisions that need to be thought through prior to the investigation. In order to write each section, you need to have worked through the key decisions in this chapter and read relevant material in other chapters. The completed template provides a written record of all these planning decisions. The sections are (1) research topic, (2) research question(s), (3) research setting, (4) researcher's relationship to the setting, (5) collaborative processes, (6) research design, (7) methods for collecting information, (8) methods for analyzing information, and (9) research timetable.

Table 5.5   Getting Permission to Observe a Colleague's Classroom

Conversation	Analysis
Joseph: I'd like to observe in your classroom to get some firsthand information about what the children are doing.	Joseph discloses wish to observe and gives a reason.
Aimee: I would have thought that my reports were detailed enough to tell you what was going on.	Aimee challenges adequacy of Joseph's reason.
Joseph: They may well be, but independent observations will provide a cross-check on what you have found. Do you have some concerns about my coming into the classroom?	Joseph acknowledges that Aimee's view is reasonable, and provides a further reason for making observations. Joseph checks his belief that Aimee is concerned about classroom observation.
Aimee: Well, I don't want anything done that could jeopardize my job here. I'm only in a temporary position.	Aimee hints at a link between being observed and job security.
Joseph: How do you think being observed might be harmful to you?	Joseph facilitates expression of Aimee's concerns about being observed.
Aimee: Well, if the principal knew that there were problems in my classroom. . . .	
Joseph: And you think he might find out through this research?	Joseph checks his understanding of Aimee's theory.
Aimee: Yes, I suppose so.	
Joseph: I certainly don't want to jeopardize your job, and I won't be talking to your principal without your permission. It's a dilemma, isn't it—I'm saying I need the observations in order to check the quality of your information, and you may be saying, "How can I trust you enough to let you into my classroom?"	Joseph lays out the apparent conflict between the two positions. Joseph attributes concerns about trust to Aimee and checks.
Aimee: Yes, that's it. Maybe if I knew a bit more about what you want to do, and we could work closely together, I wouldn't feel so vulnerable.	Aimee confirms Joseph's understanding and suggests a possible solution.
Joseph: Are you saying that if we discuss this in more detail, you might feel differently about my presence in the classroom?	Joseph tests his understanding of Aimee's prior statement.
Aimee: Yes.	
Joseph: Well, let's do that and then see how we both feel about going ahead.	Joseph suggests that they test whether further discussion can resolve the issue to the satisfaction of both parties.

In the remainder of this chapter we discuss how to record your earlier planning decisions in the proposal template. The discussion is followed by an example of a completed research proposal prepared by a group of teacher-researchers.

Research Topic

In this section, you show that you are aware of the various literatures and debates that are relevant to your topic and indicate how your project fits into this general landscape. If you are not writing a literature review as part of your project, you should have read enough, or discussed your topic with enough colleagues, to know how your study fits into the topic as a whole.

Research Question

In this section, you specify the research question(s) you are investigating and state its practical and theoretical importance.

Research Setting

The purpose of this section is to demonstrate that your research is feasible in the setting that you propose to work in. (A setting could be a classroom, a school, a group of schools, the district office, or a parent or community organization of some kind.) After a brief general introduction to the type of setting in which you are working, provide more specific detail about the practices that are the focus of your study. Who is involved in those practices and what are their relevant responsibilities? Briefly describe the history of the issue in this particular setting.

Researcher's Relationship to the Setting

In this section you should describe any involvement you have with the setting you are studying and whether this relationship poses any risks to the independence of your research. You should also briefly describe the steps you will take to reduce the identified risks.

Collaborative Processes

This section indicates how you will seek permission to conduct your research in accord with the formal processes required by either your research setting, any funding agencies, or any academic institution with which your research is associated.

Whether or not institutional approvals are required, you should also indicate the negotiation processes that you are incorporating to ensure your research is conducted collaboratively.

Research Design

Write several paragraphs describing the research design you have chosen and the reasons for choosing that design. To design the research, use Tables 5.2 and 5.3 as a guide.

Methods for Collecting Information

Explain the information you need to answer each of your research questions. Justify your methods for collecting the information in terms of the three components of a theory of action (constraints, actions, and consequences), the degree to which you need to take an unstructured or structured approach, and whether your question requires an answer at the level of espoused theory or theory-in-use or both. (An espoused theory is what people say they do and their explanations for their actions, while a theory-in-use is what they actually do and the real reasons for their actions.) If you will be sampling rather than using all the available information, you also need to describe and justify your sampling decisions.

Methods for Analyzing Information

Refer back to your design to explain briefly how you will analyze your data in ways that establish the links among constraints, actions, and consequences (we explain how to do this in Chapter 8). You should also describe how you will maximize the validity of your analysis (see Chapter 4).

Research Timetable

The last section of your proposal is a draft timetable for completing your study. The first step in making a timetable is to enter the dates of any commitments to the participants, supervisors, and funding agencies. Then, using the 40-20-40 rule, you should allocate the remaining time to the various tasks involved in planning, data collection, analysis, and reporting.

The timetable also needs to be flexible enough to take account of changes to the research question or to the research setting. Even if you have to revise the timetable several times, it is important to use it to help you make the space to complete your research in a timely and satisfying manner.

A sample proposal is provided in Figure 5.1.

SUMMING UP

The key to finding the time for research is good planning. With good planning, your research activity becomes more efficient because you know the questions that are being asked and the information that is required to answer them.

In this chapter we have discussed the seven key decisions that are involved in planning your research. These decisions focus on establishing a workable research question and choosing an appropriate research design, selecting the methods that you will use to collect the information and addressing sampling issues, deciding how to analyze the information, factoring in practicalities, and planning for collaboration. In addition, we

(Text continues on page 104)

Figure 5.1   The Four Cs Philosophy at Cockle Bay School

---

1   Research Topic

- *What is your general topic?*
- *Where does your project fit within the landscape of this topic?*

As schools today strive to differentiate themselves from others and to establish a competitive advantage, they are beginning to examine school culture and philosophy as a possible source of such an advantage. Research suggests that one of the key contributors to the impact of any philosophy is the consistency of how the philosophy has been implemented (Deal & Peterson, 1999). For this reason, schools are increasingly interested in research that looks at how to improve the effectiveness of program implementation. Our project will enable us to comment on the overall effectiveness of a particular school philosophy and on the consistency of its implementation in one elementary school.

---

2   Research Questions

- *State your specific questions.*
- *What is the practical importance of these questions?*
- *What is the theoretical importance of these questions?*

Questions

1. How is the Four Cs philosophy implemented?

2. What explains the level of implementation?

3. How adequate is the philosophy?

Practical Importance of These Questions

Cockle Bay School takes pride in its strong sense of direction and commitment to creating a quality learning environment. The effectiveness and implementation of the philosophy upon which the Four Cs are based is a critical success factor in achieving this type of learning environment. The principal's leadership style is seen as visionary by the Education Review Office (1998) and by his peers and subordinates. The Four Cs are given great emphasis through staff training, induction programs, and also annual student seminars based on this philosophy. The amount of time, effort, and expense that is placed on these four guidelines for behavior indicates the practical importance of researching their effectiveness and implementation.

Theoretical Importance of These Questions

Every school has a distinct culture, and that culture has a tremendous influence on life and learning in the school. Studies have been conducted that suggest there are two types of cultures present—simultaneously—in many organizations (Buch & Wetzel, 2001). There is said to be an "espoused culture" and a "true culture" (Schein, 1999). When there is a gap between the two types of culture, a misalignment exists that can be very harmful to the organization and its members. Through our research questions, we may be able to identify such cultural misalignments and present some initiatives or suggestions to attempt to reduce them.

Figure 5.1 (Continued)

---

3   Research Setting

Describe the setting or settings you will be working in. Give a brief history of the problem or issue as it relates to the setting. Include a description of the roles and relevant responsibilities of those who control and engage in the practices you will be studying.

Cockle Bay School is a coeducational, elementary school in East Auckland. The school has a roll of 676 and the majority of students are of European descent. There is currently a total of 38 teaching staff covering classes from Year 0–6.

The Four Cs philosophy began as a vision statement developed by a former principal. Initially he presented his Three Cs as:

1. Caring for the environment

2. Caring for each other

3. Continuous improvement

This philosophy was subsequently revised to include the fourth C:

4. Cooperation

Together these four Cs are presented at the beginning of each year to staff and students alike. Classes are required to display a copy of the Four Cs.

Any changes to the Four Cs must be discussed by senior management before being presented to team leaders and finally to the school as a whole.

The philosophy is schoolwide and attracts favorable comment from the community and from education authorities.

---

4   Researchers' Relationship to the Setting

- *What relationship do the researcher(s) have with the research setting?*
- *Are there potential conflicts of interest and, if so, how will they be mitigated?*

The researchers are three teacher-researchers conducting the research as part of a research course at the local university. Two of the three members are teachers at other schools, so there is no conflict of interest or prior relationship with the research setting. The only possible conflict of interest arises from one of the researchers being a teacher at the school in the Year 6 level. This should not pose too much of a problem except perhaps in interviewing colleagues. To avoid this conflict we will focus our research at the Year 5 and Year 2 levels. We will also exclude this researcher from the interview stage where an existing relationship might affect the interviewee responses.

---

5   Collaborative Processes

- *What permissions do you need to conduct your study? How will you obtain them?*
- *Describe any additional contracting processes you will use to:*
  - *Gain access to the required information*
  - *Involve practitioners in the conduct of your study*
  - *Increase practitioners' commitment to using the findings*

Permission for the study will need to be obtained from both the principal and the teachers involved. These will be obtained through consent forms.

Meetings will also be held with teachers to identify what they wish to learn from the study and to gain feedback on the research proposal.

Figure 5.1 (Continued)

---

6   Research Design

Explain how your research design fits the problem-based methodology (PBM) framework. Justify your design with reference to your research questions.

1. *How is the Four Cs philosophy implemented?* This question will be answered by *describing* the ways in which the principal, teachers, and students put the philosophy into practice. The consistency of implementation will be determined by seeing whether the variety of routines that teachers use are compatible with the values and principles that underpin the Four Cs philosophy. Do all teachers discipline children, for example, in the manner suggested by the philosophy?

2. *What explains the level of implementation?* The implementation of the philosophy will be explained by discovering the *constraints* that determine the level to which teachers use routines that are consistent with the philosophy. These constraints might include school policy and procedures, and teacher attitudes toward and understanding of the philosophy.

3. *How adequate is the philosophy?* Adequacy will be judged according to whether the philosophy achieves its own goals of a cooperative caring environment, and whether or not teachers believe it to be effective. This will require information on the *consequences* of the philosophy. We will focus on students' understanding of and commitment to the Four Cs and on information on student behavior that is already available in the school (for example, discipline breaches, merit awards). The researchers will also judge adequacy through the improvability criterion, that is, whether the school leadership is open to critical examination and feedback, so that the philosophy can be reviewed and if necessary changed. The following flow chart outlines how this research fits into the PBM framework.

Constraints

The constraints explain how the philosophy is implemented

Actions

What the staff do to implement this philosophy in the learning environment

Consequences

- Indicators of student behavior
- Student understanding of the Four Cs
- Degree of critical reflection on the Four Cs

Figure 5.1 (Continued)

---

7   **Methods for Collecting Information**

- *What information is required to answer your research questions? Explain whether this information concerns constraints, actions, or consequences.*

- *How will this information be obtained? Describe the sources of the information and the methods you will use to gather it.*

- *How will the information be selected from all the possible sources of relevant information?*

First, we need information about the methods of implementation of the Four Cs. We will gather this information through teacher interviews and cross-check those self-reports with some playground and classroom observations. The consistency of implementation of the Four Cs will be judged through a rating system. Two members of the team will independently rate each teacher for consistency of implementation, on the basis of their interview transcripts.

The second question will be answered by interviewing teachers about their understanding of and commitment to the philosophy. Interviews will be carried out on six teachers over two year levels: Year 2 and Year 5. These grade levels were chosen because the researchers do not teach at these levels of the school. The six teachers chosen will be those who have been at the school the longest. The principal will also be interviewed about how he interprets the philosophy in the school.

The consequences of the philosophy will be studied by (1) asking teachers and the principal about the impact of the philosophy, (2) asking students to talk about a playground incident and rating the extent to which they interpret it consistently with the philosophy, and (3) seeing whether indicators of student behavior and misbehavior (for example, discipline breaches) vary according to the level of implementation reported by class teachers.

The adequacy of the Four Cs philosophy will be evaluated by judging whether it has delivered what was intended (effectiveness), whether it has led to other positive or negative unintended consequences (coherence), and whether the school is able to reflect critically on the adequacy of the philosophy (improvability).

---

8   **Methods for Analyzing Information**

Describe how you will analyze your data. Include a description of:

- *How you will sort your data into the relevant components of a theory of action*

- *How you will ensure the validity of your analysis*

Our data will be divided into three main types. All of the information from teacher questionnaires and interviews will be sorted into reports of constraints, actions, or consequences.

The actions will be described to show the links between school policies and what teachers actually do in the classroom and playground. These patterns of activity will be explained by checking whether there are consistent links between teachers' attitudes toward and understandings of the philosophy and what they actually do. We will also establish how teacher practices are constrained by school routines and procedures. Finally, consequences will be linked to implementation practices.

Ratings of teacher implementation will be made independently by two of the three researchers. The same procedure will be used to check the reliability of the ratings of student understandings of the philosophy.

The accuracy of the researchers' description of the school's theory of action will be checked through feedback to the school. Staff will be encouraged to identify possible inaccuracies or alternative explanations that may have been missed.

Figure 5.1 (Continued)

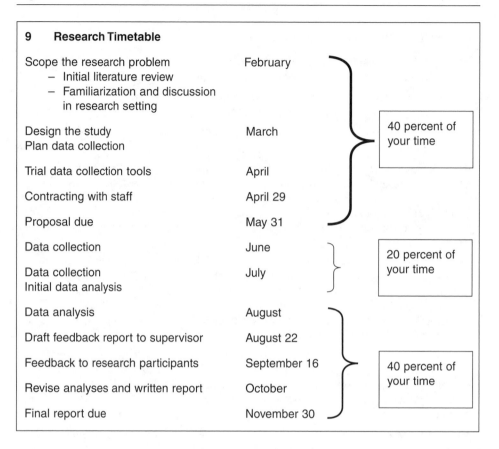

have provided a template that can be used to record these planning decisions. For those doing a formal research project, this template can be used to submit a project proposal to research supervisors, funding agencies, or governing bodies. If a formal proposal is not required, the template offers practitioners a useful way of clarifying their ideas and communicating them effectively to colleagues.

6

Purposeful Information Gathering

Interviews and Questionnaires

Teachers are continually gathering information to inquire into aspects of practice. They survey parents about what they like about the school and what they want changed; they ask students to explain how they have understood the lesson; they watch who speaks up and who is silent in the classroom. This chapter builds on teachers' existing information-gathering skills by explaining how to gather information that is directly relevant to their research questions and how to do so as efficiently as possible. The need for efficiency is suggested by our 40-20-40 rule (introduced in Chapter 5), where 20 percent refers to the proportion of your project that should be devoted to information gathering.

The chapter develops themes that were introduced in Chapter 5 about how to decide what information is required and how to collect it. If you have followed the planning process in Chapter 5, you will have already selected the appropriate methods to collect information on actions, constraints, and consequences (the three components of a theory of action) and will now be ready to develop the data collection tools for your chosen methods. In this chapter, we focus on designing data collection tools for two methods that are commonly used in problem-based methodology (PBM) studies—interviews and questionnaires. We discuss interviews first, followed by questionnaires. In Chapter 7, we discuss several other methods that are common in PBM studies—observations, rating scales, documents, and diaries. We encourage you to use more than one of these methods so that you can verify the information collected. We therefore recommend that you read both chapters, even if at this stage you are planning to collect information using only interviews and questionnaires. We also encourage you to read the section in the following chapter on testing your data collection tool, as this section applies equally to interviews and questionnaires.

DESIGNING INTERVIEWS

Learning how to develop and conduct a successful interview is an important skill, as much teacher work depends on the ability to get good information from talking with people. Job interviews and teacher evaluations are examples of structured, formal conversations in which it is important to obtain high-quality information. Listening to parental concerns, questioning students about their understanding of a lesson, or talking to a senior manager about the merits of purchasing a particular resource are examples in which it is just as important to get high-quality information, even though the conversations will be relatively unstructured and informal. Teachers who learn how to conduct successful research interviews are likely to become better listeners and better information gatherers in many of these on-the-job situations.

In the first part of this section on interviews, we discuss how to decide what information is needed. In the subsequent parts, we discuss how to write the interview questions, how to sequence and group the questions, and how to conduct the interview itself.[1]

What Information Do You Need?

An effective planning process clarifies the information that is needed to answer the research questions. As discussed in Chapter 5, you may have already made decisions about how the research question links to one or more components of a theory of action, about whether exploratory or checking questions are required, and about whether information is needed on the practitioners' espoused theories, theories-in-use, or both. Once these decisions are made, it is relatively easy to write the interview questions.

We review the process of moving from research question to interview question by reflecting on our study of copying among Chinese university students studying in New Zealand (Robinson & Lai, 1999). The study was motivated by Viviane's concern at the number of Chinese students who were coming before the university's discipline committee for copying in tests and exams. Mei, herself Chinese, was also aware of some peer

---

1. An excellent classic text on interviewing is Kahn & Cannell (1957).

subcultures among Chinese students where copying of assignments was taken for granted. As we began to explore the issue, we realized that while many university staff had strongly held views about why this happened (difficulties with the English language, family pressure to succeed), it was important to test these theories by asking students themselves. If we knew more about why students copied, we could collaborate with them to change their practice.

The first of our research questions ("How do these Chinese students complete their assignments?") required information about actions, while the second question ("What explains their completion strategies?") required information about the constraints that explained their assignment completion strategies (Table 6.1).

Table 6.1   Planning an Interview Schedule

Research Questions	Relevance to Theories of Action	Type of Question	Possible Interview Questions
1. How do these Chinese students complete their assignments?	Actions	Exploratory	"Take your last assignment in math. Can you tell me how you completed that assignment?"
1.1 Do they copy?	Actions	Checking through a follow-up probe question	"Copying sections of friends' assignments sometimes happens in this course. Did you copy any part of this assignment?"
2. What explains their completion strategies?	Constraints	Exploratory	"What factors led you to complete the assignment as you did?"
2.1 What explains their copying?	Constraints	Exploratory	"Why did you copy this assignment?"
2.2 How do students feel about copying?	Constraints	Exploratory	"How do you feel about the fact that you copied that assignment?"
2.3 What knowledge do students have of university regulations?	Constraints	Checking	"Do you know the university's regulations on copying?" "How important were they in your decision to copy/not copy?"

Since we were exploring how the students completed their assignments rather than directly testing whether they copied, careful descriptions were needed of exactly how they completed their work. Similarly, we needed to explore the students' own explanations for their strategy rather than ask questions that checked the relevance of others' explanations (the role of language, family pressure, and knowledge of the rules). As already noted, careful exploration provides sufficient information to be able to check the relevance of particular actions or constraints. The reverse, however, does not apply. If we had simply checked whether particular strategies or actions were relevant, we would not have known whether there were other factors that were more important than those we had investigated.

The links that are described in Table 6.1 between our research and interview questions became clearer as we tried to write the actual questions and as we tried them out before we began the interviews.

It is important to point out that this exercise in establishing whether you need information about constraints, actions, or consequences should also be used when developing questions for any other method of collecting data. You would devise a table similar to Table 6.1, but you would replace the final column with questions that match the method you are using (for example, "rating scale questions" or "questionnaire items").

Wording the Interview Questions

Since the wording of interview questions depends on exactly what one wants to know, there can be no rules about how to write interview questions. There are, however, a number of very useful guidelines.

Exploratory Questions and Checking Questions

One of the most common distinctions made in discussions of interviewing is that between the structured and the unstructured interview (Denzin & Lincoln, 2000, pp. 649–656; Selltiz, Jahoda, Deutsch, & Cook, 1959, pp. 255–268). In the *structured interview,* the purpose is to check the applicability of the interviewer's ideas. Thus the interview is organized around the theory of the interviewer that the interviewee is invited to react to. In the *unstructured interview,* the purpose is primarily to discover the espoused theory, the theory-in-use, or both, of the interviewee. In the unstructured interview, therefore, there will be many more exploratory than checking questions.

Exploratory and checking questions were introduced in Chapter 5. Exploratory questions, typically worded as open questions, explore others' views by inviting them to construct a response using their own ideas and language. Open questions are defined as those that cannot be answered with a simple "Yes" or "No" or by choosing between fixed alternatives. Checking questions, typically worded as closed questions, tell us how the interviewee reacts to the ideas of the interviewer by asking questions that invite a "Yes" or "No" answer. Note how the four questions in the left-hand column of Table 6.2 can be answered by a simple "Yes" or "No" or by selecting one of the interviewer's alternatives.

Questions about who, what, why, and how are very useful openers for exploring another's views. They are sometimes called "reportorial questions" because reporters often use them when interviewing people. Notice

Table 6.2 Comparing Closed and Open Questions

Closed Questions	Open Questions
Is it difficult to do this job?	How are you finding this job?
Did you change your reading program to fit the new school policy?	Why have you changed your reading program?
Have you decided to talk to the student or refer him to the counselor?	What have you decided to do?
Did your counselor suggest that?	Who suggested that you do that?

that all the questions on the right-hand side of Table 6.2 start with these words.

In deciding whether or not to use closed or open questions, you also need to think very carefully about how you are going to analyze the data. While open questions have the advantage of letting you discover how interviewees think about the issues, rather than how they respond to the way you think about the issues, they are more difficult to analyze. We shall explain more about how to analyze answers to open questions in Chapter 8.

Direct Questions and Indirect Questions

A direct question *directly requests* the information the interviewer requires. An indirect question requires the interviewer to *infer* the relevant information from the answers supplied. Indirect questions are particularly useful when the issue is a sensitive one or when the interviewer believes the interviewee might feel pressured to give a particular reply. For example, if you want to know how much responsibility a teacher feels for his students' learning, an indirect question is probably preferable to a direct one. Teachers who are asked a direct question like "How much responsibility do you feel for your students' learning?" are likely to indicate that they take considerable responsibility, as that is how teachers are supposed to feel. A better approach would be to ask the question indirectly by inviting the teacher to explain the achievement level of his students. The interviewer can then use the teacher's answers to infer the extent to which he takes responsibility for his students' learning.

Questions That Seek Information About Facts

Strictly speaking, interviewing is an inappropriate method to use when research questions require information about facts. There is much research evidence that people's reports about such matters are not predictive of what is actually the case (Argyris, 1982; Nisbett & Ross, 1980). Facts are therefore best obtained by appropriate observations, not by asking people what they think or believe to be the case. When observations prove impossible, then interview questions can be substituted as long as techniques are used that get as close as possible to the facts of the matter. It is important for PBM researchers to be skillful in the use of these techniques when their research questions require the analysis of relevant theories-in-use.

In general, these techniques involve helping the interviewee to be as specific as possible. This means helping interviewees to move down the ladder of inference (discussed in Chapter 3) from abstract conclusions to concrete examples and illustrations. This will enable the interviewer to judge the likely validity of the claims made by the interviewee.

Imagine a teacher-researcher who is studying a new leadership initiative in his district. He interviews one principal who declares, "I always consult my staff about important matters of policy." If the teacher-researcher does not obtain some specific examples, he will be unable to make up his own mind about whether the principal can be accurately described as consultative. All he will be able to do is report the principal's *perception* that he is consultative.

Helping interviewees to be more specific, without alienating them in the process, is one of the most challenging aspects of interviewing. There are several possible techniques that can be used, which we discuss next.

Repeated Probe Questions. The first response of an interviewee is usually very vague and abstract. Only after repeated requests for examples or clarification will an approximation of what occurred be reported. Consequently, a range of probe questions should be employed. In the following example, a skilled interviewer uses several different types of probe questions to help an interviewee become more specific.

Interviewer:	Mr. Richards, we have discussed briefly this professional development initiative and the way it operates. Will you now please tell me what you do as facilitator?
Facilitator:	As facilitator, I am naturally responsible for many things.
Interviewer:	So what are some of those responsibilities?
Facilitator:	Well, I must see that things go all right.
Interviewer:	Can you give me an example?
Facilitator:	I must see that we get the right programs in place.
Interviewer:	Can you elaborate on what you mean by "getting the right programs in place"?
Facilitator:	Now, that is hard to say.
Interviewer:	Let's take another task. What did you do in the last meeting you facilitated?
Facilitator:	Well, that was on Wednesday. I began by asking the teachers if they had been able to complete the classroom observation exercise we had discussed the previous time. . . .

The interviewer in this example is able to shift from one question type to another until he finds one that succeeds in drawing out more detailed answers.

Critical Incident Method. In this method a particular incident is identified and recalled in detail. The incident is selected because it is considered to be typical or indicative of the issues or practices that are relevant to the research question. For example, a teacher-researcher who is interested in teacher stress may ask colleagues to identify an incident that typifies the stress that they experience. The incident would then be recalled through a series of questions about when it happened, what happened, where, who was involved, and what was the outcome.

Interviewer: Can you think of an example of something that happened recently that typifies these stress factors that you have been describing?

Teacher: My departmental head makes unreasonable demands all the time.

Interviewer: Okay. So it happens a lot. Is there one recent example that stands out for you?

Teacher: Well, last week she asked me for another set of plans for the unit on democracy that we will be teaching next semester.

Interviewer: Well, let's focus on that request. What exactly did she ask for?

Teacher: She wanted to see that I had completed the revisions.

Interviewer: When had she asked for these?

Teacher: Oh, at the last minute—our meeting had been the day before and she was asking for them the next day.

Interviewer: And what exactly did you have to do to complete them?

Since critical incidents usually involve more than one person, the account given by one interviewee can be checked by interviewing other participants about the same incident. If those participants' accounts are sufficiently similar, the interviewer can be confident that the events happened as described. Once the factual matters are clarified, the interviewer may continue to probe the incident to discover the significance it holds for the teacher and why it is perceived as stress inducing. The interviewer will also have sufficient detail about the incident to be able to make an independent judgment about whether or not the demand seems unreasonable.

Role-Playing Techniques. This is another technique that can be used to obtain more detail about what actually took place or was said in a specific situation. While the information obtained is still a construction rather than an actual record of what took place, it is likely to give a more accurate picture than a generalized summary. In a role-play, the interview shifts unobtrusively from talking about what happened to reliving it. For example, an interviewer could encourage more detail about what happened in a staff meeting by saying the following:

Interviewer: Why don't you show me what happened in the meeting? You said you had described the budget plan and some staff objected. What did you actually say?

Principal: I said we had to make cutbacks and the department heads did not want to listen.

Interviewer: Well, I'll pretend to be those department heads and you be you. [Interviewer then expresses her objections and the principal replies.]

The role-play technique allows the richness of an interaction to be analyzed in far more detail than would be the case if the interviewee only gave a brief summary of what happened.

Sequence and Grouping of Questions

A well-constructed interview has a flow and a logic that makes sense to the interviewee. Questions should be organized to arouse interest, maintain motivation, facilitate recall of information, and overcome any suspicion. Here are some guidelines for ensuring a smooth flow through the various interview items:

- *Group similar items together.* For example, if you are asking high school students questions about smoking, you could put all the reportorial questions (how many, where, when, and who with) in the first section and checking questions about possible constraints in the next section.
- *Locate sensitive questions in the appropriate context.* If you put sensitive questions first, participants might be put off the entire interview. If you put them last, however, participants may feel a bit misled and choose not to answer them. The best solution is to put them in the most logical place. For example, if you wanted to ask students some sensitive questions about constraints on their smoking ("How much do your parents know about your smoking?" "Could they stop you from smoking?"), you should place these with other questions about possible constraints on smoking.

Conducting the Interview

It is the responsibility of the interviewer to coach the interviewee into providing information that is relevant to the research question. This is done by being clear about the purpose of the interview and by giving feedback that helps the interviewee to stay on track. Thus the interviewer will need to control the sequence, pace, and relevance of the information provided by the interviewee. Skillful exercise of control by an interviewer does not jeopardize the interviewer-interviewee relationship. After all, the interviewee has agreed to participate, and is likely to appreciate guidance on how to organize what they have to say. On the other hand, interviewers also need to be open to changing their approach to pursue leads that turn out to be relevant even though they were not anticipated.

Introducing the Interview

If at all possible, you should establish a relationship with your interviewees before the interview takes place. If participants know about you and your research beforehand, the interview is likely to be more comfortable for everyone. The following steps are a useful guide to introducing the interview itself:

- *Introduce yourself, or reintroduce yourself,* as necessary. Make sure that the interviewee knows the role you are playing in the interview. For example, if they know you as a colleague, clarify your role as a researcher on this occasion.
- *Introduce or reintroduce your project.* Check what the interviewee knows about the project, including how they would like it to be of benefit to them. Answer any further questions. Check the amount of time available to the interviewee and tailor the interview accordingly or reschedule if needed. Remember that a lengthy interview is not necessarily better than a shorter one!
- *Complete any formal documentation,* for example, consent forms.
- *Explain how the information will be used and kept confidential,* if that is what is desired.
- *Explain the main topics* that will be covered in the interview.
- *Request permission to take notes and/or use a tape recorder.* Explain how using the tape recorder enables you to listen more carefully and to keep an accurate record of what is said.
- If the interviewee agrees to the use of the tape recorder, *chat with the interviewee* while you set it up. *Test* whether or not it is working properly by saying the date, place, and project name and inviting the interviewee to state their name (or pseudonym) and position. Listen to see if your voices have been recorded, and if so, that both your voice and the voice of the person you are interviewing can be easily heard on tape. Proceed with the interview.

Asking the Questions

As you ask the questions, listen intently so that you can determine whether or not the interviewee has provided the information you need to answer your research question. For example, has he or she provided enough information to enable you to form your own opinion about the actions that have taken place? Have they provided sufficient detail about why those actions take place, and why the alternatives do not, so that you will be able to identify the relevant constraints?

In order to answer these questions, you must actively analyze the interview data during the course of the interview. The purpose of this on-the-spot analysis is to check whether (1) you have understood what the interviewee means, and (2) whether what has been said answers your question. The following provides some hints about how to maintain the relationship, check understanding, and analyze interviewee answers while continuing to maintain the flow of the interview:

- *Adopt a seating arrangement that is comfortable* for you and your interviewee. A quiet room where interruptions are unlikely is preferable. Adjust your nonverbal behavior—for example, eye contact—to suit the culture of your interviewee.
- *Test your understanding* of what is said whenever you feel uncertain. Ask for examples so you do not have to guess at an interviewee's meaning:

  "I'm not sure if I understood you correctly. Can you please clarify?"

  "Can you please give me an example of what you mean by that?"

- *Repeat back* to interviewees what they have said, to ensure your notes are correct or to prompt them to clarify a point:

  "I would like to summarize what you've said so far to check whether I've understood you. You talked about how you first decided that the school needed a new direction. . . ."

- *End your summary with a question* that invites the interviewee to comment on the accuracy of your summary or to modify what they have said:

  "Have I understood you correctly?"

  "Do you want to modify any of that?"

- *Avoid inserting your own opinions* into your summaries of the views of the interviewee. The purpose of a summary is to check your understanding of their opinion, not to endorse it or to change it.
- If the interviewee confirms that you have correctly understood their views, then a *learning conversation* on alternative views may be warranted, if such discussion has been agreed to in the original negotiation. (See Chapter 3 for examples of how to conduct such learning conversations.) Such discussion may include critique of existing practice and discussion of how it could be improved using an agreed criteria for evaluating the existing practice.
- *Avoid asking loaded questions.* Questions are said to be "loaded" when they incorporate unwarranted assumptions. For example, the question "How far behind are you in essay preparation?" presumes that the interviewee is behind. Such an assumption is unwarranted if the interviewer has no grounds for assuming that this is true. Take a second example: "Given all the problems with the policy, will you implement it?" This question is also loaded if the interviewer is incorrect in assuming that the interviewee thinks there are problems

with the policy. It may be just the interviewer who holds that opinion. If, however, this question follows a series of prior questions that have established that the interviewee does perceive this to be the case, then the question would not be a loaded one.

- *Avoid asking double-barreled questions.* "Double-barreled questions" include two or more questions in the one sentence. If all the component questions are important, they should be asked and analyzed separately. For example the question "How useful and interesting was the course?" should be replaced by two separate questions.

Closing the Interview

Leave time at the end of the interview to summarize your understanding of any remaining sections of the interview, and to discuss what will happen to the information that has been supplied. Some specific suggestions follow:

- Ask the interviewee whether he or she has said all that he or she wanted to say.
- If you are going to produce a transcript of the interview, ask the interviewee if he or she would like the opportunity to check it.
- Label the tape carefully with the names of the participants, date, and name of the project.
- Confirm any arrangements you have negotiated for follow-up or for further involving the interviewee in checking drafts of the research report.
- Close the interview by thanking the interviewee for his or her time and effort.

It is a good idea to schedule time to review an interview record as soon as possible after it is completed. Ask yourself whether you got the information you need in order to answer your research questions. If you did not, then change your interview questions so that you will get better information next time. If you can pay a typist to transcribe the interview, you can review the full interview record rather than just your notes. Allow approximately four hours of transcription time for every hour of interview.

DESIGNING QUESTIONNAIRES

Questionnaires have a lot in common with structured interviews because the wording and sequence of the questions are determined in advance. The differences are that participants provide a written rather than oral answer, and the person conducting the research does not need to be present at the time. This means that a questionnaire must be very clear and easy to complete, as there is usually no opportunity for the person conducting the research to clarify the questions. While it takes effort to develop a good questionnaire, they can, unlike interviews, be administered to large numbers of people relatively cheaply.

The questions that make up a questionnaire are usually referred to as "questionnaire items." Many of the points we made earlier about developing interview questions apply equally to questionnaire items. There are, however, some additional points that are worth noting.

Deciding Between Closed and Open Questions

In the section on interviews, we explained the difference between open and closed questions and how they apply to the interview situation. Open questionnaire items allow respondents to write what they wish to say in response to an item. The following box illustrates an open questionnaire item:

Q1. What difficulties, if any, have you experienced in trying to implement the new music curriculum? (Write your answer below)

_____

_____

_____

_____

Closed items, on the other hand, require respondents to express their answers by selecting from a range of predetermined alternatives. A closed item that addresses the same research question might look like this:

Q1. What difficulties have you experienced in trying to implement the new music curriculum? (Check all that apply)

a. Insufficient knowledge of the new curriculum documents ☐

b. Insufficient knowledge about the topics the new curriculum requires me to teach ☐

c. Insufficient expertise in the music skills the new curriculum requires me to teach ☐

d. Insufficient resources to teach the new curriculum ☐

e. Insufficient time to teach all that is required ☐

f. Disagreement with the underlying philosophy of this curriculum ☐

g. Other . . . ☐

There are advantages and disadvantages with both open and closed items. While open items provide participants with more freedom of expression, you have little control over the richness and relevance of the information provided. In the open questionnaire example, your colleagues might write very little about the difficulties they have experienced. A possible disadvantage of the closed item, however, is that the validity of the conclusions drawn depends on whether the seven alternatives accurately capture the range of difficulties that teachers actually experience. This is why all such items should be trialed to see whether they capture the range of teacher experiences. Sometimes you have no choice but to use a lot of open items because you have too little prior knowledge of a topic to write likely response alternatives.

Open items are harder to complete because they demand much more time commitment of respondents than closed items, so it is important to determine beforehand how willing your research participants are likely to be to write extensive answers to open questions. However, closed items can force the respondent to choose an option even when he or she knows little about the issue or has no opinion. (This is another reason why it is important to pretest your questionnaire and to provide an option where respondents can signal that they have no opinion on the matter.)

When designing closed questionnaire items, you should ensure that the response categories provided are non-overlapping and exhaustive. By "non-overlapping" we mean that a person should be able choose only one category (unless you have allowed them to choose more than one), and by "exhaustive" we mean that most people's responses should fit into one of the response categories provided. Here is an example of response categories that are both overlapping and nonexhaustive:

What is your age?

Under 20 ☐

20–30 ☐

30–40 ☐

40–50 ☐

The response categories are overlapping because people who are exactly 20, 30, or 40 years old can check more than one box. The categories are also not exhaustive, because there are no categories for respondents over 50. It is better to rewrite these response categories as follows:

Under 20	☐
20–29	☐
30–39	☐
40–49	☐
50–59	☐
Over 59	☐

It is also important when writing closed items to ensure that all response options directly address the same question. Take, for example, the question in the following box:

Q1. How much experience of data analysis did you have prior to attending the training program?

1. No experience at all ☐

2. Theoretical experience only ☐

3. Practical experience only ☐

4. Some practical and theoretical experience ☐

The question stem is about the amount of experience, yet some of the response alternatives have introduced a second question about the type of experience. This means the question is now double-barreled, because Option 1 is about the amount of experience while Options 2–4 are about the type of experience (practical or theoretical). If information is needed about both amount and type of experience, then two separate questions should be written, as shown on page 119.

Given the advantages and disadvantages of both open and closed questionnaire items, it is worth considering using a combination of both. Closed items save time, while open items recognize that you cannot always anticipate what is important. In addition, research participants may feel constrained by a questionnaire that does not allow them to write comments.

Clearly Understood Questions and Instructions

Practitioners are far more likely to give thoughtful answers if questionnaire items have been carefully worded and the instructions are clear. The following offer some useful guidelines:

- *Provide clear instructions.* Tell participants how to answer each question. This is particularly important for closed questions for which

Q1. How much experience in the analysis of student achievement data did you have prior to attending the training program? (Check one)

a. No experience at all ☐

b. Limited experience ☐

c. Moderate experience ☐

d. A lot of experience ☐

If you have had no experience with data analysis, please skip Question 2.

Q2. What type of experience did you have prior to attending the training program? (Check all that apply)

a. Studied it in courses ☐

b. Analyzed data from my own students ☐

c. Analyzed departmental data ☐

d. Analyzed schoolwide data ☐

participants have to choose a response category. If you want them to pick one alternative, then you should write an instruction like "Check the one category that best reflects your opinion." On the other hand, if more than one response category could apply, the instructions should read "Check all that apply."

- *Avoid jargon.* Check before administering your questionnaire that people understand the language you are using in the same way that you do. The best way to avoid problems with jargon is to try out your questions with people who have a similar background to those who will complete the final version of the questionnaire. For example, if you ask your colleagues whether an assessment should be moderated using interscorer agreement, you need to check that they understand such jargon.

- *Explain key terms and concepts.* Several years ago, Viviane asked teacher-leaders to list the various literacy (reading, writing, and spelling) programs that were operating in their school. The information was important because it seemed that additional government funding was encouraging a proliferation of such programs (Robinson, Phillips, & Timperley, 2002). She soon discovered that since teacher-leaders had varying understandings of what constituted a "program," it would have been impossible to aggregate the data obtained from each teacher. The solution was to provide a clear and credible definition of what counted as a program, so that each person was more likely to respond in the same way. As always, however, you need to be guided by your research questions. You do not need to provide definitions when the purpose of the questionnaire is to explore others' understandings rather than test reactions to your own definitions. For example, a New Zealand anti-bullying program begins by asking teachers and students in each participating school to indicate which items in a list of behaviors constitute bullying. They are also asked to indicate the frequency of each behavior. This information is then fed back to the school to stimulate debate about what counts as bullying, perceptions of its frequency, and the adequacy of the school's anti-bullying policy and practices.

- *Avoid asking questions that people do not know the answers to.* Sometimes questionnaire items are inappropriate because you have incorrectly assumed that participants have detailed knowledge or opinions about the topic. For example, if you are asking teachers their opinion on a particular district policy, it is important to ensure that teachers have sufficient knowledge of the policy to be able to respond to your question.

There are many other technical details that are relevant to the design and wording of questionnaire items. A useful discussion of the topic can be found in Oppenheim (1992). The sequence and grouping of questions in the questionnaire are also important, and the points on sequence and grouping discussed earlier with reference to interviews are equally applicable to questionnaires.

A Questionnaire Example

Finally, we discuss an extract from a simple questionnaire that could be used in the second phase of the study we described in Chapter 5 into why students drop trash in the playground. Imagine that the principal has learned a lot from the first phase, in which students interviewed each other. She may have learned, for example, that some students simply did not notice the trash, and that others who did took it for granted that the school grounds would be dirty. She may have also learned that students treated different types of trash differently. She wants to explore these perceptions with a wider group of students while still exploring students' beliefs about why they continue to litter. Three possible questionnaire items are reproduced for additional critique:

Extract From Draft Questionnaire on Playground Trash

1. *Do you consider trash a problem at this school? (Please circle)*
   Yes No

2. *How often do you drop trash? (Please circle)*
   Most of the time Sometimes Occasionally Rarely

3. *What type of trash do you drop? (Please circle)*
   Paper Food/fruit Plastic

Here are our comments on the extract:

- Item 1 is a good closed question, but it does not tell you why they do or do not think it is a problem. It would be good to follow up with an open question asking students to state their reasons.
- The response categories for Item 2 are unsatisfactory. First, the categories assume that everyone drops trash to some degree. There should be a category for those who believe they do not drop trash in the playground at all. Second, the differences among "sometimes," "occasionally," and "rarely" are unclear and are likely to be understood differently by different people.
- The principal wanted to know the type of trash dropped because she had learned from Phase 1 that items that could be recycled in the school's recycling scheme (bottles and cans) were dropped less frequently than the nonrecycled items (food, fruit, and paper). There are several problems, however, with the way Item 3 is worded. First, the instructions do not make clear whether more than one category can be circled. People are likely to drop more than one of these types of trash. Second, fruit is a subcategory of food, so it should not be mentioned separately. Third, the categories are not exhaustive, because there are other types of trash besides those mentioned.
- The layout of the questionnaire is cramped. The response categories for Items 2 and 3 are too close together, making it difficult for students to circle one without accidentally circling part of another. It would be good to redo the format of the questionnaire for ease of responding.

Our revisions are presented in the following text box. We have altered the questionnaire to show how information about constraints on dropping trash could be gathered, as well as information about behavior.

SUMMING UP

Purposeful information gathering requires you to collect information that is trustworthy and relevant to your research questions. In this chapter we have focused on designing instruments for two methods that are commonly employed in PBM studies—interviews and questionnaires. For each method we have offered advice on how to construct an effective instrument and have provided examples to illustrate the points we have made.

We emphasized the importance of planning for a well-designed interview and discussed how to write, group, and sequence interview questions. We finished with a discussion on how to conduct the interview itself. In addition, we discussed the relative merits of open and closed questions and the importance of ensuring questions and instructions are

Extract From Questionnaire About Trash

1. Do you consider trash in the playground a problem at this high school? (Please circle)

   Yes   No

   Please state your reasons: _____

   _____

   _____

   _____

   _____

2. What percentage of the times that you have some trash do you put it in the trash can? (Please check one box)

   80–100%   ☐

   60–79%   ☐

   40–59%   ☐

   20–39%   ☐

   0–19%   ☐

3. If you never drop trash at school, please explain below why you do not:

   _____

   _____

   _____

4. If you do drop trash at school, please explain below why you do:

   _____

   _____

   _____

5. What type of trash do you drop? (Please check all the boxes that apply to you)

   Paper   ☐

   Food   ☐

   Plastic   ☐

   Cans   ☐

   Bottles   ☐

   Other (please state) _____

clearly understood. Many of the points discussed for designing interviews also apply to questionnaires.

We also encouraged you to use more than one method so that you can verify the information you collect. For this reason we recommended you read this chapter in conjunction with the next one, which discusses some other methods of data collection that are commonly used in PBM studies.

7

Purposeful Information Gathering

*Observations and Other
Data Collection Methods*

In the previous chapter, we discussed how to design interviews and questionnaires—two common methods of collecting information in research that uses problem-based methodology (PBM). In this chapter we continue by examining other common methods of collecting information in PBM—observations, rating scales, documents, and diaries. It is important to emphasize that any of the methods we discuss in this chapter can be used to gather information on actions, constraints, or consequences. The chapter ends with a discussion of how to trial your data collection tools.

OBSERVATIONS

Teachers rely on informal observation to find out what is happening during their lessons or in the playground. They might also make more formal observations, such as when observing a beginning teacher or taking a running record of the reading of a six-year-old child (Clay, 2002). Doing research can increase practitioners' power of observation by making it more systematic, focused, and accurate.

There are many different types of observation, and choosing among them is a matter of finding the most practical way of gaining the information required by your research question. The key decision to make is whether you are using observation to explore what is happening or whether you are using it to check whether particular things are happening. For example, if you sense that there is a lot of bullying in the playground but are not yet sure about what is really going on, you should start by taking an unstructured approach that does not prejudge the specific types of behavior to be observed. In other words, start by exploring what is happening. Once you have a sense of the types of bullying that may be happening, you could then design a much more specific observation form that specified categories of bullying and allowed you to measure it more precisely. You would then use this observation form to check whether certain types of bullying were happening.

Observations provide an important check on whether what is espoused is actually happening. For example, if a science teacher claims that he interacts with his female students as much as his male students, you can observe several science lessons to check whether this is the case.

Observations That Explore What Is Happening

This type of observation is equivalent to the unstructured interview—you know the broad areas of information you require, but you do not predetermine the details of the observation.

To continue the bullying example, you could start by sitting in a central spot and taking notes about anything that happens that might be relevant to the issue of bullying. You could also experiment with using a Dictaphone as you watch or walk around the playground.

There is an art to taking a record of a stream of events and activities. If observations are to provide high-quality information, you must make a clear distinction between your record of what is happening and your inferences about what it might mean. This means using clear, unbiased language and eliminating evaluative words like *nice, sloppy, aggressive,* and *democratic,* as these words may have different meanings for different people. Two observers, for example, may not agree that a child who does not tuck in his school shirt is "sloppy." As far as possible, record the words spoken and the action taken.

This point is the same as the one we made when discussing the ladder of inference (see Chapter 3). Inferences about the meaning and worth of what is happening (the top of the ladder of inference) must be defensible in terms of the observations you have made (the bottom of the ladder of inference). If your notes do not record exactly what you saw, you will not be able to defend your interpretations.

When you make careful distinctions between your observations and your interpretations, you often gain important insights that motivate change. This is what happened to Rachel, a beginning teacher who tape-recorded the beginning of her lesson so that she could study how she gave instructions to her class. She had concluded that her instructions were clear. When she was given feedback by her mentor, she was prompted to go back down the ladder of inference and make a record of what she actually said to her students. She learned that there was a considerable gap between the information at the bottom of the ladder (her actual instructions) and the conclusion she had previously drawn ("I give clear instructions"). In her portfolio she wrote, "I am surprised when students do not understand my instructions—I assume they are clear. *The problem is they are clearer to me, in my head, than they are when expressed to others.*"

However you record observations, make a physical distinction between your description and your interpretation of what happened. One way of doing this is through a split-page technique in which the observational record and possible interpretations are kept in separate columns of a page:

Description of the Incident		Inference
Words	*Action*	
Jonathan asks Mary to share her lunch with him.	Jonathan pushes Mary as he says this. Mary looks around. Mary gives him the lunch and looks down.	Mary is being bullied into sharing her lunch.

Another strategy is to insert comments into a transcript or observational record by using a different colored font or typescript, such as "Jonathan asks Mary to share her lunch with him. Jonathan pushes Mary as he says this. Mary looks around. Mary gives him the lunch and looks down. *My guess is that she is being bullied to share her lunch.*" Whichever strategy you use, keep your notes of what you heard and saw physically separate from your interpretations, and yet in close enough proximity to them to make it easy to check one against the other. This technique can also be used for transcripts of recordings.

Observations That Check What Is Happening

If the purpose of your observation is to check rather than explore what is happening, then much more precision is needed in the design of the observation tool. Two main decisions are needed: what to observe and how to observe it.

What to Observe

Broadly speaking, your research question tells you what to observe. If your question is "How are teachers implementing a literacy program?" then you need to observe their implementation of the program. But what would you actually be looking for? Some prior work would be needed to identify the types of planning, teaching, and assessment activities that were relevant. For example, the program might require that teachers teach reading in a way that encourages children to self-correct. But what would an observer actually see if the teachers were doing this?

Before observations began, you would not only have to identify implementation activities, but define them well enough to enable two different observers (one of whom could be yourself) to agree whether a teacher was or was not teaching in ways that encouraged self-correction. The process of defining categories often takes much longer than the observation process itself, but it is worthwhile because it forces you to clarify what it is that you are interested in. This means that definitions should not include words that mean different things to different people. For example, you might say that self-correction is encouraged when teachers give the child a chance to discover their own mistakes. But another person watching the same teacher, or analyzing the same tape of a reading lesson, might disagree about when the teacher did "give the child a chance." You would be more likely to agree if a more specific definition was used, such as "Teacher waits at least five seconds, or until the child has read the whole sentence before identifying a mistake." In our experience, the creation of specific definitions involves learning conversations, as teacher-researchers often disagree on how to define an action to be observed. Addressing these differences requires each teacher-researcher involved in the research to explain the differences in definition, agree on exactly what is causing the difference, and create a new definition, which may be sourced from prior research. (See Chapter 3 for more detail on how to conduct such learning conversations.)

The level of precision required in an observational study varies according to the purpose of the study. If a teacher wants to check her sense that a group of boys is "nearly always off task," then she does not need highly precise definitions. A working definition such as "doing or not doing what they are supposed to be doing at the time" is good enough. However, if the teacher wishes to use this information to change the way group work is undertaken in her school, a more precise and agreed definition of what counts as "off task" is required, so that colleagues will not dismiss the findings as not capturing what they mean by the term.

If you are intending to be more precise in your definitions, it is useful to find out whether there are published observations in the area you wish to research. Some of these observations, such as the Observation Survey of Early Literacy Development (Clay, 2002), have precise definitions of what to look for that are based on years of research. Students' understanding of punctuation,[1] for example, is assessed by a series of structured questions on different aspects of punctuation. Teachers are asked to point or trace with a pencil a full stop (period) in a story, ask the child "What's this for?" and observe the answer. Adopting or adapting a relevant published observation tool can be an efficient way of working out how to conduct your own observations.

---

1. Punctuation is part of the survey assessing students' concepts about print.

How to Observe

Decisions about how to observe particular actions and events depend on their duration and frequency. For events that have a defined beginning and end, an event-recording system is appropriate. An event-recording system records every instance of the behavior. For example, a teacher who is eager to develop cooperative team behaviors in her class might want to record for a particular group of students how often they asked each other questions. Question asking is a discrete activity, whose frequency can be recorded in a simple chart like that following:

	Session 1	Session 2	Session 3
Students	*Questions Asked*	*Questions Asked*	*Questions Asked*
Derwent	||| 3		
Sally	| 1		
Melissa	ⅢⅠ 5		
Jonah	ⅢⅠ| 6		
Selina	| 1		

Event recording would also be suitable for recording such things as how often certain people spoke at meetings, the completion of homework, and the number of times that foul language was used by a student.

For actions that do not have a defined beginning and end, or that last a long time, a time-sampling rather than event-recording method is appropriate. In a time-sampling method, the observer asks whether or not the behavior occurs within a particular time interval. The easiest way to describe the techniques of time sampling is to use the example of on-task activity. A teacher is concerned about the low level of on-task activity of four or five students in his class. He decides to collect some more systematic information to check whether or not he is correct in thinking that these particular students are often off task. One method he could use is that of momentary time sampling. At five times in the lesson he observes each of the students in turn and records whether they are on or off task at that precise moment. The teacher could record this in a simple chart like the one following, where ✓ means that the student is on task and *x* means that the student is off task:

	Time 1	Time 2	Time 3	Time 4	Time 5
Kaylyn	✓	✓	✓	x	x
Jaya	✓	✓	x	x	x
May	x	x	✓	✓	✓
Jason	✓	x	x	x	x
Pearly	✓	✓	✓	✓	x

If the teacher had more time, he could use an interval rather than a momentary time-sampling system. This would involve locating each student, watching them for a predetermined time interval (say 5 or 10 seconds), and then recording whether the student was on task for the full interval. Such information can be very useful if discussed with the students concerned. If they and their teacher can identify the constraints that produce the off-task behavior, they might be able to alter the behavior in ways that improve the situation.

You will need to think ahead about how you can integrate conducting observations with your daily responsibilities. There are many ways of achieving this integration. One of the most common ways in New Zealand schools is to integrate observation in the professional development of groups of teachers. This enables the work of collecting and discussing observational data to be shared among its members. If, for example, the group wants to study the type of feedback that its members give their students during a lesson, a schedule could be developed that enabled one group member to observe another's teaching. The observer could sit at the back of the classroom and record the teacher's feedback to students on a predesigned sheet. Alternatively, the observer could videotape or audiotape the lesson and record the frequency and type of feedback on the same sheet.

It is also possible to conduct observations in your own classroom even if you do not have the time or the desire to use a video or tape recorder. For example, the sweeps of on-task behavior described earlier can be managed while teaching if the times for the recordings have been preestablished and a discrete timer is used to indicate when an observation is due.

How to Moderate Your Observations

Most teachers recognize that the assessment of students is subject to various types of error and inconsistency. For example, if one teacher assesses a child's reading by providing numerous prompts and another does not provide prompts, then the scores of those teachers' students should not be compared, because the scores were obtained under quite different conditions. Most schools take steps to reduce such errors and inconsistencies by using various systems of moderation. For example, grading criteria are developed so that similar descriptors are assigned by teachers to similar levels of achievement. Special steps are taken in the administration of school- or department-wide tests so that students take the tests under standardized conditions.

The aforementioned issues of error and inconsistency are also relevant to observations. Observations are susceptible to the "eyewitness effect," where different people observe the same event or action but see different things. Steps need to be taken to reduce the probability of error occurring—or, to put it positively, to increase the reliability of the observational data. There are many factors that cause observational data to fall below an acceptable level of reliability. The definitions of what is being observed may be inadequate, so that it is unclear whether or not the behavior should be counted. One observer may be able to see the events or behavior better than another, or one observer may lose concentration. If your observations are going to be used to make a decision that affects others in important ways, you should take as many precautions as possible to ensure that the data are collected reliably.

Some of you might see issues of reliability and moderation as too theoretical and academic to be of direct relevance. The following example, however, shows how teachers' knowledge of these concepts can act as a catalyst for change. Mei worked with a group of teachers to check the impact of a literacy program on student achievement. The participating schools decided to use the Observation Survey of Early Childhood Literacy (Clay, 2002) to gather these data. Since the survey requires teachers to make on-the-spot judgments while they are listening to a child's reading, Mei emphasized the importance of moderating the teachers' assessments.

Joanne Milich, the assistant principal of Mary McKillop School in Auckland, explains how she moderated her colleagues' observations and what the school learned from the exercise:

> When talking to other administrators in the district and listening to how they conducted the "six-year observation survey" assessment, I realized that there was a huge discrepancy in the way they were conducted. We all had to be scoring assessments the same way. We all had to have the same understanding of what children were expected to achieve so that we could get comparable results. So we started discussing how to do so, and organized workshops with a trained nationwide assessor to help us administer and score the assessments reliably. Then, Mei helped us organize a professional development exercise where two school administrators would score the same test simultaneously and calculate interrater reliability scores.[2] For each relevant section of the survey, this meant dividing the number of agreements over the total possible score in the survey. The results of the exercise indicated that almost all of us were scoring the assessments reliably and we could be assured of the quality of the data collected.
>
> Participating in the districtwide moderation highlighted issues in our own school. We have always talked about the discrepancies in reading assessments from class to class, but nobody knew how to go about getting reliability across teachers. (We didn't even know the word *reliability*!) Without this professional development, we would have talked and talked but we definitely would not have known how to address it. We now check for reliability in all our assessments.

---

2. Interrater reliability scores reveal the extent to which two people rating the same performance, behavior, or piece of work agree on the score, grade, or rating to be given. Higher scores indicate greater agreement between the two independent raters.

RATING SCALES

In PBM projects, teachers frequently want to know what people's attitudes are toward particular constraints, actions, or consequences. For example, a teacher might wish to examine the consequences of a new math program on parents' satisfaction with their children's interest and achievement in the subject.

While unstructured interviews or questionnaires could provide rich descriptions about how parents feel about these matters, the information gained is very difficult to summarize in a succinct way. Without some form of quantification, it is also very difficult to make comparisons, such as that between satisfaction with student achievement and student interest. Rating scales make it possible for people to express their attitudes and evaluations in numeric form, and numbers are much easier to summarize and compare than a lot of words. While there are many types of rating scales, the examples we are about to present are Likert scales, one of the most popular types of rating scale for teacher-researchers. (See Oppenheim, 1992, for more information on different kinds of rating scales.)

In the following two rating scales, parents are asked to select the number that best represents their views.

Example 1

How satisfied are you with your child's level of achievement in math?

1	2	3	4	5
Very Dissatisfied		Neither Satisfied nor Dissatisfied		Very Satisfied

Example 2

How satisfied are you with your child's level of interest in math?

1	2	3	4	5
Very Dissatisfied		Neither Satisfied nor Dissatisfied		Very Satisfied

These two rating scales could be incorporated into either an interview or questionnaire. After a few simple calculations, the teacher could provide a numerical summary of all the ratings (mean, median, and range of the ratings) and compare the results for achievement and interest. She might discover, for example, that while parents are very satisfied with the achievement level of their children, they are somewhat dissatisfied with their children's interest in the subject. As this is clearly an unintended consequence of the new teaching method, the administrator could use this information to find ways of teaching math that maintain good results without turning students off the subject.

Rating scales look simple but are deceptively difficult to create. In what follows, we discuss the main decisions that you will face when constructing rating scales. Further, more technical, information is available in Babbie (1990) and Burns (1994).

In Likert scales, each response option on the numerical scale is assigned a number. There are four main decisions required in constructing this type of scale:

1. How many numbers or points on the scale will I use?

2. Will my scale have a midpoint?

3. What descriptors will I use on the scale?

4. Do the descriptors on the scale logically match the question?

There has been some attempt in the research literature to identify the ideal number of points on the scale, but as is the case for most research decisions, what is best depends on the circumstances of the particular study. Scales of fewer than 3 points usually provide too little information. Scales of more than 10 points are usually too demanding of the participants. They also assume that people can reliably make all those distinctions, and in the case of attitudes and evaluations, that assumption is usually false. Michael Scriven, in his *Evaluation Thesaurus,* recommends that scales of 5 and 7 points usually work well (Scriven, 1991, p. 300).

There is also a debate about whether or not a scale should have an odd or even number of points. Odd numbers provide a midpoint, whereas an even number of points on a scale force the respondent to make a judgment one way or another. This latter option, however, also has its disadvantages, as respondents may wish to evaluate an idea or object as neither positive nor negative. In such cases, scales without a midpoint introduce inaccuracy into the evaluation.

If a midpoint is used, it should not be confused with a "no opinion" option. The parent who is neither satisfied nor dissatisfed holds a genuinely neutral opinion, and this is not the same as having no opinion. A "no opinion" option should be provided as a separate check box, or as part of a comments section below the scale itself.

The third main decision to make is how to describe the points on the scale. It is usual to provide a brief description that conveys the extent, level, or frequency of what is being evaluated. The more points in the scale, the harder it is to find language that communicates varying levels, frequency, or strength of the single idea or dimension that the scale represents. That is why some specialists recommend that a descriptor is used for the endpoints and midpoints only.

In writing descriptors for scale points, keep in mind that the words must reflect the order conveyed by the numbers on the scale. For example, in the following scale, the descriptor "Not that important" may not be understood by respondents as *less* important than "Somewhat important."

Example 3

How important is it to involve students in establishing classroom rules?

1	2	3	4	5
Not at All Important	Not That Important	Somewhat Important	Important	Very Important

Another point to notice is the descriptor used for the midpoint. While the number 3 can be seen as midway between the highly negative and positive ends of the scale, the descriptor "Somewhat important" invites a positive evaluation. Since there are three positive and two negative descriptors, the scale is biased toward positive evaluations! The examples in Table 7.1 provide clues about how to write better descriptors.

The fourth main decision is to ensure that the descriptors on the scale match the rating scale question. If you asked the question "How satisfied are you with the science resources?" your descriptors must describe some degree of satisfaction such as "Very satisfied" or "Dissatisfed," rather than "Yes," "No," or "Undecided." Similarly, if you asked someone how often they perform an action, you need descriptors that describe the frequency of the action, such as "Very often." The best way to ensure that the descriptors match the question is to check whether the answer would make sense in a normal conversation. For example, if you asked the question "How well do you know your students?" you would expect answers that range from "Very well" to "Not well at all," so you would design a rating scale that provides such descriptors.

Rating scales can provide high-quality information that can inform schools' decision making. The following example shows how rating scales can be integrated into schools' decision-making processes. Mei worked with a group of schools who wanted to be linked through an electronic network. A panel of teachers, administrators, and principals from the participating schools was set up to interview short-listed information technology companies. The panel needed to design a systematic and fair way of comparing potential providers. The panel began by specifying the constraints that they wanted the successful provider to satisfy and then constructed a series of rating scales to measure the panel's confidence in each provider's capacity to meet the specified constraints. A seven-point scale was used, with one indicating low confidence and seven indicating high confidence. There were three reasons for choosing to use a rating scale:

Table 7.1 Examples of Descriptors for Rating Scales

	Poor Descriptors	Better Descriptors	Comments
1.	1 2 3 4 5 6 7 Extremely Dissatisfied — Neither Satisfied nor Dissatisfied — Very Satisfied	1 2 3 4 5 6 7 Extremely Dissatisfied — Neither Satisfied nor Dissatisfied — Extremely Satisfied	In the scale on the left-hand side, the descriptor for 1 is more extreme than the descriptor for 7. This presents two problems. First, people can express extreme dissatisfaction but not extreme satisfaction. Second, people are more likely to choose 7 on the scale if it is labeled "very satisfied" than if it is labeled "extremely satisfied." This asymmetry in the scale on the left-hand side can be corrected by balancing the language at each end.
2.	1 2 3 4 5 Poor Average Excellent	1 2 3 4 5 Poor Satisfactory Excellent	The descriptors confuse ranking language "average" with grading language "excellent" and "poor." A student may be average for the group and still poor when graded against an achievement criterion. Alter by using the same type of descriptor (in this case grading language).
3.	1 2 3 4 Hardly Ever Usually Mostly All the Time	1 2 3 4 5 Never Hardly Ever Some of the Time Most of the Time All the Time	The descriptors do not suggest a clearly ascending order of frequency, as the relative frequency is unclear. Is "usually" less frequent than "mostly"? They are also unbalanced with 4 (all the time) being more extreme than 1 (hardly ever). A five-point scale should also be used, as there is too large an interval between "hardly ever" and "usually." Correct by using words that describe a better sequence and by balancing the descriptor at each end.

1. The numerical rating scale enabled the 12 panel members to express their judgments in a standardized manner. The scores could also be quickly totaled and compared.

2. The seven-point scale allowed individuals to make greater distinctions among providers than did a scale with fewer points.

3. An odd-numbered scale was chosen so panel members could express genuine uncertainty about the suitability of each applicant.

Without the rating scale, it would have been extremely difficult to ensure a fair and consistent process for making this important decision, because the panel would not have had an accurate comparison across providers.

DOCUMENTS

Documents are commonly used in schools to gather information on school practices. Reports to the school board about student achievement, student report cards, written school and district policies, teachers' planning books, minutes of meetings, and e-mail trails about key decisions are stored either electronically or manually within schools and district offices. These documents may be a valuable source of information for your research question.

If you choose to retrieve information from documents, you need to decide which ones are relevant and what information needs to be extracted from them. Your knowledge of school operational procedures is one of the best ways of identifying the necessary documents to use for checking. You could also ask the participants in your research which documents are appropriate.

In most cases, the documents you will need to examine and the information you will need to extract from them is obvious from your research question. For example, you may want to examine whether teachers report student achievement accurately in report cards. The relevant documents, therefore, are the report cards, and the information you need from the report cards are the sections that report student achievement. You will also need to define what constitutes "accurate" reporting of student achievement. If teachers do not compare students to national norms, is that considered "accurate" reporting? In other words, you will need to go through a similar process to that described in the section on "What to Observe," where you define specifically what you want to extract from the document.

You can also use documents to check or explore constraints, actions, or consequences that are not an explicit part of your research question. To illustrate, if teachers report that they do something because a written policy requires it, you could check the policy to see if that constraint is actually specified in the policy. If you want to check a teacher's claim that she always submits reports that refer to student achievement, you would examine her reports to verify her reported action. In this case, you would decide what counts as "absent" or "present" (for example, does one sentence on student achievement in a report count as "present"?) and then check every report to see whether this achievement information was included.

There are particular problems to be aware of in using documents. First, schools may not provide a complete record of the information you need to answer your research questions. Minutes of key meetings may be missing, or the records of student achievement may not provide the information you require. Second, you should investigate the context in which the documents were produced. For what purpose were they compiled? Who produced them and how accurate are they likely to be? If you seek answers to these questions, you will be in a better position to judge the completeness and accuracy of the information. For example, a senior high school teacher analyzed the school detention records as part of a review of the school's detention policy. He wanted to know how detention rates varied across different teachers so that he could identify teachers who needed extra support with classroom management and those who might be examples of good practice who could assist those who needed help. Before completing this analysis, however, he checked the context in which the detention records were produced and satisfied himself that they comprised an accurate record of student detentions.

Third, it is important to remember that because documents are reports of events, activities, and their outcomes, they may not be entirely accurate. There may be a considerable gap, for example, between what a policy document specifies and how the policy was implemented. Similarly, agendas and minutes do not always give an accurate record of what happened in a meeting.

One of the benefits of attempting to use existing school documents for inquiry purposes is that you learn how to make future documents and records more useful for school, parent, and teacher decision making. For example, Heather Hampton, the principal of an Auckland elementary school, learned through a PBM project conducted in her school that parents found it difficult to understand the way her school reported student achievement. She wanted parents to better understand their children's achievement so that they could make better educational decisions for their children, so she used the research to identify the areas of the report that parents found difficult to understand, and changed these areas. For example, she replaced words that were "teacher jargon," such as "oral language," and changed the diagram the school used to display student achievement because parents had found it was confusing. (More details of the changes are reported in Marino, Nicholl, Paki-Slater, Timperley, Lai, & Hampton, 2001.)

DIARIES

While diaries have a long history as a means of communicating and reflecting on personal experience, they have only recently been accepted as a research tool (Anderson, Herr, & Nihlen, 1994; Bell, 1999). Like interviews, diary techniques can be described as structured or unstructured.

The unstructured diary is particularly useful in PBM research as a way of understanding how people experience particular life events.

An unstructured diary approach is used by Ngaire Hoben, a teacher educator at the University of Auckland. For several years, Ngaire had noticed the varying quality of feedback, supervision, and mentoring that her beginning English teachers experienced during their school placements. She decided to research the issue and involved her students in developing a diary that they could share with her. The diary was organized around key questions that prompted students to reflect on the quality of their experiences during school placements, including the role of their associate teacher. The following boxed text shows the instructions she gave to her student teachers about how to keep a diary.

Instructions for an Unstructured Diary Given to Student Teachers at the University of Auckland Following Their First School Placement

You have now completed seven weeks in a school—the first of the big hurdles in your career as a teacher. This journal entry invites you to reflect on the experience.

Many of you expressed hopes that your associate teacher would prove to be a role model for planning, classroom teaching, and class management. You had hopes that he or she would have time for you, would provide helpful feedback including constructive criticism, and that you would be welcomed as a colleague in the classroom.

- To what extent were your hopes in regard to your associate realized?
- Were you able to establish the sort of relationship you wanted to?
- How hard is it to maintain relationships over two or three associates?
- What did you learn from your associate that you would implement in your own classroom or that you would emulate as a teacher?

Ngaire used the diaries to learn how to give her students better support for their school placements. In other words, Ngaire used the diary to uncover constraints that would help her improve the way she and her university colleagues placed and supported students in schools.

Structured diaries provide a record or log of selected activities. For example, a teacher may use a structured diary to help her monitor how she allocates time to particular activities during the course of a lesson or teaching block. Such a diary could help teachers match their planned and actual allocation of teaching time. Teachers may also ask students to keep diaries about such activities as enjoyment and completion of homework or their experience of peers during lunch breaks. This often enables teachers to uncover actions and constraints that they may not be privy to. For example, a student writes about staying in the library during lunch breaks because she does not have any friends and does not want to look "friendless" in front of her classmates. This diary entry has identified the action (staying in the library) and the constraints (no friends but does not want to look "friendless") that led her to stay in the library.

Structured diaries are a form of self-observation. As such, the same care needs to be taken in their planning as in the design of an observation schedule. Decisions need to be made about precisely what should be recorded in the diary. For example, if you want students to record how much time they spend on their homework, they need to understand what counts as homework. The form they use should also indicate whether they should record total time or the time spent on each separate homework activity. Keeping a diary takes considerable effort. Students not only have to do their homework, but they have to keep a record as well! Students are far more likely to cooperate if they understand what they have to do, and more important, believe in its value. Talk to students beforehand about the purpose of the information, and check that the diary or log you have planned will work for them.

In any diary research, there are problems with representativeness. Are the teaching plans that have been recorded typical? Was it more difficult for the students to complete homework this week because of participation in the sports competition? This is a sampling problem and can be addressed in the same way as any other sampling problem (see Chapter 5). The time period should be chosen to provide the information needed to answer the research question. If a typical pattern or record is required, then the diary period should be selected with this in mind. One way of determining typicality is to check beforehand whether or not those involved think the selected period fits this criterion.

Diaries are susceptible to the problem of reactivity. This means that the very act of keeping a record leads the diarist to change their pattern of activity. Students do more homework simply because they are keeping a record that they know will be seen by their teacher. If teacher and students have discussed the research beforehand, this may not be a bad thing. They could then discuss why homework time had increased and how that increase could be sustained. If, however, the purpose of the research was not to change behavior, but simply to get an accurate description of what typically happens, then such reactivity is a problem. One way to overcome it is to engage with participants in learning conversations such as those described in Chapter 3. Explain why you do not want people to change their behavior and why the best answer is a truthful one, even though it might mean that no homework was completed for the whole week!

TRIALING YOUR DATA COLLECTION INSTRUMENT

After you have designed the data collection tools you are planning to use, you need to trial them to make sure that they produce the information you require. The need for this "pilot testing" is obvious when the possibility for misunderstanding is high. However, even with groups that you think you know well, there is the possibility that the instrument you have created will be misunderstood or that the situation is different from that which you anticipated.

Pilot testing proved to be crucial when Mei was investigating how young adults allocated time to three important areas of their lives. Her initial intention was to ask participants to estimate the percentage of time they spent in the three areas. When she trialed this way of gathering information, she found that the young people were unable to estimate time accurately. Every participant overestimated the time they spent in each area, so that their total came to more than 100 percent of their time. If she had not trialed her way of gathering information, the findings would not have been valid.

So, what do you do when trialing an instrument? First, decide who to involve in your trial. It is a good idea to select individuals who are similar to those you will involve in your final study. It is even better if those individuals can also provide you with constructive feedback on the strengths and weaknesses of your instrument. Second, administer the instrument to the people you have selected. Their reaction to the instrument, as well as their answers to the questions, will tell you whether it is working as you intended.

After you revise your instrument based on feedback from the trial, you might want to give both the original and the revised versions of the instrument back to the original people in the trial and ask them whether they think the changes reflect your discussion. If you have made major changes to your instrument, you should trial your instrument again with at least one other person. Once you are satisfied that the instrument will provide you with the information you need, you can start collecting data for your inquiry. It is important not to be discouraged if people misunderstand the instructions or questions and do not provide the information you anticipated. Trialing is an important step in the information-gathering process and helps ensure that the information you collect for your project will be relevant and trustworthy.

SUMMING UP

This chapter continues the theme of the previous chapter—namely, the design and use of data collection methods that will enable you to collect information that is trustworthy and relevant to your research questions. Whereas the previous chapter considered interviews and questionnaires, here we have focused on observations, rating scales, document analysis, and diaries, which are also appropriate for PBM studies.

We have offered advice on how to construct an effective instrument for each method, and have provided examples to illustrate the points we have made. In addition, we have emphasized the importance of trialing your data collection instruments once they have been developed. Such pilot testing provides a check that your instruments are working as intended and ensures that they produce the information you require to answer your research questions.

8

Purposeful Data Analysis

The process of analyzing information gathered through interviews, observations, and fieldwork is the most exciting part of doing research and signals that you have begun the final 40 percent of your project. This is the stage at which you use the information to propose answers to your research questions. In order to do this task, you need to be able to recognize, retrieve, and organize those pieces of information that are meaningful in terms of your research questions.

While most data analysis happens after the information is gathered, it should begin while information is still being collected. It is too late once all your teacher interviews have been completed, for example, to discover that the information is too sketchy to provide convincing answers to your questions. These are the sort of difficulties that can be picked up at an early stage if analysis is begun as soon as one or two interviews have been completed. You then have time to change your mind about the information you require and to try out different approaches to the analysis. None of this is possible if the report is due in a few days' time!

The goal of the data analysis phase is to provide valid answers to your research questions. In problem-based methodology (PBM), answering most research questions involves describing one or more components of a theory of action (constraints, actions, and consequences) and identifying relationships among them. Some research questions also require evaluation of the theory of action.

Some research questions can be answered by mapping only one or two of the components of a theory of action. (See Chapter 5, Figures 5.2 and 5.3, for revision of these points.) For example, if your question is about what is happening, or what is believed to be happening, then analysis of actions, or perceptions of actions, is all that is required. Other research questions require mapping the entire theory of action so that the relationships among constraints, actions, and consequences are made explicit. In these cases, the goal of the data analysis is to draw the theory of action in a one-page diagram such as that shown in Figure 8.1. If you can explain and defend your diagram, then your analysis has been successful!

Figure 8.1   A Theory of Action to Describe and Explain Teacher Reporting of Student Achievement to Parents

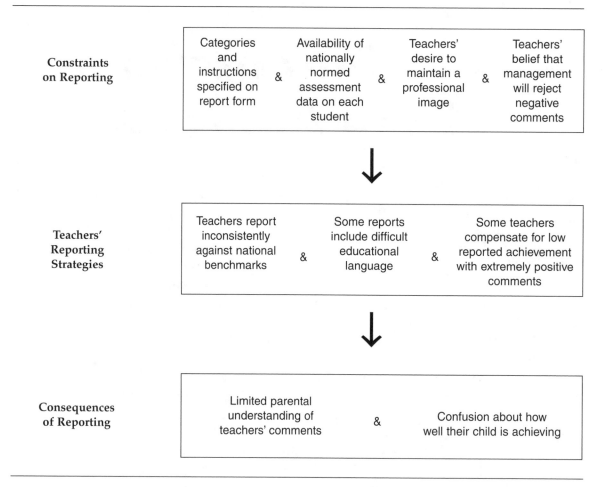

Figure 8.1 summarizes the theory of action that describes and explains how teachers in an inner-city multicultural elementary school write reports to parents about their students' achievement (Robinson, 2002). (See Chapter 2 for a description of this case.) The researchers wanted to know whether the school reports helped parents understand how well their children were achieving. They examined samples of school reports and interviewed teachers and school administrators about how reports were written. They also interviewed and surveyed parents about how the reports were understood.

The theory of action in Figure 8.1 provides answers to the following research questions:

1. How do teachers complete written reports to parents?

    This is answered by the three reporting strategies summarized in the middle row of Figure 8.1.

2. What are the constraints that explain these particular reporting practices?

    The answer to this question is provided by the set of constraints in the top row of Figure 8.1.

3. What are the consequences of these reporting practices for parental understanding?

    This is answered, in summary form, in the bottom row of Figure 8.1.

In order to complete the type of analysis summarized in Figure 8.1, the following steps need to be taken:

Steps of Data Analysis

1. Read and sort the information.

2. Determine the starting point of the analysis.

3. Analyze actions.

4. Analyze constraints.

5. Analyze consequences.

These steps are explained and illustrated throughout the remainder of this chapter. The final section of the chapter illustrates the process of evaluating a theory of action.

READING AND SORTING THE INFORMATION

Researchers are frequently advised to read and reread the information they have gathered before beginning a detailed analysis. This enables researchers to get a sense of the whole, so that recurring themes and possible relationships can be kept in mind while more detailed analyses are completed. It is also a good idea, even at this early stage, to focus on the relationships in your data, rather than on the isolated pieces of information, by sketching some possible theories of action.

With large data sets, involving numerous documents, interview transcripts, or questionnaires, it may be impractical to start by reviewing all the data. In such cases, it is sufficient to sample your information, taking care to include transcripts and data sources that are likely to reflect the variety of information gathered.

Once a sense of the whole has been gained, the next step in the analysis process is to sort your information according to whether it

- Describes or evaluates actions
- Provides a possible explanation of actions
- Describes possible consequences of actions

Not all three types of information may be relevant to your research question. The third category, for example, is not relevant to a question that does not concern itself with the description or evaluation of consequences. In such cases you would not sort any information into that category, nor refer to it when writing about or discussing the research.

Identifying the information that belongs in each category is easy when different methods or questions have been used to gather information about actions, constraints, and consequences. In the study summarized in Figure 8.1, for example, information about how teachers wrote reports was available from an analysis of the reports that they had completed. Information about why they wrote the reports as they did was found in their answers to particular interview questions. Information about the consequences of teachers' reporting for parental understanding was found in parents' answers to a questionnaire about how they understood the reports and in their replies to selected interview questions.

Sorting which pieces of information relate to constraints, actions, and consequences is a bit more complicated when information has been gathered in a less structured manner. One interview transcript, or even one section of a transcript, could cover all three categories. In such cases, you could use the approach described in the following box.

Analyzing Teachers' Talk in Professional Development Meetings

Brian Annan, a school improvement coordinator, examined the kinds of professional conversations teachers had with each other during professional development meetings. There were two primary sources of data—transcripts of the meetings themselves, and transcripts of interviews with the teachers and the professional developer. Brian coded each paragraph of the meeting and interview transcripts with a C for constraint and an A for action. Once he had done this preliminary sorting, he reviewed all the A paragraphs in the transcript and wrote a description of the kinds of conversations that occurred. He then reviewed all the C paragraphs and wrote a page that explained what they chose to talk about.

Notice that at this early stage of analysis, one is identifying *possible* constraints and consequences. It is important to be open to being wrong and to realize that initial ideas are likely to change. The process of developing and validating a theory of action continues throughout the analysis phase of research.

Some research questions require information about the practices of more than one group of people. In such cases, initial sorting into constraints, actions, and consequences should be done separately for each group. This approach allows for the possibility that the practices of each group are different and that different constraints are operating. For example, you might be interested in how experienced teachers and beginning teachers write school reports. By sorting the constraints, actions, and consequences for each group of teachers separately, you will be able to examine whether the way reports are written and the reasons for doing so differ according to teacher experience.

DETERMINING THE STARTING POINT OF THE ANALYSIS

Once your information is sorted, it is usually best to start by analyzing actions. A description of actions provides an anchor point for a subsequent search for the constraints that explain those actions. Similarly, if your research question asks about the consequences of particular actions, then a careful description of the actions guides the search for their consequences.

An exception to this rule is when you want to discover which actions have produced particular consequences. A group of teachers might want to raise student achievement by identifying effective teaching practices and discarding ineffective ones. They cannot start by describing actions, because they do not know how to identify those that are effective and ineffective in terms of their impact on student achievement. They should begin, therefore, by identifying contexts in which there are contrasting levels of student achievement. They can then treat these varying levels of achievement as the possible consequence of some, as yet unknown, teaching practices. The second step in the analysis, therefore, is to search for any teaching practices that might be responsible for the different levels of student achievement.

ANALYZING ACTIONS

The purpose of this step in your data analysis is to describe actions in a way that is relevant to your research question. This usually means completing the following three steps:

1. Identifying the relevant features of the actions

2. Counting the extent to which the relevant features are present

3. Summarizing the actions

We discuss each of these in turn next.

Identifying the Relevant Features of Actions

There is an infinite number of ways that any action or set of actions can be described. Researchers have to make decisions about the features of actions that they are going to highlight in their description. The way teachers write reports, for example, can be described in terms of the length of their comments, the color pen they use, or the proportion of comments that are made about student academic work or behavior. As Figure 8.1 shows, Viviane used three particular features to describe teacher report writing: whether or not they reported against national benchmarks, the difficulty level of their language, and the use of positive comments in relation to student achievement. Those particular features were highlighted because they were predicted to explain how well parents understood their child's report. In other words, the goal is not just to describe action, but to describe it using features that are likely to be useful in answering the research question.

In Chapter 5, we introduced the distinction between exploratory and checking research questions. This distinction is also important in determining the relevant features of action. In the reporting study discussed here, we had decided in advance, based on earlier research and on a literature review, that those three features of reporting were likely to be important in explaining parental understanding. In this case, therefore, we were checking whether certain features of reporting were present, rather than exploring in a more open-ended fashion. Checking whether predetermined features are present is also common in research on implementation. A professional developer, for example, may want to know whether the strategies she has taught teachers to employ are being used in the classroom. Her description of teachers' activity will, in this case, be organized around the particular features that were emphasized in the professional development.

Rather than checking whether particular features of activity are present, some research questions call for a more exploratory approach. Instead of bringing predetermined categories to the data, the researcher explores the data by identifying themes and patterns that appear relevant to the research question. The description is then organized around these emergent themes and patterns.

The distinction between emergent and predetermined analytic categories is a blurred rather than a sharp one. This is nicely illustrated in the following account of how Brian Annan, the school improvement coordinator we introduced earlier, developed his categories for different types of teacher talk. (You can read a report of this research in Annan, Lai, & Robinson, 2003.)

Developing Categories of Teacher Talk

An Auckland elementary school was part of a school improvement initiative where most of the professional development occurred in teacher clusters. These clusters met regularly to discuss strategies for improving schooling in their communities. Brian Annan, the school improvement coordinator assigned to this initiative, was concerned about the type of teacher conversations that occurred in the clusters. He believed that improvements would occur only if teachers talked about how to improve their own practices. He decided to study the teachers' talk by seeking permission to tape and analyze several cluster meetings. Once the tapes were transcribed, he had to develop a way of analyzing them that showed him whether these conversations were focused on teachers' own practice.

Brian began by reading all the meeting transcripts and searching for patterns in what he read. He and his colleagues noticed several different types of talk (actions). First, they noticed that a lot of the talk was not about school at all, but about teachers' personal lives. This led to the distinction between non-school and school talk (Figure 8.2). Second, they made a distinction between school talk that was and was not focused on teaching. They then subdivided the teaching talk category into non-learning and learning talk. ("Learning talk" was defined as talk that analyzed and evaluated the impact of teaching on student achievement, and challenged teachers to develop more effective practices to improve student learning.) This distinction was a particularly important one for Brian, because he wanted as much professional development time as possible to be focused on how to understand and strengthen the relationship between what teachers taught and what their students learned and understood.

Once they had developed and defined these categories, Brian and his colleagues reread all the transcripts and checked to see which types of talk teachers were engaging in. They counted the number of times a particular type of talk was present or absent in order to answer their original question about whether teachers were engaging in the types of conversations that they believed were most likely to improve teaching.

Figure 8.2   Categories of Teacher Talk

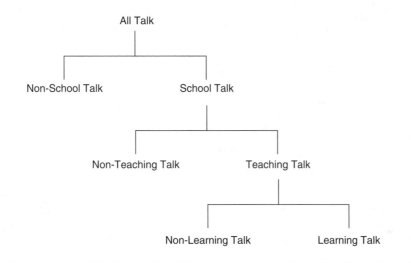

SOURCE: Adapted from Annan, Lai, & Robinson (2003).

The last paragraph in this example illustrates how the process of exploring is often completed by checking. Exploratory questions about what is happening are answered by identifying relevant features of the activity. These are described by codes or categories that are then used to check the relative frequency of the identified features.

If members of a teacher research team have differing views about what features of action need to be described, they should resolve their differences through a learning conversation. This is what happened in John Ackroyd's research, which, as we discussed in Chapters 3 and 4, was investigating whether his school's teacher evaluation policy focused on teaching and learning. The team wanted to check whether the policy had a "direct" or "indirect" focus on teaching and learning, but the team could not initially agree on how to distinguish between them. John described part of the process this way:

> Even when we knew exactly what we meant by a direct and indirect focus on teaching and learning, we ended up disagreeing when we tried to check how these definitions applied to the policy. So each team member went away and counted the statements in the policy which they believed matched each definition. Then, as a team, we discussed what each member had counted. Because we still disagreed, we ended up discussing whether we should use a different definition of what was direct and indirect. In the end, we developed a new way of checking for direct or indirect features.

(We described the steps you can take to resolve similar issues using learning conversations in Table 3.2.)

Finally, when analyzing actions, you need to distinguish between reported and actual actions. While observations produce data on what actually happened, interviews, diaries, and questionnaires produce reports of action that will need to be verified by cross-checking against other relevant sources of information. These sources could include meeting minutes that record that the action took place and interviews with other persons with relevant experience. The more that people's reports of actions check out with one another, the more confident you can be that their reports describe what actually happened.

Counting the Relevant Features of Action

Counting or quantifying information is important, even when your data source is primarily textual rather than numeric. First, much of the language we use to describe actions, such as "Most people do . . . ," and "This action hardly ever occurs . . . ," implies that some counting has gone on. Second, counting provides a disciplined way to check the validity of your initial descriptions of your data. It forces you to take all the relevant information into account, rather than just those examples or extracts that attract your attention as you read over your notes and transcripts. Third, counting provides a more precise and readily shared language than vague phrases like "many teachers" or "most students."

In some instances, however, a qualitative description of the relevant features of the action may suffice. This is usually true when the research describes and explains the action of an individual. For example, if you are describing the actions of a student who copies assignments and decide that the relevant features are what assignments were copied, how the copying took place, and the percentage of the final grade the copied assignments were worth, you could state, "The student only copied math assignments that were worth less than 10 percent of the final grade. He would copy all his friend's answers without changing any of them." Counting may also be unnecessary when rich qualitative descriptions of the actions provide convincing evidence of the validity of the conclusions drawn. (See Chapter 4 for more information about procedures to increase the validity of qualitative analyses.)

It is important to note that this section focuses on how to make decisions about what to count rather than on statistical or data presentation techniques. We recommend that you read books such as Leedy and Ormrod (2001) and Gay and Airasian (2003) to learn more about using statistics in your work,[1] and read Bell (1999) to learn about how to present information. Remember that problem-based methodology is open to both qualitative and quantitative information, and to the use of statistics to analyze information that is in quantitative form.

We next outline some of the decisions you will need to make in order to count relevant features of action. If a structured approach to data collection was used, many of these decisions will have been made prior to data collection. If data were collected in an unstructured way, then decisions about how to count actions will need to be made at this stage. There are three main decisions to be made if you want to quantify your descriptions of action:

1. Count the presence/absence or frequency of action.

2. Determine the unit of analysis.

3. Decide whether to associate actions with people.

Count Presence/Absence or Frequency of Action

Sometimes all we want to know is whether or not something occurred, rather than how often it occurred. Some actions are so unusual or powerful that a single occurrence in a meeting or a class period will have an impact. A teacher-researcher may want to eliminate any instance of verbal abuse by students, and so a simple count of whether or not it occurred in a lesson would be sufficient. Similarly, a teacher may want to monitor whether or not a student who is very shy is able to ask for help. A single

---

1. For a helpful introductory statistics tutorial, see Lauer (2004).

instance of this behavior over a series of lessons would represent considerable progress.

An example of how you could count and present such data using the verbal abuse example is as follows:

Lesson	Verbal Abuse Occurred in the Lesson (✓ = Yes, x = No)
Math	✓
Science	x
Geography	✓
Art	✓
History	✓

One of the dangers of counting the presence rather than the frequency of an action is that important variations are lost. A teacher who implemented a new strategy once in her lesson (the bare minimum!) will look no different from a teacher who used the same strategy five times. For example, if you look at the following checksheet, you will see that every teacher attempted to use the new strategy. If you were merely counting the presence or absence of the strategies, you would report that all teachers used the new strategy. However, when you compare the number of times they used it, you can see that there is a large variation in the number of uses, particularly between Joseph, who used it 10 times, and Jeff, who used it only once. This may not be a problem, however, if the researcher's concern is whether or not teachers *can* use the strategy, rather than how often they use it.

Teacher	Number of Times Strategy Is Used	
Joseph	ⅢⅢ ⅢⅢ	10
Kim	ⅢⅢ Ⅰ	6
Jeff	Ⅰ	1
James	ⅢⅠ	3

Determine the Unit of Analysis

In order to count an action, you need to be able to distinguish it from the stream of ongoing events and activity. If you cannot identify the beginning and end of an activity, then it is impossible to get an accurate frequency count. In the language of research techniques, you need to decide on the *unit of analysis*.

Sometimes activities have natural beginning and endpoints, so it is relatively easy to demarcate their occurrence. For example, a teacher may be working with his students on a project that involves increasing their care of the school grounds. They develop an observation schedule that counts, over a half-hour period, the number of students they see putting trash into one of three trash containers. The act of putting trash into a container is a relatively discrete one, and thus over a period of time, two different observers of the same events should be able to get the same or nearly the same frequency counts. Compare this case with a project designed to increase the interaction of learning disabled and non-learning disabled children. What counts as one interaction? If two disabled students talk to a non-disabled student, is that one interaction or two? If they stop talking because they stop to listen to the teacher, is that two interactions or one continuous interaction?

The key point to remember in deciding such questions is that there are no standard answers. Each researcher must establish their own answers using the following as rules of thumb:

- Construct rules about how to count that suit the practicalities of the situation.
- Write the rules down so that you can apply them consistently.
- Test whether or not your rules work by seeing whether two analysts arrive at the same or very similar counts.

The unit of analysis problem must also be solved before coding records of interviews, meetings, or conversations. To illustrate this latter process, we return to the previous example where Brian Annan, the school improvement coordinator, was studying what teachers talked about in their professional development meetings. He had already reviewed the transcripts and defined the categories of talk that he was interested in. His next step was deciding how to define a unit of talk. He could decide that every sentence was an instance of teacher talk and code each sentence into one of the categories. On the other hand, he could treat each speaker's turn as the unit, regardless of the number of sentences they spoke on each occasion. In this case, every turn taken by a speaker would be coded into one of the categories. A third option would be to treat a change in category as the unit of analysis. Every change in type of talk would be coded, even if it occurred within a single sentence.

Once again, there are no hard and fast rules for deciding whether a unit of analysis for coding speech should be each change of speaker, every new sentence, or every change in speech content that could be coded in a new category. Two key considerations are the level of precision required and the accurate representation of the main patterns of talk. The smaller the unit, the more precisely one can count the way the various categories are represented. Precision is not everything, however. A teacher could speak one sentence on how to administer a test and repeat himself in the next two sentences. If the sentence was the unit of analysis, this would be scored three times under non-teaching talk in Brian's coding. If the larger units (a speaker's turn, or change of category) were used, these three sentences would be scored once. In this case, the choice of unit depends on whether or not the researcher wants to emphasize how talk uses up air time, or how it communicates ideas. If the use of air time is seen as important, then the three sentences should be scored separately. If the researcher is interested in ideas, then it makes sense to treat these three sentences as one procedural idea. Once again, there is no one right or wrong answer. What is important is to make a decision, justify that decision in terms of the research question, and try it out.

Decide Whether to Associate Actions With People

Some research questions require information about not only what happened, but also about who did what. In this section, we consider two ways in which actions are associated with people:

1. Counting the proportion or percentage of a group who did something

2. Counting actions performed by people with certain characteristics

Teachers quite often want to know that all or nearly all of their students have completed an activity. Professional developers often want to know what proportion of the teachers who attended a course have implemented the instructional strategies that they were taught. This type of analysis requires each action to be associated with an identified individual, so that the proportion of the group who engaged in the activity can be calculated. It tells us about the spread of the activity across a defined group and gives us quite different information from an analysis that counts the total number of actions regardless of who performed them. Consider a counselor who has just led a course for senior students who have volunteered to be mentors for the new freshman class. One of the skills he has taught the senior students is the use of open rather than closed questions. He tapes the last four discussions of the group, when they have been instructed to practice using open questions, and counts the number of open and closed questions that the seniors ask. His results are summarized in Table 8.1. (Note that he included the total number of questions each student asked because each student asked a different number of questions.)

If the counselor was interested only in the totals, he could consider his training a success, as the senior students ask 25 percent more open than closed questions. (To obtain this percentage, subtract the total number of closed questions from the open questions, divide by the total number of questions and multiply by 100. The calculations are $[50 - 30/80] \times 100 = 25\%$.)

An analysis that associates actions with people, however, tells a different story, for it shows that 5 of the 11 students still use as many or more closed than open questions. If asking more open than closed questions were the standard for passing this aspect of the training, then one has to conclude that the course was not successful with approximately 45 percent of the students. (To obtain this percentage, divide the number of students

Table 8.1   Number of Closed and Open Questions Used by Senior Students

Student	Number Closed	Number Open	Total Questions
Angela	3	0	3
April	2	6	8
Liz	2	0	2
Maggie	0	8	8
Sharmila	2	2	4
Ben	6	2	8
Junior	3	7	10
Lawton	3	10	13
Malo	4	1	5
Timothy	4	8	12
Tipene	1	6	7
Total	30	50	80

($n = 11$)

who asked as many or more closed questions than open questions by the total number of students and multiply by 100 [$5/11 \times 100 = 45\%$].) This type of analysis is particularly important for practitioners who are concerned about the well-being and performance of individuals rather than just the average performance of the whole group.

In Table 8.1, the counselor has associated the actions with individual students. It is sometimes useful to group individuals in ways that explore or check the relationship between groups and the actions. The selection of groups may be determined before the data are collected, based on prior research or experience. On the other hand, the groups may suggest themselves as the counselor explores the data. He may have developed the impression, for example, that his male students are more likely to use open questions than his female students. This hunch could be checked by reanalyzing the data in Table 8.1 as shown in Table 8.2. To reanalyze the information, the counselor added up the number of open and closed questions the girls and boys made separately.

Table 8.2   Number of Closed and Open Questions by Gender of Senior Students

	Number Closed	Number Open	Total Questions
Girls ($n = 5$)	9	16	25
Boys ($n = 6$)	21	34	55
Total	30	50	80

Table 8.2 is deceptively simple. On first sight, it might look as if the boys do ask more open questions than the girls (boys asked 34 open questions and girls asked 16). The problem with this analysis is that it has used the raw frequencies without taking into account that there are more boys

(n = 6) than girls (n = 5) in the group.[2] The boys' total might be greater simply because there are more of them. A fair comparison between boys and girls requires calculation of the average number of open questions asked by the students in each group. The resulting figures of 5.7 and 3.2 open questions for boys and girls, respectively, suggest that boys do ask more open questions than girls. To obtain these figures, you would divide the number of open questions in each group by the number of students in that group. For example, the calculation for the girls' group is 16/5 = 3.2.

There is still more work to do, however, because the analysis so far has also failed to take into account that the male and female students asked very different total numbers of questions. The greater number of open questions per male student may reflect the greater total number of questions (open and closed) that they asked. What is also needed is an analysis of the relative proportions of closed and open questions asked by male and female students. When the open questions are calculated as a proportion of each group's total number of questions, the proportions turn out to be almost identical, in this case .64 of girls' questions are open as compared to .62 of boys' questions. (To obtain this percentage, divide the number of open questions in each group by the total number of questions in each group. For example, the calculation for the girls' group is 16/25 = .64.)

The correct conclusions to draw from Tables 8.1 and 8.2 are the following:

1. On average, boys asked more open questions than girls.

2. On average, boys asked more total questions than girls.

3. The proportion of open and closed questions asked by boys and girls was very similar.

The conclusions drawn from Table 8.2 could be further tested with the use of a simple statistical test called *chi square*, which is designed to show whether differences between groups are statistically significant (for a readable account of descriptive statistics including chi square, see Salkind, 2004). Before using such statistics, however, it is important to understand how to interpret the distribution of data in a table such as Table 8.2. One test of such understanding is whether or not you can describe what a table is telling you, as we have done for Table 8.1 and 8.2.

Summarizing Actions

The last stage of the analysis of actions involves writing a short summary of your findings. The summary describes those features of the data that are relevant to the research question and that need to be explained by a subsequent constraint analysis.

Quantitative data are summarized in tables with the main points of the table elaborated and highlighted in the accompanying text. Qualitative

---

2. "n = 11" tells you the number of students (11) involved in this analysis.

data (that is, information that has not been counted) are also summarized by describing the main patterns of activity, including how they are associated with particular groups or individuals.

We recommend tables or graphs for counted data because, if well constructed, they communicate a lot of information simply. It is important when constructing a table to think of the main points you want to make and then organize the table in a manner that communicates them clearly. For example, if you want to make a point about individuals, then you should organize your table by individual; if you want to make a point about categories of action, then those same categories should be used in the table. Table 8.1 illustrates how a table contains both information about the individual students (for example, April, Liz) and the categories of action (closed and open questions). (For further details on how to decide what to put in the rows and columns of your table and how to order the information, we recommend you read Wainer, 1992.)

Keep tables simple by avoiding numerous subcategories of information. Such information quickly becomes meaningless, particularly when there are very small numbers involved. Similarly, avoid using several decimal places. They suggest a level of precision that is usually inappropriate for the methods that are used in teacher research. Round your averages and other calculations to the nearest whole number or to one decimal point. Describing the average experience of a group of teachers as 8.35 years does not make a lot of sense and is harder to remember than an average of 8 years. On the other hand, the use of two decimal places may be justified if, for example, one is reporting test scores of a large group of students and the difference between a score of 12.23 and 12.98 has some practical or statistical significance.

The relationship between tables and text is important. The text should highlight and explain, rather than repeat, the key points of the tables. For example, the text that accompanies Table 8.2 should explain how the data support the three conclusions that were drawn earlier, namely, that the boys asked more questions than the girls, that they also asked more open questions, and finally, how the relative proportion of open and closed questions was no different for the two groups.

Finally, keep all your raw data and analyses so that you can return to them when you revisit different aspects of your analysis. Keeping good records also enables you to share your work and get help from others.

ANALYZING CONSTRAINTS

In Chapter 2, we explained how teaching practices can be understood as solutions to practical problems about what to do. Since there are usually many different ways of solving any particular problem, the way we understand these practices in PBM is to understand why a particular solution, rather than any of the plausible alternatives, is being used. This explanatory process involves undertaking a constraint analysis; that is, discovering the constraints that have ruled in this solution while ruling out the other possibilities. For example, if we want to understand why a teacher persists in using only two reading groups in her Grade 2 class, when all her colleagues use three or four, we need to understand the constraints that rule in the use of two groups and rule out using more than two. We can discover the relevant constraints by asking the teacher herself and by observing the context of the relevant activity. The teacher may explain, through an interview or questionnaire, that she uses two groups because she needs to keep a close eye on the children as they are not well enough behaved to work independently of her supervision. According to the teacher herself, the constraint that explains her use of two reading groups is the children's behavior.

The reasons that people give for their own actions constitute the constraints that form part of their espoused theory of action, and it is very important to distinguish them from the actual constraints on their action. Sometimes people's reasons turn out to be accurate when checked against information gained from other sources. Sometimes they turn out to be inaccurate, because people are either not aware of the relevant constraints, or they do not wish to reveal those constraints that, in their eyes, make them look bad.

How can you test whether people's espoused theory identifies the real constraints on their action? To return to the example of the reading groups, you could check the teacher's reasons in an interview situation by asking questions like "If you were more confident that the children would behave when working independently, would that enable you to run more reading groups?" or "Is there any other reason that would stop you doing that?" Such questions ask teachers to reflect on the constraints they have put forward by considering whether they accurately describe all the conditions that are important to them. These questions can be anticipated and asked during the interview or can be asked during any follow-up sessions with the teacher. As you will not always be able to anticipate what information you will need to check constraints, you may have to go through additional cycles of data collection and analysis before confirming a constraint set.

A further type of check comes with detailed knowledge of the teacher's context. Such knowledge suggests other possible constraints, each of which needs to be checked against the facts of the situation.

In short, the skill in constraint analysis involves using the following to suggest and test possible constraints on action:

- Teachers' own explanations
- Your knowledge of the research context
- Your knowledge of similar contexts

In Table 8.3, we have suggested some possible constraints on the teacher's use of only two reading groups, and some practical ways in which their validity could be checked. Some of the constraints could be suggested by the teacher herself; others may be suggested by the teacher-researcher. In either case, their validity needs to be carefully checked.

Table 8.3   Checking Possible Constraints on Action

Possible Constraints on Teacher's Use of Two Reading Groups	Suggested Checks
Children are too badly behaved to work without close supervision, and the teacher can supervise two groups more closely than four.	• Ask teacher to imagine her class as well behaved and independent. Would she then use four groups? • Help teacher to satisfy this constraint by becoming more skilled in instructional routines and classroom management. Check whether teacher then uses four rather than two groups.
Reading resources are inadequate to run more than two different groups.	• Check how other teachers resource four reading groups. • Check availability of surplus reading resources. • Check willingness of teacher to change if administrators supply additional materials.
More time and effort is involved in organizing a reading program for four rather than two groups.	• Ask teacher to talk about the costs/benefits of running four rather than two reading groups.

As a result of the checking described in Table 8.3, the researcher will be able to establish whether the constraints reported by the teacher provide valid explanations of her use of two reading groups.

In the remainder of this section we provide a guide to the process of constraint analysis. While we describe some broad steps and guidelines, keep in mind that what you are trying to achieve is a consistent and logical explanation of particular actions.

There are four broad steps in a constraint analysis:

1. Identify possible constraints.

2. Label the proposed constraints.

3. Develop the constraint set.

4. Construct group or organizational constraint sets.

Identifying Possible Constraints

Start by clearly describing the actions you want to explain and keep in mind as you work backward that you are searching for the problem for which these actions are the solution. Since constraints are conditions that rule in possible actions and rule out others, it is often extremely helpful to also describe some of the solution alternatives that have been ruled out. For example, in Table 8.3 the questions about why four reading groups are not used (an alternative solution to the problem of how to organize reading) provide vital clues about the constraints that have ruled in the use of two groups. A good constraint analysis is sufficiently specific to explain why one solution to a problem rather than another has been employed.

The raw data for a constraint analysis are all the pieces of information that were identified through the sorting process as sources of possible constraints. If the analysis involves checking a previously established list of possible constraints, this information will be examined for the degree of support for the items on the list. If the analysis is exploratory, then the search is for conditions that might explain the particular action, strategy, or policy under consideration.

Analysts of qualitative data are often urged to search for repeated themes in their data. However, repetition is not always a good guide to the identification of constraints. Something might be mentioned by many people as being important, yet they may be incorrect in their beliefs, in which case, these themes represent what people believe are the relevant constraints and may not be the actual constraints. On the other hand, the actual constraints may be so taken for granted that they are not explicitly talked about. For example, people may not be aware of the way actions are constrained by personal qualities, or if they are aware, they may prefer to speak about constraints that are less threatening. For all those reasons, repeatedly nominated constraints should be taken notice of, but the fact of their repetition is no guarantee of their validity.

The validation of a constraint involves the processes described in Chapter 4 on validity. The analyst uses multiple data sources to check that the constraint has explanatory power while at the same time staying alert for any disconfirming evidence. The analyst plays devil's advocate by asking questions such as the following:

- Was this constraint present when the action did not take place?
- Has the action occurred when the constraint was not present?
- Would the proposed constraints also rule in the plausible alternative solutions?

Such questions provide logical and empirical checks on the strength of the relationship between the proposed constraints and the actions that the analyst is trying to explain.

Practitioners who are skilled in constraint analysis reap important practical benefits. A teacher who through careful observation, questioning, and logical reasoning comes to understand the actions of her students will be able to win their confidence and to collaborate with them in removing or lessening the impact of the constraints that limit their success. Similarly, as this next account shows, a careful constraint analysis helps practitioners to target resources in ways that are effective and efficient because they understand precisely what has to change in order to gain improvement.

Careful Constraint Analysis Has Practical Payoff

Mei, in her role as professional developer in a school improvement initiative, was required to make an application for further funding to help teachers use student achievement information to improve teaching and learning. Mei collected data on teachers' existing capacity by asking them to write a case study describing an example of how they had analyzed and used achievement data to improve teaching practice. In reviewing these cases, Mei uncovered four major learning needs. Rather than just ask for money to address these needs, she wanted to know more about why, after all the professional development teachers had already received, they were still unable to demonstrate these particular skills. In other words, Mei wanted to understand more about the constraints on learning these particular analysis skills, so that she could provide a better targeted development experience.

One of the skills that practitioners were unable to demonstrate in their written cases was providing evidence for their causal explanations of student achievement. Practitioners would claim, for example, that low achievement scores were due to an invalid assessment tool, without providing any evidence for this claim.

Mei started her analysis by raising and discounting several possible explanations for the absence of evidence in teachers' cases. One explanation she considered was that the teachers typically employed data-free explanations of student achievement. She discounted this explanation, however, because in a prior oral mastery task, teachers had provided evidence for their causal claims.

On reviewing the notes she had made during this oral task, however, Mei noticed that she had written about how teachers provided evidence only when prompted to do so. This made her think that the reason why they did not provide evidence in their cases was not that they did not have any, but that they were not skilled in writing about that evidence unless prompted or helped to do so.

Mei checked the validity of her belief that the main constraint on providing evidence was teachers' inability to write about it by taking the following steps:

1. In follow-up sessions with the case writers, she asked for evidence for their causal explanations. Under those circumstances, all practitioners could provide evidence through critical incidents and/or appropriate school records.

2. She asked teachers directly whether writing about their evidence was a problem for them, and they confirmed that it was.

3. Mei checked the professional development curriculum already delivered to the teachers, and noted that nothing had been taught on writing in an evidence-based style.

From these three checks, Mei concluded that the main constraint on teachers' case writing was not their inability to think in an evidence-based way, but their difficulty with writing about evidence. She then designed a new segment of training that focused on how to write reports for funders and administrators in which statements about local needs and resource requirements were backed up with evidence.

This example illustrates how a constraint that is suggested by one type of evidence is validated by checking against information gathered by a different method. As always, however, rigor must be achieved in a practical way. Teacher-researchers do not have time to check all their proposed constraints against three or four different types of data. Much of the checking can be done, as Mei did, through "thought experiments" by asking what would happen if the suggested constraint on the action was not present, or whether the action still happens even though the proposed constraint is absent. Thus much of the validation process is a matter of critical thinking—of progressively developing and revising your interpretations of your data. Critical thinking is stimulated by considering the arguments that are mounted by your most skeptical audience. Those arguments provide tough tests of the validity of your constraint analysis, and if you can convince those audiences, you are likely to have an adequate explanation.

Labeling the Proposed Constraints

The next step in a constraint analysis involves labeling the proposed constraints. This involves identifying and naming the relevant features j177of the proposed constraints in a way that makes it easier to understand how the constraint explains the relevant action. For example, you want to know the reason why a group of teachers does not keep up-to-date with the latest relevant research. Several teachers you interviewed mentioned that the latest research was "not useful" and "less relevant to practice." You group these ideas under a heading of "relevance," but are unsure about how to word the label. There are several possibilities:

1. Relevance of research

2. Perceived relevance of research

3. Low perceived relevance of research

The first label indicates that one of the qualities that these teachers take into account when deciding what to read is the relevance of the research. The label is inadequate, however, because it does not communicate the judgment that explains lack of professional reading. Without this judgment we do not understand the link between relevance and the action of not reading the research. The second label suffers from the same limitation. It is an improvement on the first, however, because it describes the constraint as the *perceived* relevance of published research rather than the relevance. This is an appropriate change given that the constraint is based on teacher interviews and their perceptions of relevance. The constraining factor may be the teachers' understanding of the research and its potential usefulness, rather than the actual relevance of the research. The third label is preferable to the other two, because it makes explicit that the data comprise perceptions of relevance and it also describes the judgment that has been made about the degree of relevance. The label conveys that (1) these teachers want their reading to be of relevance, and (2) that they have judged recent published research to be of little relevance to their work. Hence the label conveys the link between the constraint and the action to be explained (lack of professional reading).

Developing the Constraint Set

Once you have identified and labeled a list of possible constraints, you need to examine how the constraints work as a set to explain action. This means discovering the relationships between the various constraints and understanding how these relationships lead to the action in question. Constraints do not operate independently of one another. It is the combination of constraints and the relationships between them that explain action. That is why an adequate constraint analysis must go beyond the creation of a list, and show how the constraints work together as a set to rule in the action and rule out the alternatives.

Imagine a school administrator charged with drawing up a budget that saves money over the previous year. There may be 10 realistic ways in which he can achieve this. Imagine, in addition, that he is also required to maintain high levels of morale among the teaching staff. There may also be 10 realistic ways of adequately satisfying the second constraint on his budget. The point of the example is that there are likely to be far fewer than 10 ways in which *both* constraints can be satisfied. The constraints are in tension, in that many of the actions that would satisfy one constraint are ruled out because they do not satisfy the other to an adequate extent. If you do not understand the relationship between these two constraints, you will not be able to explain why strategies that would produce higher savings or higher levels of morale have not been adopted.

The tension between constraints is often so strong that a trade-off is required, which results in one being satisfied to a far greater extent than the others. In our study on reporting, for example, we discovered that while teachers claimed to write reports that were both accurate and positive, their actual report writing satisfied the accuracy constraint to a far lower degree than the constraint to be positive. The reason was not that the teachers set out to deliberately deceive, but that they lacked the skills and understandings required to craft comments that were simultaneously honest and positive in tone. To them, "being accurate" was more than in tension with "being positive"—they saw them as in conflict when reporting on an underachieving student. When these tensions and dilemmas are accurately and respectfully identified and discussed, it is highly likely that teachers will be able to take the next step of planning improvements in their practice. The analysis has, quite literally, pointed the way to improvement.

So far we have described and illustrated two of three strategies that we employ in formulating a constraint set—identifying the relationship between the various constraints, and identifying their relative importance.

In the remainder of this section, we describe the third strategy—checking the adequacy of the constraint set by eliminating alternative actions. A constraint analysis is complete when it shows why the observed action was the only possible alternative given the constraints that were operating. If the constraint set fails to exclude other actions or strategies, then it is incomplete and should be revised.

In our study on student copying (Robinson & Lai, 1999), we discovered that our constraint set did not provide an adequate explanation of the copying of one student. In our original constraint set we suggested that his copying of friends' assignments was constrained by (1) his desire to get good grades, and (2) his desire to learn from model answers. This analysis was incomplete, however, because these two constraints could also be satisfied by asking friends to help him develop his own model answers. Why did he just copy the model answers from his successful friends? In a follow-up interview, we posed this alternative action to the student, and he explained that he would rather appear smart and lazy than hardworking and stupid. Hence he copied rather than asked for help in developing model answers. We drew the constraint set for this student's copying as follows:

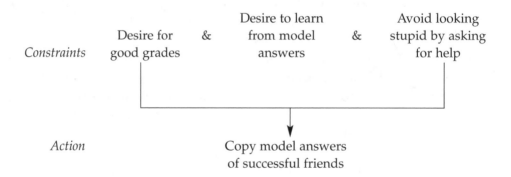

This example illustrates an important point—often when developing the constraint set you may need to identify and label new constraints. You may also have to revise the way you have labeled the constraints. Hence the process of developing a constraint set often involves returning to the first two steps of identifying and labeling the possible constraints.

In summary, once a list of possible constraints is proposed, a constraint set is developed using three strategies: identifying the relationship between the constraints, identifying their relative importance, and checking that the constraint set eliminates all the alternative courses of action. The result is a causal account that explains what led people to act as they did, whether or not they were aware of the factors that led them to do so.

Constructing Group or Organizational Constraint Sets

An individual's actions are understood by creating a constraint set for that individual; a group's actions are understood by creating a constraint set for the group; and organizational action is understood by creating a constraint set that shows how organizational values, culture, and other conditions lead to particular patterns of activity.

One way of creating a group constraint set involves creating separate constraint sets for each member and then seeing whether the constraints are sufficiently similar across all members to collapse them into one. For example, in our study on why students copied assignments (Robinson & Lai, 1999), we created six separate constraint sets for each participating student. Then we looked for commonalities across the constraint sets and noticed that most of the constraint sets had two constraints in common: the need to be efficient when completing assignments and the desire to obtain good grades. We could then use these two constraints to explain the copying of all but one of the groups.

A constraint set for an organizational action can be constructed by tracing the interrelationships between the constraint sets of different organizational groups. Such analyses show how the actions of one group constrain the actions of another, in a cascade of interdependent patterns. We have previously discussed how the way teachers reported to parents was constrained by the school management's requirement that there be no negative comments (Robinson & Timperley, 2000). A further question can be asked, however, about the origins of this requirement. This question is answered in PBM by treating the instruction to report positively as an action that is explained by discovering the constraints that led management to issue this instruction. This example nicely illustrates how one group's actions act as constraints on the actions of another.

An Exercise in Constraint Analysis

The following exercise[3] shows how a constraint set is constructed from interview data to explain aspects of teachers' interactions with students. The teacher in charge of learning support at an Auckland high school was curious about the effectiveness of the school's new policy on placing students who were learning disabled (LD) in the same classes as their peers who were not learning disabled (NLD). He decided to involve his colleagues in an informal evaluation of how this mainstreaming policy was working. One of the questions he asked was whether teachers talked to the LD students about the lesson content or whether interactions between these students and their teachers were largely nonacademic.

The teacher-researchers developed a simple observation schedule that they used to code every teacher's interaction with individual students as either academic or nonacademic. This enabled them to compare the extent of academic and nonacademic interactions across both LD and NLD students in six classrooms. The teachers then prepared the summary of their observations that is presented in Table 8.4. The main conclusion they drew from the table was that, with the exception of Charmaine, teachers

---

3. The exercise is based on the published report of Lai, Sinclair, Naidoo, Naidoo, & Robinson (2003), but some details and data have been changed to simplify and clarify the exercise.

Table 8.4   Percentage of Teacher-Student Interactions That Are Academic

Teacher	Learning Disabled Students	Non-Learning Disabled Students
Daniel	5	40
Robin	17	60
Tipene	15	58
Stella	25	53
Ursula	10	20
Charmaine	50	48

had a much lower percentage of academic interactions with students with learning disabilities than with students who were not learning disabled.

Table 8.5 presents those extracts from the transcripts of each teacher's interview that suggest possible constraints on their academic interaction with students with learning disabilities.

Table 8.5   Extracts From Teacher Interviews Suggesting Constraints on Academic Interaction

Teacher	Interview Extracts
Daniel	I'm there to provide support for the LD students, to help them feel good about education and learning. Sometimes it's hard, because they do everything so badly, but I try and find something they can do well and comment on that, like the effort they make and how neat their work is. Mary [teacher aide] works with the LD kids on all the "heavy learning." I think that's why they've hired her. If I had more time in class, I would help them, but Mary is doing a fantastic job so I can concentrate on teaching the non-LD kids.
Robin	It's not my job to teach them so to speak. Mary [teacher aide] teaches them. I'm to be their cheerleader. I only have a limited number of hours in each class. Since they have a teacher aide to teach them, I focus on the non-LD kids.
Tipene	The school put Sushila [teacher aide] in my class, so I'm assuming that's her job—to work with the LD kids and help them with the material. If I had more time, in an ideal world, yeah I'll help them, but as it is I don't have enough time to work with my non-LD kids.
Stella	Not wanting to be non-PC or anything, but I don't have the time to teach the LD kids. I don't have enough hours as it is to help the regular kids.
Ursula	It's not my job to teach academic stuff to LD kids. They've got the teacher aide. I'm here to make sure they feel good about their studies. There aren't enough hours in a day to teach two lots of kids who are so different. I don't have the expertise anyway.
Charmaine	It's my responsibility to help these students understand the content of the lesson. I talk to the LD students to make sure they understand what I mean. I also make sure they have the instructions clear before I leave them.

Here is how we suggest you go about constructing a constraint set for each of the six teachers interviewed, beginning with Daniel.

Identify Possible Constraints. The process of identifying possible constraints begins by listing the relevant actions you are trying to explain. In this case, start with the data on Daniel's interaction with his students. Table 8.4 shows that he has a much lower percentage of academic interactions with students with learning disabilities than with those who do not have such disabilities.

The next step in identifying constraints is to study the extracts from Daniel's interview and list the relevant constraints. Daniel mentions four constraints:

1. Providing support to LD students

2. Helping LD students feel good

3. Teacher aide helps with all "heavy learning" for LD students

4. Limited class time so he concentrates on non-LD students

Label the Constraints. In this step, label the possible constraints in a way that enables you to understand how the constraint set explains the relevant action. In this example, the descriptions of the four constraints are sufficiently detailed to be used as the initial labels.

Develop and Verify the Constraint Set. Begin by working out how the constraints work as a set to explain the action. This involves clarifying how each constraint rules actions in and out. The first proposed constraint—being supportive—does not necessarily preclude academic interaction. After all, many good teachers provide support by explaining lesson content clearly to their students. Why is it that Daniel's idea of support rules out giving academic support? The answer seems to lie in Daniel's belief that to be supportive involves giving positive feedback that makes people feel good. Since his LD students are not succeeding academically, he believes he can give them little by way of academic support. Instead, he supports by praising such things as effort and neatness of work.

Daniel's perception of the role of his teacher aide also rules out his engagement in academic teaching of LD students. He believes such teaching ("heavy learning") is the aide's role. The fourth constraint on academic interaction is time—given the aide's role, Daniel's priority for academic interaction is the NLD students.

It is useful at this stage to draw a picture to show the relationship between the various constraints and the action. This gives you a summary of how the constraints work as a set to explain Daniel's actions.

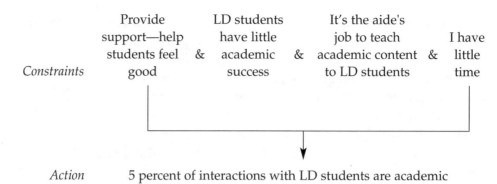

It is also useful to write a summary that briefly describes the constraint set and shows how it explains the teacher's interactions. A summary of Daniel's constraint set is as follows:

> Daniel seldom talks with the LD students in his class about academic matters because he believes his role is to help them feel good about their learning. Since his LD students seldom succeed in academic tasks, he provides support by focusing on nonacademic matters such as their effort and the neatness of their work. Daniel's conception of support is further reinforced by the role he attributes to the teacher aide—he perceives her role as helping students with the "heavy learning." Finally, given the limited class time, he believes it more important that he teach the NLD students, particularly since he sees the aide's role as teaching the LD students.

Now that the first draft of Daniel's constraint set has been developed, begin verifying the constraint set. To do so, identify any features of the constraint set that need further checking. The analysis thus far is based only on Daniel's self-report. A number of Daniel's claims could be relatively easily checked. First, the observation notes could be used to check Daniel's claim that his interactions with LD students provide nonacademic support. Second, does the teacher aide confirm that Daniel sees her role as teaching the LD students? Third, why does Daniel say that the aide's role is to teach, and that she is doing a fantastic job, when he also claims that the students seldom succeed on academic tasks?

Once you have completed Daniel's constraint set and are satisfied that it is an accurate explanation, repeat the process of identifying, labeling, developing, and verifying constraints for the remaining five teachers. The following five diagrams convey the main constraints that are operating for each of the remaining teachers. Remember there is no one right way to identify and label constraints. The key to an adequate constraint analysis is to make sure you have captured the meanings and the conditions that produce the actions you are trying to explain.

Robin

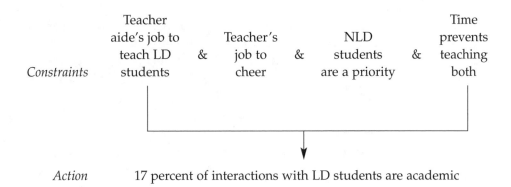

Constraints   Teacher aide's job to teach LD students   &   Teacher's job to cheer   &   NLD students are a priority   &   Time prevents teaching both

Action   17 percent of interactions with LD students are academic

Tipene

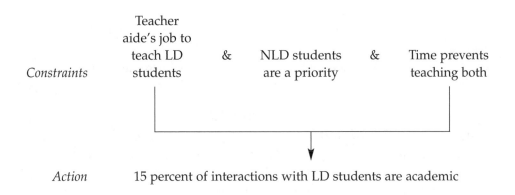

Constraints   Teacher aide's job to teach LD students   &   NLD students are a priority   &   Time prevents teaching both

Action   15 percent of interactions with LD students are academic

Stella

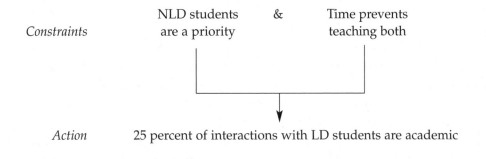

Constraints   NLD students are a priority   &   Time prevents teaching both

Action   25 percent of interactions with LD students are academic

Ursula

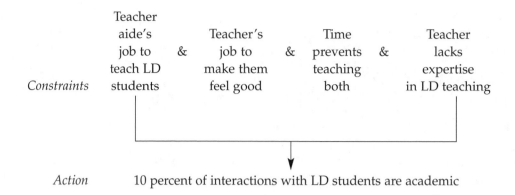

Charmaine

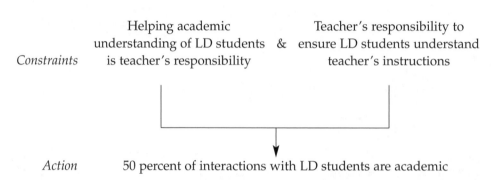

Construct Group or Organizational Constraint Sets. Finally, consider whether you can claim to have found a common explanation for these teachers' interactions. You should exclude Charmaine from consideration, because her pattern of interaction with students is clearly different from those of her five colleagues. Ask yourself whether there are sufficient commonalities across the remaining five individual constraint sets to enable them to be collapsed together. You could argue that there is a common explanation for the interaction patterns of these five, because they have similar beliefs about the respective responsibilities of the teacher and teacher aide and about time limitations. The constraint of expertise should probably not be included in the group analysis since it applies only to Ursula. This exception could be noted in the explanatory text. Since Charmaine does not belong to the same group as the other five, her constraint set would need to be discussed separately. As such, you would present and discuss the group's constraint set followed by Charmaine's constraint set, and discuss the difference between the two.

The following diagram conveys the constraint set that is operating for all teachers except Charmaine. (The percentage of academic interactions is obtained by adding up the percentage of academic interactions across all five teachers and dividing by 5.) In explaining the diagram you should make clear that it is a generalization that allows for some individual variation in the importance placed on each constraint by each teacher.

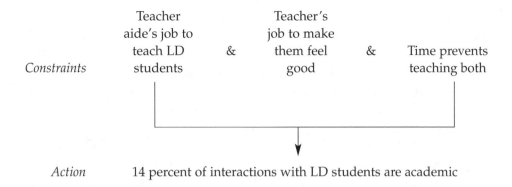

ANALYZING CONSEQUENCES

For many research questions, you need to go beyond the description and explanation of action by investigating its consequences. If you have information about consequences, you can evaluate the effectiveness of the actions that produced them. For example, while you may know from careful observation that teachers are implementing a new curriculum, you cannot evaluate its impact without collecting and analyzing information about the consequences of the implementation.

Analyzing consequences is very similar to analyzing actions. All the steps for doing so are virtually identical to those of analyzing actions, and we recommend you follow the same process of exploring and/or checking, counting, and summarizing actions when analyzing consequences. Decisions may have been taken at the planning stage about what consequences to study, in which case the analysis checks the extent to which they are present. Alternatively, the analysis explores the data to locate the major consequences of the selected practices. It is well known that most planned human activity produces as many unintended as intended consequences. This is especially true in complex systems such as schools. Teachers intend their instruction to have certain impacts on students. As well as evaluating the extent to which these impacts are evident, it is often important to identify any unintended consequences of those activities. Where does one begin to look for such consequences? There are two sources of guidance: practitioner experience and previously published research.

It is particularly important when analyzing consequences to establish the causal link between the actions and their claimed consequences. Establishing causality is notoriously difficult in educational and social research. The classic way of doing so is to run an experiment in which one group receives an intervention and another similar group does not. If the two groups are otherwise comparable, the intervention can be described as causing any resulting differences between the two groups (Campbell & Stanley, 1966; Cook & Campbell, 1979). Since practitioners are seldom able to run experiments, they need alternative ways of establishing causality, even though those ways may not provide the same level of certainty as the classic experiment.

Fortunately, running experiments is not the only way to establish causality in educational research. It is also established by intensive investigations of the processes that link elements together (Maxwell, 2004). The causal claims gain credibility by providing detailed descriptions of *how* the elements are linked and by showing that the proposed cause is more likely than other alternatives. In short, by disconfirming other possibilities, we gain more confidence in the proposed causal link.

A group of teacher-researchers were invited to evaluate how an urban elementary school reported students' progress to their parents. They learned through parent interviews that many parents had difficulty understanding their child's reports (Marino, Nicholl, Paki-Slater, Timperley, & Hampton, 2001). Their spontaneous comments about the educational "jargon" in the reports suggested a causal link between the teachers' use of jargon and the parents' ability to understand. Some of the school's teachers disagreed with the teacher-researchers' analysis—the difficulty, they claimed, was not the jargon but parents' overall low proficiency with the English language. They argued that the best solution was to have the reports translated and explained by a community worker.

Since these two different possible causes of the misunderstanding suggested quite different ways of improving the reporting process, it was worth seeing which was most likely to be correct. The teacher-researchers met with a group of parents and asked them to explain words and phrases that had been classified as educational jargon, and those that had been classified as nonjargon. Parents could understand almost all of the nonjargon words and few of the jargon words. This suggested that it was the jargon rather than overall English proficiency that was the cause of parents' difficulty with the reports. The teacher-researchers could now more confidently claim that the use of educational jargon caused parental misunderstanding.

EVALUATING PRACTITIONERS' THEORIES OF ACTION

In Chapter 2 we stressed that PBM is explicitly evaluative. This means that once a theory of action is made explicit, it is evaluated so that people can decide whether or not improvement is needed. We have already said a great deal about how theories of action are evaluated in PBM. In Chapter 2 we proposed four standards for judging the adequacy of theories of action: accuracy, effectiveness, coherence, and improvability. These standards provide a neutral platform against which a range of alternative theories of action could be evaluated. The standards are neutral in that they say, for example, that a theory of action for school reporting must be effective without specifying in advance what counts as effective. In Chapter 3 we explained and illustrated how theory evaluation can be done collaboratively as part of a learning conversation.

We now conclude this chapter on analysis of findings by showing how the theory of action portrayed in Figure 8.1 could be evaluated. The figure is the end result of the researchers' analysis. It describes how the staff at a multicultural elementary school have understood and solved the problem of how to report to parents. (Please assume that the school has agreed that the figure is an accurate portrayal of their reporting practice.)

The first question to ask in evaluating the theory portrayed in Figure 8.1 is whether it is accurate. Note that this question does not refer to the accuracy of the researchers' description of the schools' practices (this has already been established), but to the accuracy of any claims that are made within the theory itself. Are some of the beliefs and factual claims mistaken? For example, the figure shows that teachers' desire to communicate positive messages about students was partially motivated by their belief that their principal would not accept any negative comments. While the teacher-researchers confirmed with the principal that she was insistent on a positive tone, she was more open than her teachers believed to comments that honestly described low achievement. What she wanted, in addition, was constructive suggestions about improvement. This subtle change in the accuracy of the teachers' understanding opened up new possibilities about how to formulate an improved theory of reporting. They could be more frank about low achievement *and* satisfy their principal's policy on reporting.

The effectiveness standard is used to ask whether the theory delivers what is important to the school. Does the teachers' way of reporting enable them to simultaneously appear professional and positive about their students? In many respects the answer is "No." One could argue that writing in jargon to a lay audience is not professional. Similarly, reports that include mixed or confused messages could be seen as unprofessional. These criticisms are further supported by the consequences for parents, which were some confusion and limited understanding of the teachers' comments. The current theory of action fails to meet the effectiveness standard.

The coherence standard takes the evaluation out of the staff's own frame of reference and asks, "Is what staff themselves want desirable?" What other values might be important? The coherence standard enables a researcher to argue that there are additional or different constraints that are relevant to the evaluation. In this case, the staff's practices were not constrained by a requirement for valid and accurate reporting. The need to include this additional constraint was debated with the school staff and accepted by them. This acceptance involved substantial learning conversations with the school staff about how they could reframe their understanding of "being positive" so that they could resolve their dilemma of how to be both positive and honest when reporting on underachieving students. The school staff now had a more adequate theory of reporting—one that met the additional constraint of providing honest information.

Finally, the improvability standard led to a discussion of the school and teachers' ability to learn and make improvements over time. Is the school open to the possibility that the parental confusion and limited understanding is causally related to its own reporting practices and not to the cultural and linguistic background of the parents? Does the school test the degree to which parents understand the reports? Is there critical debate about what constitutes "professional" in respect of reporting? Does the principal realize that her "Be positive" message is interpreted by staff in ways that produce some mixed messages and inaccurate reporting? The answer to this question cannot be gleaned from the summary presented in Figure 8.1. It becomes apparent in dialogue with staff and in their openness to critical examination and revision of their theories. In this case, the staff did have the capacity to critically reflect and to invite outsiders to help them in the process. The result was a revised theory of reporting that placed much more emphasis on parental understanding, accurate information, and constructive suggestions about how parents and teachers could work together to help underachieving children.

SUMMING UP

The point of data analysis is to provide compelling answers to your research questions. For PBM researchers, this involves revealing the theory of action that controls the practice being investigated. In this chapter we have discussed the steps you will need to take in order to complete this type of analysis and to demonstrate its validity.

A successful analysis enables you to answer your research questions by showing the relationship among the relevant constraints, actions, and consequences. With practice, you will be able to perceive patterns in the data, discern the meanings of constraints, and identify causal relationships far more efficiently and quickly than you are able to do the first time you construct a theory of action. Whether or not you wish to conduct formal research projects, these analytical skills will enhance your ability to reflect on and improve your own and others' practice. You will also have a basis for evaluating the inevitable differences that arise in a healthy professional community. Those differences will be seen as theoretical rather than personal and as potentially resolvable by using the four standards of theoretical adequacy we discussed in this and earlier chapters.

9

Communicating Your Research

This chapter continues the collaborative theme of this book by talking about how to negotiate the content of research reports as well as how to write them. We begin by discussing the importance of involving research participants in negotiating and checking findings and provide a step-by-step guide to this process. We then address the task of writing a research report by outlining the benefits of writing up research, presenting and discussing the key components of a formal research report, and offering advice on how to manage the writing process.

NEGOTIATING AND VALIDATING YOUR RESEARCH FINDINGS

In problem-based methodology (PBM), or any form of truly collaborative research, the first audience for your research findings should be the people who contributed the information. Teacher-researchers have an ethical obligation to respect and acknowledge the contribution made by participants and to check that they are comfortable with how their information has been interpreted. Participants should also be involved in any decisions about how the research will be used and disseminated. Even when your research has largely been centered on your own practice, colleagues who have acted as collaborators or "critical friends" (Costa & Kallick, 1993) should be the first audience.

Feedback to research participants serves methodological as well as ethical purposes. Teacher-researchers' accounts of theories of action include descriptions and explanations of others' behavior. As discussed in

Chapter 4, steps must be taken to increase the validity of such accounts. One way to do this is to share the initial findings with research participants and seek feedback on their accuracy. Do participants agree with the description of their teaching? Do they agree with how it is explained? Even if you are studying your own practice, you should ask a critical friend to check your account of your own teaching.

Once participants agree that their practice has been accurately described and explained, they should be invited to discuss the teacher-researcher's evaluation of that practice. Many teachers are wary of offering or receiving evaluative feedback because they have experienced it as an overly personal and controlling process. This is not how evaluation is used in PBM. First, it is not people or isolated practices that are evaluated but theories of action. (See Chapter 2 for a discussion of how theories of action are evaluated.) This means that evaluation happens after the reasons for current practice are understood. Second, the basis of the evaluation is, whenever possible, negotiated in advance. Third, the evaluation is reciprocal and is conducted as part of a learning conversation in which the relative adequacy of the current and proposed alternative theory of action is debated.

In summary, the feedback meeting is not a one-way critique but rather an opportunity for mutual critique and learning. The result should be a shared understanding of what is happening, why, and of its adequacy. Given the importance of gaining participant feedback on initial research findings, we have compiled the following guide to the feedback process. This guide offers specific advice on how to conduct a feedback session, and can be modified to suit both the stage in the research process at which feedback is sought and the formality and informality of the occasion.

Although the guide provided in Table 9.1 is largely self-explanatory, there are a number of points that are worth emphasizing. First, the four purposes of feedback (Table 9.1, 1a–1d) indicate that the aim is to increase validity and commitment rather than to defend the draft research findings. The values of a learning conversation, namely, openness, respect, and validity, are crucial to achieving these purposes.

Second, a feedback session can become tedious if you do not add value to the audience. This happens when the audience is told what they already know or when you present raw data without explaining what you make of it. Thus, careful preparation is crucial so that you are clear about the main messages you wish to communicate. It is these messages that need to be disclosed and checked rather than raw data. The raw data may become important in showing how particular conclusions were arrived at—that is, in showing how links were made between the top and bottom rungs of the ladder of inference (Chapter 3).

Third, disagreements should be treated as theory competition rather than personal criticism. You may find it helpful to use the ladder of inference as a visual aid during feedback sessions as a way of locating where the disagreement lies. By moving down the ladder of inference, each party can identify how they reached their differing views. This builds mutual

Table 9.1   Guidelines for Feedback of Initial Findings to Research Participants

1. **Why give feedback?**
   a. To fulfill ethical commitments to research participants
   b. To increase the validity of the research analyses and conclusions
   c. To develop a shared understanding of how the problem has been understood and resolved
   d. To increase commitment to the improvement of practice

2. **Whom do I give it to?**
   a. The people you gained initial agreement from who are responsible for the practices you have investigated
   b. The people who provided the information you collected
   c. Discuss with participants whether to privide individual or group feedback
   d. If multiple audiences, decide the appropriate order for feedback

3. **What do I feed back?**
   a. The material you would like to check
   b. Checking can occur at many levels:
      i. Checking what occurred
      ii. Checking your understanding of others' theories of action
      iii. Checking your evaluation of others' theories of action
      iv. Seeking reactions to your suggested alternative theory of action
   c. The material to be checked should be easily understood. Do not present raw data or numerous overheads. Use a diagram to show draft analyses of theories of action.

4. **How do I present my findings?**
   Introduce the findings.
   a. Restate the research question(s), for example, "What classroom assessments do teachers use in math?" "What use is made of the results?"
   b. Review why the question was important to the audience.
   c. Explain or review how the questions have been investigated by discovering and evaluating the relevant theory or theories of action.
   d. Explain or review the idea of a theory of action and its components (constraints, actions, and consequences).
   e. Disclose and explain your evaluative perspective, for example, "We were interested in how teachers used the assessment results to improve their teaching." In most cases this evaluative perspective should have been negotiated at the outset with your research participants.

   Present the findings (use a diagram).
   f. Describe the relevant actions. (Describe what assessments are given by teachers and how they interpret and use the results.) Give two or three summary statements only, and be prepared to provide more supporting evidence if asked.
   g. Describe the set of constraints that explain the actions. This analysis should show that you have understood why things happen as they do. Check.
   h. Describe the intended and unintended consequences of those actions. Check the accuracy of your claims.
   i. Disclose your evaluation of the existing theory of action. This should be clearly based on the evidence you have already presented.

5. **What happens if we disagree?**
   a. Agree on what it is that you disagree on.
   b. Agree on what it is that you agree on—the common ground.

(Continued)

Table 9.1 (Continued)

> c. Treat disagreements as theoretical differences.
> d. Give the reasons for your own views and ask for those of the audience.
> e. Use the ladder of inference to examine the adequacy of the reasons.
> f. Agree on how the difference could be tested and resolved and determine if there is an interest in doing so.
>
> 6. **What happens if we agree?**
>   a. If there is sufficient agreement, collaborate in the redesign of the practice.
>   b. Discuss how the new practice will be evaluated in the next cycle of the research and determine if there is an interest in doing so.

understanding and reduces defensiveness. If people feel understood, they do not have to fight back!

Fourth, the feedback process can be an important catalyst for change. If participants agree with the analysis and the evaluation of their current theory of action, teacher-researchers and research participants can collaborate in the design of improved practice.

In Chapter 3, we illustrated what we meant by a learning conversation with an excerpt from a feedback session. The excerpt shows how the teacher-researcher avoided imposing his own evaluative framework by explaining how the school's current practices did not enable it to achieve one of the principal's own goals (better achievement for low-track students). The principal's and teacher's shared desire for improved achievement levels then became the basis for collaborative discussion about how to improve the school's approach to the problem of assigning students to instructional programs.

If you reach sufficient agreement with research participants, you can plan how to disseminate your findings to other relevant audiences. By involving research participants in dissemination, you model the collaborative process that is central to PBM. Such collabroation also builds a professional community that conducts and uses research to investigate and improve its own practice.

Dissemination of your research through discussion with other professionals does not require that you write a formal research report. Nancy Fichtman Dana and Diane Yendol-Silva (2003) discuss how teacher-researchers can share their work through posters, PowerPoint presentations, and dedicated faculty meetings. There are considerable benefits to be gained, however, from writing a formal research report, and it is to these that we turn next.

WHY WRITE UP YOUR RESEARCH?

There are three compelling reasons for writing about your research. One is that written reports require a sharpness of thought and expression that is often not required in informal reporting and discussion of research. In an informal discussion, you can have several attempts at explaining the aims of your research, and no one may notice that each version was slightly different. This variation would be unacceptable to both the writer and the readers of a written research report. It would be taken as a sign of vagueness or even confusion. The discipline of writing helps practitioners to think and write more clearly. The well-known educational ethnographer Harry Wolcott expresses the relationship between thinking and writing as follows: "The conventional wisdom is that writing reflects thinking. I am drawn to a stronger position: Writing *is* thinking. Stated more cautiously, writing is one form that thinking can take" (Wolcott, 2001, p. 22). In short, learning to write about practice has spillover benefits for the way you think about practice.

The second reason for writing up your research is that it creates a public record that contributes to the body of knowledge about your topic. The report enables the research to live beyond the time, place, and persons who were initially involved. Depending on the audience, the written report may be useful to teachers who deal with similar practical problems, or to those who are interested in it from a more theoretical point of view. In either case, the impact and contribution is greater because there is a permanent record that can be accessed by more people over a longer period of time than is possible with an oral presentation. Sharing insights gained locally can improve practice on a wider scale as other readers recognize how the research can be applied to their own situations.

A third compelling reason is that a written report on your research provides tangible evidence of your accomplishments—accomplishments that are a source of pride and of further research and career opportunities. A written account of teacher research also demonstrates its practical possibility and encourages other teachers by showing what a colleague in a similar situation has accomplished!

WHAT TO INCLUDE IN YOUR RESEARCH REPORT

A report should be written with a particular audience in mind, because its style, length, and organization will vary accordingly. Writing styles vary enormously across different types of publication. A practitioner journal may encourage authors to adopt a personal tone so that readers can understand how they experienced the process of completing the research. The editors of a more academic journal, on the other hand, are usually not interested in the personal learning journeys of authors—what they want is a fairly dispassionate account of the methods used to answer the research questions and of the research findings.

Given this variation, it is important to decide at the outset who the audience is and the type of publication that is read by that group. Once this decision is made, the best strategy is to locate examples of such publications and use them as a guide to the style, length, and organization of your report.

In the remainder of this section we discuss the organization of a research report. While there is variation in the type of section headings that are appropriate to particular types of report, most reports are structured around the following questions:

Questions for Structuring a Research Report

1. What motivated the investigation? What questions were being asked?

2. Why is the question important? What is its practical and/or theoretical significance?

3. How did you go about answering the question?

4. What did you find?

5. What is the significance of what you found? What action will be taken as a result?

6. What further research will inform the improvement effort?

With these questions in mind, in what follows we outline the sections that are typically included in more formal research reports. By "formal" we mean those written by graduate students in research classes, and those that teachers often publish in professional journals after review by professional colleagues. For a more informal report writing style and organization, we suggest you refer to the account of teacher writing given by Nancy Fichtman Dana and Diane Yendol-Silva in *The Reflective Educator's Guide to Classroom Research* (2003). We have used a more formal model with our teacher-researchers so they could have the opportunity to publish their work in peer-reviewed professional journals and to make an easier transition to academic publishing if they wished to do so.

Components of a Formal Research Report

The following eight headings are typical of those included in a more formal report. There is considerable overlap between them and those suggested for a research proposal (Chapter 5). In many of these sections what you write will be a revision and elaboration of what was included in the proposal.

1. Abstract and/or Executive Summary

2. Introduction

3. Research Setting

4. Research Approach
   - Methodology
   - Participants
   - Data Collection Instruments
   - Analysis
   - Procedure

5. Research Findings

6. Discussion Including Limitations of the Research

7. References

8. Appendices

Abstract and/or Executive Summary

The abstract is a brief (100–150 words) outline of the aims of the research, the methods used, the main findings, and conclusions. It is usually written last, after you have written the entire report. A good abstract tells the reader what was done and what was found. Since important decisions may be made about your research on the basis of the abstract alone, it is important to write it well. Colleagues will decide whether the study is of sufficient relevance and interest to read the whole report, funding agencies could decide on the basis of your abstract whether to provide further funding, and conference organizers will use the abstract to decide whether your work deserves a place in the program.

An executive summary is usually much longer than an abstract and thus can include more reference to the background context and literature and more discussion of the findings. Executive summaries often accompany reports to superintendents and boards of education, and may be read in place of the full report.

The following example of an abstract is adapted from a study of the use of achievement data for school-based curriculum review (Robinson, Phillips, & Timperley, 2002). This example illustrates many of the features of a good abstract. In particular, it begins by identifying the wider context and relating this context to the particular study that is the focus of the research article. It then describes how the study was conducted and what was found. Finally, the abstract concludes with a brief description of the study's implications.

Many school reform initiatives now require school leaders to make curriculum and resourcing decisions on the basis of evidence about their likely impact on student achievement. In this paper, we discuss the implication of this policy demand in the context of a descriptive study of schools' capacity to collect, analyze, and use collective achievement data to inform curriculum review and revision. The study of 47 teacher leaders in 26 elementary and middle schools showed that there was extensive assessment in literacy. However, school leaders typically did not use such data to evaluate their literacy programs. When data were used, they were likely to be incorrectly interpreted. The implications of the study are discussed in terms of how reform policies and initiatives can build local capacity for data-based review and revision of teaching programs. (Adapted from Robinson, Phillips, & Timperley, 2002)

Introduction

The purpose of the introductory section of a report is to place the research project in a much wider context. The challenge for the teacher-researcher is to show how a small-scale investigation conducted in a specific setting has relevance and significance for a much wider audience.

It is often possible to demonstrate this relevance because theories of action that operate in one local context can resemble those found in other contexts. This is because there are common constraints of policy, resources, and cultural values and beliefs operating across many educational contexts. The more practitioners become aware of these constraints and their impact, the more they can work together to alter them if they believe that an improved theory of action is required. Table 9.2 suggests how the introduction to a project report can be written to make clear the link between a small project and a wider topic that is of more general interest.

The example in Table 9.2 is based on the work of Claire Sinnema, an elementary teacher who became aware through her graduate studies that

Table 9.2 Components of the Introduction to a Research Report

Structure	*Illustrative Example*
1. Outline the problem, challenge, or issues that are relevant to your project: • What is problematic? • What are the debates? • Refer to relevant published research.	Annual teacher evaluation is compulsory in this district, yet: • Little is known about what is discussed in these evaluation interviews • Its impact on improving teaching and learning is unknown • It is resource-intensive
2. State the specific research question(s) that guided your investigation.	What do teachers talk about in their evaluation interviews and why?
3. Discuss the significance of the question to the issues/problems described in #1: • What is the relevance of your question to the broader issue? • What difference will finding an answer make, both in your setting and more widely?	Knowing what is talked about is a first step to finding out whether teacher evaluation has an impact on teaching and learning. Explaining the degree of focus on student learning and achievement will provide guidance about how to make teacher evaluation serve teachers and students better.

much teacher evaluation in New Zealand schools was not focused on the improvement of teaching and learning. After several attempts to link her small study to the wider debates on teacher evaluation, she wrote an introduction to her final research report based on the points described in the right-hand side of the table. She used the literature on teacher evaluation to show that even though many writers and policymakers intended evaluation to contribute to teaching and learning, little was known about whether it did. She argued that her research question was relevant because it was important to know whether evaluation practice served the purpose intended by the policy. It was also important to investigate why teachers talked about certain topics rather than others in their evaluation interviews.

Discussion of literature is typically included in the introduction and discussion sections of a report, though brief references may also be included in other sections when, for example, the author is defending the choice of research method. Next, we identify a few of the main points to keep in mind when using published research in your report. Further guidance on using the literature and on literature reviews is available from Hart (1998) and Leedy and Ormrod (2001):

1. Be scrupulous about the accuracy of your use of others' research. If you have misunderstood or misrepresented others' work, readers might lose confidence in your whole report.

2. Evaluative comments about others' work are appropriate as long as you have understood the work in the first place. Explain why you are critical or approving.

3. Use others' research rather than summarize it. When you are clear about the point you want to make, use the research to help you make that particular point. If you tell readers the relevance of the research to your particular question, they will not be left wondering why they are reading a series of boring paragraphs that begin with "Smith says . . . Green says. . . ."

4. Avoid multiple lengthy citations of others' work. Since the purpose of the project report is to make your views clear, long quotations are distracting. Use short direct quotations when they communicate a point you would want to make in a particularly compelling way. The following quote from Leedy and Ormrod (2001) makes exactly this point in a succinct and compelling way: "As important as what others say about their studies, and perhaps even more important, is what *you* say about their studies. Your emphasis should always be on how a particular idea or research finding relates to your own problem—something that only you can discuss" (p. 86). Quotations from the original are also appropriate when you are critiquing a document or text. In all cases, check that the quotation is an exact copy of what has been published and that it is appropriately referenced.

Research Setting

This section describes the setting in which you conducted your research. Give enough detail to enable the reader to understand how your particular setting might be similar or dissimilar to their own situation. For example, if your research is on the use of information technology, give enough detail about the school's information technology resources, and how they are organized and used, so that your reader can judge whether your findings are likely to be applicable in their situation.

You should also describe any features of the setting that may not be familiar to your audience, but that they need to understand in order to make sense of subsequent sections of the report. For example, it might be important to describe the history of the practices you are investigating so that the reader understands some of what has led to the current situation. In the example used in Table 9.2, it would be important to explain how New Zealand's policy on teacher evaluation gives teachers considerable freedom to determine the focus of their evaluations.

Research Approach

This section describes and justifies the decisions you made about how to conduct your study. In Chapter 4 we explained how the validity of findings is judged by the quality of the process used to obtain them. This is why it is important in this section to tell the reader exactly how you selected, gathered, and analyzed your information. The following subsections are typical of those that are usually included.

Methodology. In this section you explain why you have taken the overall approach you have. In the case of PBM, you would explain that your decision to describe and evaluate relevant theories of action was based on a desire to contribute to the understanding and improvement of practice. Research that describes and evaluates relevant theories of action provides opportunities for deeper understanding of why problems have been solved in particular ways, and for reflection on the adequacy of those solutions. The contribution of PBM to improvement is also enhanced through collaborative analysis and evaluation of the theories of action relevant to the research question.

Once you have justified your choice of methodology, explain how the research questions were answered by describing the relevant components of the theory of action (see Table 5.2). In the following example, we use the study discussed in Table 9.2 to describe how the research questions were answered by investigating the relevant components of the theory of action for teacher evaluation.

The first research question asked about the degree to which teachers' evaluation interviews were focused on the impact of their teaching on student learning and achievement. This required accurate descriptions of what was talked about (actions) and evaluation of the extent to which the talk focused on the teaching-learning relationship.

The second question asked why teachers talked about what they did. This involved discovering the constraints that explained what they talked about, and identifying those that ruled in and ruled out talking about the relationship between a teacher's own teaching practice and his or her students' learning.

Participants. Readers need to know who was involved in your study and how these participants became involved. Describe the research participants in ways that are relevant to the research question. For example, if you are researching teachers' use of information technology and believe that years of experience makes a difference to its use, then you need to describe participants' years of experience. If experience of teaching is unlikely to be relevant, you do not need to describe it. If you had to select a sample of people to interview or observe, then describe and justify your sampling decisions. All this information enables readers to judge whether those who participated in your research had some special characteristics that limit the extent to which your findings are likely to be applicable to their situation.

Data Collection Instruments. Describe, in turn, each instrument you used for collecting data (put copies of all instruments in the appendices). For example, describe the questions in the interview schedule, demonstrating how the questions were designed to provide information that was relevant to your research questions. If relevant, you should also explain how the instruments were developed and trialed.

Analysis. The analysis section of the research proposal signals much of the material that should be included in this section of the report. Make sure that you describe your analysis procedures in a way that shows how they help you to provide answers to your research questions. For example, the analysis section of the report on Claire Sinnema's study on teacher evaluation could include a statement like the following:

> The extent of focus on teaching and learning in the evaluation interviews was determined by averaging the amount of time that each teacher reported spending on this topic.

Include in this section any steps you took to increase the validity of the information you gathered and the conclusions that you reached. For example, since teachers' reports of the content of their evaluation interviews may not be entirely accurate, you should report here any steps you took to check their accuracy:

> Teachers' reports of the proportion of time that was spent on various topics were cross-checked against the parallel reports of their

evaluator. Where there were discrepancies between the two reports, we noted the discrepancy and used the longer estimated time in our calculations.

The analysis of qualitative data needs to be clearly described to show how various sorts of bias were avoided. As explained in Chapter 4, this bias involves selecting evidence that supports the author's points, while overlooking evidence that challenges them. Describe how you took account of any disconfirming evidence by, for example, identifying quotes from transcripts that did not fit a general pattern, or by deliberately identifying rival explanations for emergent findings.

Procedure. Detail how your research was conducted, from pilot test (if any) to actual study, including feedback. This is where you describe the informal or formal agreement you negotiated to do the research, the ethical procedures, the feedback processes you used, and any subsequent follow-up.

Research Findings

Generally, this section should describe the findings in a clear and straightforward manner. Discussion of the practical and theoretical significance of the findings should be saved for the subsequent discussion section. This separation enables readers to draw their own conclusions about the significance of the findings before they read those of the author.

Organize the results so that questions about what happened (actions) are answered first, followed by questions about why (constraints) and questions about consequences. This sequence enables you to make an argument about the causes and consequences of particular actions. Conclude this section with a summary showing the interrelationships between the various components of the theory of action. The argument could also be reinforced by including a diagram of the whole theory of action (see Figure 8.1 for an example).

Display the evidence associated with each main finding so that the reader can judge its validity, and use the ladder of inference to show how you moved from evidence to conclusion. For example, you should defend your analysis of constraints by describing how alternative explanations were considered during the analysis process or in a feedback session and shown to be less plausible than those being presented.

Display quantitative evidence in tables, graphs, and charts, and explain them briefly in the text. There are a variety of ways of displaying qualitative evidence, but the following points will enhance the credibility of your report:

- Identify each main pattern of evidence and illustrate it with typical quotations.
- Briefly describe any important idiosyncratic evidence that does not fit each main pattern and illustrate it.

- Provide sufficient context in the sentence leading up to the quotation so the reader knows where it comes from.
- Ensure that the quotations you select from transcripts, tapes, or documents clearly illustrate the point you want to make.
- Ensure that all quotations are accurately copied from the original.
- Quotations may be edited to increase comprehension, but edits should not alter the meaning of the quotation. Edits should be indicated by an appropriate textual convention, for example, square brackets ([ ]) to indicate paraphrasing, or an ellipsis (. . .) to indicate a deleted section.
- As part of checking draft reports with research participants, ensure that speakers are comfortable with how you have quoted them. In small local projects, speakers are readily identified even when quotations are made anonymous.
- Do not overuse quotations. The focus of the paragraph should be the point that you are making about the quotation rather than the quotation itself.

The following extract from a study of reporting to parents (Marino, Nicholl, Paki-Slater, Timperley, Lai, & Hampton, 2001) shows how quotations add to the richness and credibility of a research report:

The majority of parents (9 of the 14 interviewed) expressed their appreciation of the school's efforts to report achievement against national standards. As one mother explained, "This report has its good parts. It gives an accurate account of where my child is at in each subject. In the old report, the 'excellent,' 'very good,' 'good' did tell me what he was excellent in—but compared with who?"

Five of these parents indicated that they also wanted local benchmarks, such as the class and/or school. In contrast, five parents preferred school or class norms only, or no comparative benchmarks at all.

All interviewed parents put considerable effort into understanding the report card and how well their children were performing. They looked to the report card and parent interviews to help them understand where their child was at and what they could do to help. One mother said, "In talking to the teacher and looking through his books, I can see he's improved. What I'm interested in knowing is how confident he is and where he needs help."

The main problem parents encountered, however, was how to interpret the report. The graphs showing the curriculum levels were new and unfamiliar as a form of reporting. As one father said, "I get muddled about the curriculum. I'm not sure what the curriculum level means." In addition, many parents had difficulty accessing the professional language used in the report. One mother, for example, expressed a wish that the reports would be written in "plain English." (Marino et al., 2001, p. 9)

The range of quotations in the extract presented enriches the report and gives the reader confidence that all parents' views have been fairly represented.

Discussion

This is not a repetition of the results but a discussion of them at a different level. In this section, the focus shifts from a close examination of the data to the big picture, by linking the findings to the original research question and the literature (prior research) and discussing their implications.

The discussion section starts with a summary of your answers to the research question. The next part of the discussion should address any aspect of your study that limits its internal or external (generalizability) validity. This may include limits on the validity of some data (for example, overreliance on teachers' self-reports), insufficient in-depth interviewing and hence limited understanding of some constraints, or a biased sample of interviewees. It is important to avoid taking a formulaic approach to the discussion of these limitations. For example do not say, "A limit of this study was its small sample size," unless you can explain exactly how the small sample limits what you can claim to have found.

The best way to approach the limitations section is to write about possible objections that others may raise to your findings and show how you have addressed them or could do so in a subsequent study. Some objections are justified and cannot be adequately answered. The best way to deal with those is to acknowledge the relevant limitation and be more modest about what you would otherwise claim.

Once you have summarized the main findings and addressed likely objections, you are free to discuss the wider implications of your study. Consider the usefulness of the study. To what extent did the research make an impact on practice? Were the collaborative processes sufficient to increase participants' understanding of their own practice and their involvement in its evaluation and revision? What changes, if any, were agreed to, and what action was taken? What further research will be done to continue the evaluation and improvement of the new theory of action?

References

There are many different styles for writing reference lists and referring to them in the body of the report. The best approach to choosing the appropriate referencing style is to adopt the one used by the publisher, agency, or professional association that is most relevant to your work. Whatever style you choose, the golden rule is to reference with accuracy and consistency. The numerous conventions that make up a style have evolved to ensure that readers can retrieve the material you have used as efficiently as possible.

Two of the best known style guides are the *Publication Manual of the American Psychological Association* (American Psychological Association, 2001) and *The Chicago Manual of Style* (University of Chicago Press, 2003).

The manual of the American Psychological Association (APA) has been followed in this book because it is particularly suited to empirical research and is followed by most academic and professional journals that report empirical research.[1]

Appendices

Finally, your appendices should include sample participant information forms, sample consent forms, all data collection instruments used, and any detailed supplementary tables and evidence that back up material included in the main body of your text. In general, use appendices for material that supplements your report but would be distracting if included in the main body of the text.

MASTERING THE WRITING PROCESS

Writing a substantial report can be a daunting task, even for experienced researchers. Novice writers may experience psychological barriers to getting started, fearing that they lack the skill or the time to complete the task. However, there are techniques to help you get under way and produce an interesting report that others will want to read. You may even set your sights on publishing your report in a professional journal. In what follows, we focus on how to master the writing process by scheduling time, making a plan, creating and linking interesting paragraphs, and striking the right tone.

Scheduling Time

Allowing plenty of time for writing is essential because writing several drafts is an inevitable part of the process. You will have written, or at least sketched the first of these drafts as part of your preparation for the feedback meeting. You should then plan to write a full draft, get critical feedback from colleagues, and then rewrite the report once more. However lengthy the process seems, it will be considerably shorter for those of you who completed a formal research proposal (Chapter 5), since many sections of the final report will simply comprise revisions and elaborations of sections of the proposal.

If your report is submitted to reviewers from a publisher or funding agency, they may suggest further revisions. This process of revision and rewriting is a very powerful form of professional development. It is no different, in principle, from how teachers encourage their students to become writers—through conferencing, feedback, and revision.

---

1. A useful guide to using APA style can also be found at the following Web site: http://owl.english.purdue.edu/handouts/print/research/r_apa.html
Further information is available at the APA style website http://www.apastyle.org

Some practitioners (and academics) believe that they cannot succeed with their writing unless they have dedicated blocks of time, such as study leave or holiday breaks. If such leave is possible, then take full advantage! If it is not, then do not be discouraged because research on academics has shown that the most productive ones are those who do not wait for large blocks of time but who incorporate writing into their daily routines. Whether your writing routine is best scheduled for 5:30–7:00 A.M. in the morning, 8:00–10:00 P.M. at night, or some other time, the important point is to find a time that you can stick to.

Making a Plan

When writers struggle to find the right words, the cause of the difficulty is often that they are unclear about *what* they want to say rather than *how* to say it. This difficulty is overcome by making a plan that identifies the main points to be communicated before trying to write. The headings discussed in the previous section provide the skeleton of your plan. The flesh consists of the points you want to make and the argument or evidence that backs them up.

Under each heading, list your main points and check that they are relevant to the main purpose of your study. Identify the evidence or argument that you will use to back up each point. No matter how interesting a quote might be, it doesn't deserve space in your report unless it serves the point you wish to make.

Once you have listed the main points, check their sequence. Is it clear to you and the reader which are the main points and which are the subpoints? You can check the adequacy of your outline by trying it out with a colleague. As you tell the story out loud, you can both judge whether it has a beginning, a middle, and an end and a minimum of distractions that interrupt its narrative flow. Can your colleague, after listening to your story, clearly identify the purpose of your research, how you pursued it, what you found, and what it all means? Some revision to your plan may be needed before you have a compelling sequence of relevant points. On the other hand, you should not strive for perfection, because that will prevent you from getting started. The test of the adequacy of your plan is the quality of the draft itself. Careful planning does not ensure a perfect draft, though it should reduce the number of revisions required.

If planning is not your preferred style, then plunge straight into writing a draft, but be prepared to go through the same process of revision and rewriting after you have committed words to paper.

Maintaining Interest

Your report starts with a statement of the problem, challenge, or issue that motivated your efforts. Assuming that the reader is also interested in this problem, how do you maintain their interest through the whole report?

A good report has a narrative structure—that is, it tells a "story" that establishes the importance of your research question, proposes an approach to answering the question, and then moves through a series of arguments that make a compelling case for the final position taken. The connectedness of the narrative is established by being aware of what you are going to say next and summarizing the main points of each section. In addition, narrative flow is maintained by being explicit about the relevance of every paragraph to the case you are building about the answer to your research question.

Good paragraphs are the basis of good writing. They include *one* point, an elaboration of the point, and an indication of how the point is relevant to the question being asked. These three qualities are summarized by the PER rule.[2]

The PER Rule

Point	This is usually stated in the first sentence of the paragraph. The point is made by you, not by other authors or research participants. This means you should not start a paragraph with the names of authors or with quotes. You should start with what *you* want to say about your research.
Elaboration	The point can be elaborated with arguments that explain more about what you mean, with qualitative or quantitative evidence drawn from your study, or with practical examples. This is where you use your evidence to back up your point.
Relevance	Indicate how the point made and elaborated in the paragraph is significant to the question or argument you are addressing. This is crucial to maintaining the narrative flow of your report. The reader should not be left wondering, "Why am I reading this?"

Since writing is an art and not an exact science, there will be variations in how points are made and elaborated and in how their relevance is demonstrated. In some cases, the point may be made toward the end rather than at the beginning of the paragraph, and its relevance may be implied rather than directly stated. In all cases, however, the reader must be in no doubt about what the point is and what its relevance is to the question that motivates the whole research project.

One of the most common faults in research writing is the inclusion of too many points in one paragraph. This often means they are not sufficiently explained and their relevance is unclear. The example in Table 9.3 provides a good model of paragraph construction. It is taken from the report of a group of teacher-researchers who studied the attitudes of dance students toward the theoretical components of their program (Hill, 2003).

---

2. We are indebted to our colleague Alison Jones for her notes on the PER rule.

Table 9.3 Using the PER Rule

Paragraph	PER Rule
One of the major challenges in designing a degree-level performance program in the arts is how to integrate theoretical and practical study in a way that motivates students (Fortin, 1993; Hagood, 2001; Lazaroff, 2001).	*Point:* Integrating theoretical and practical study in the arts is a challenge.
Students faced with theory that is taught outside the context of its practical application may lose interest and see the theory component as of little relevance to their learning.	*Elaboration:* This explains the nature of the challenge in terms of student motivation and perceived relevance.
The purpose of our study was to find out more about how theory and practice were integrated in our degree-level dance program, and how the students experienced both types of learning.	*Relevance:* Relevance is suggested by showing how theory-practice integration is an issue for many degree-level performance programs, including the author's own setting.

SOURCE: Hill (2003).

Each paragraph must be linked to the one that precedes and follows it. These links are not hard to make when the points that belong under a particular section or heading have been planned in advance. In a section discussing the impact of an innovative teaching program on student achievement, for example, the point being made in one paragraph might be that several studies suggest that the program has a positive effect. The next paragraph that deals with the less favorable research might start with "Contrary to these positive findings, several more recent studies have raised questions about the effectiveness of this approach. . . ." A third paragraph that suggests how these apparently contradictory findings may be resolved might start with "There are two possible explanations for these apparently contradictory findings. . . ."

Appropriate Tone

We have emphasized that writing a research report involves asking an interesting question and proposing an answer. Given this stance, it does not make sense to adopt a highly impersonal or neutral tone in your writing. The use of the impersonal "The authors noted . . ." or the passive voice "It was found that . . ." does nothing to add objectivity to your report. As discussed in Chapter 4, questions of objectivity are inextricably tied to validity, and that has nothing to do with whether or not you use the personal pronoun.

Although we agree with the use of the personal pronoun when reporting teacher research, its use does not excuse polemic or bias. The latter is evident when the writer makes a point by assertion rather than argument. Assertions are bald statements of one's position, without declaring the grounds for the position or acknowledging the possibility of alternative views or interpretations. In an argument, the author discusses the possible limitations of and alternatives to the proposed position.

The need to come to a conclusion about what your research means does not mean you have to be more definitive than is warranted. In many cases, your findings, like others' research on the same topic, will not be clear cut. In such cases you can still take a position by, for example, providing an explanation of your conflicting findings, proposing a further study, or describing what you and your colleagues learned from the process.

The values that inform a learning conversation provide a good guide to the tone of a written report. Respect for those involved in your study is demonstrated by accurately describing their theories of action before making any judgments about their practice. When participants' perspectives are ignored, the result is a report that fits the "Describe, Criticize, Recommend" (D-C-R) mode rather than the collaborative mode of "Describe, Explain, Evaluate, Recommend" (D-E-E-R) (see Chapter 3) that is central to PBM. We illustrate the difference in tone between these two approaches in the following boxes. The first version describes and criticizes the actions of teachers and makes no attempt to explain the constraints responsible for their current practice. The result is a judgmental piece of writing that is likely to alienate teachers rather than strengthen collaboration and improve practice.

In the second version, the same description of the teachers' reporting is provided, but it is embedded in the theory of action that explains why the situation arose. Rather than a source of condemnation, the report now provides insight and conveys respect for what the teachers are up against. The researchers' evaluation of the theory of action remains the same, but the explanation provides crucial clues about how the situation can be improved. A new theory of reporting that shows how the idea of being positive can be integrated with the new constraint of accuracy will be a far more powerful catalyst for improvement than the somewhat patronizing recommendations included in the first version.

POOR: Describe, Criticize, and Recommend (D-C-R)

Though teachers have valid information on students' achievement, the information on the reports is not accurate and is of little use to parents. Most school reports still tell parents that their children are progressing well even if they are achieving below the district average. Despite the school changing its assessment practices and introducing a new report, parents are still not receiving accurate and honest information. The school is accountable to parents. It should ensure that parents are told how their child is achieving in relation to an understood benchmark.

> **BETTER: Describe, Explain,**
> **Evaluate, and Recommend (D-E-E-R)**
>
> On the whole, these teachers use positive categories and positive written comments when reporting their students' achievement to parents. This holds true even for students who are achieving below age-related benchmarks. Our interviews revealed several reasons why teachers tended to underreport their students' low achievement. First, their principal had given them clear messages about the need to be positive on the reports. This left teachers in a dilemma about how to be positive about the achievement of underperforming children while at the same time trying to provide accurate information. Second, the school assessment policy and practice was unclear about the need to report against benchmarks and about which benchmarks were appropriate. This meant each teacher decided what was "excellent," "good," or "poor" performance. Third, there was strong pressure in this economically disadvantaged school community to celebrate success rather than report failure. Reports were treated as one means of celebrating what a child could do, thereby building esteem, confidence, and family pride.
>
> During the feedback session, staff agreed that their approach to reporting should be revised so that more accurate and consistent messages could be communicated. We then discussed how to do this. . . .

The same values that are important in a learning conversation are also important in communicating research findings. We have already explained, using the examples, how respect for research participants is communicated. In addition, a concern for the validity of the research itself is conveyed by careful writing and the avoidance of exaggerated language and rhetoric. A report should be a type of conversation with the reader—one that gives them sufficient evidence and argument to enable them to judge the validity of the findings for themselves.

Finally, a good report invites the reader to see the research topic and question as timely, worthwhile, and of significance for their own work. The most successful are those that take an open, dispassionate tone by indicating the relevance of the arguments and evidence to the question and the proposed answer. They also inspire others to take up the challenge of continuing the investigation!

SUMMING UP

We have emphasized throughout this chapter how the communication of your research is another opportunity to strengthen its validity, deepen collaboration, and make collective decisions about how to improve practice. By feeding draft research findings back to participants, you not only give back to those who have helped you, but you also invite reciprocal feedback about how well you have described, explained, and evaluated the practices you have investigated. This feedback is an important way to increase the validity of your study. One indicator of successful collaboration is that the research participants trust the findings sufficiently to want to act on them.

If you want your research to contribute to the wider professional dialogue about the improvement of educational practice, it is useful to create a permanent written record of your work. To assist you in writing up your research, we have discussed and illustrated the key components of a formal research report that is suitable for publishing in professional journals. Finally, we offered some advice for effectively managing the writing process to help you produce an interesting research report that convinces readers of the relevance of your research question and the usefulness of your findings.

PART III

Practitioner Research and School Improvement

10

Integrating Practitioner Research Schoolwide

At the beginning of the book, we proposed that it is both realistic and desirable to incorporate a research role into the work of practitioners. In order to benefit from a strengthened research role, however, practitioners need to adopt a research approach that is simultaneously rigorous and relevant to the context and complexity of their situation. We introduced problem-based methodology (PBM) as an appropriate framework for such an approach. We now turn to the question of how to embed research activity into practitioners' roles so that it is sustained over time and makes a discernible difference to the quality of teaching and learning.

The current research literature suggests that a culture of inquiry is needed if changes such as the introduction of practitioner research are to foster deep and ongoing improvements in teacher and school practice (Toole & Seashore Louis, 2002). However, it is also true that critical aspects of a culture of inquiry are strengthened through the use of PBM. Thus a reciprocal relationship exists between fostering a culture of inquiry in schools and using PBM to incorporate research into teachers' work.

This chapter illustrates this reciprocal relationship—particularly its benefits for improving the quality of teaching and learning—with the example of a government-funded school improvement initiative in Auckland, New Zealand. It will demonstrate how PBM can strengthen a culture of inquiry and how a culture of inquiry, in turn, provides an environment for developing the research skills of practitioners. In order to understand this illustration, we need to explain what is meant by a culture of inquiry and expand on how PBM is both consistent with, and strengthens, such a culture.

CULTURE OF INQUIRY

There is no simple definition of a culture of inquiry. Nor is there a simple checklist of the components of such a culture (see, for example, the various definitions discussed in Toole & Seashore Louis, 2002). The definition we adopt in this chapter is that of Toole and Seashore Louis (2002). They describe a culture of inquiry as "a school-wide culture that makes collaboration expected, inclusive, genuine, ongoing, and focused on critically examining practice to improve student outcomes" (p. 247). In their view, such collaborative communities, often referred to as "professional learning communities," are not comfortable collaborations through which teachers merely share ideas but are opportunities for rigorous investigations of schoolwide teaching and learning.

Toole and Seashore Louis's focus on the relational aspects of collaboration is consistent with PBM. PBM emphasizes how relationships of mutual respect (as seen in learning conversations) are essential for examining and resolving differences between competing theories of action (Chapter 3). There is the expectation in PBM of inclusive, genuine, and ongoing collaboration.

The second part of Toole and Seashore Louis's definition requires the critical examination of practice to improve student outcomes. This is also consistent with PBM's focus on evaluating theories of action to improve practice. However, Toole and Seashore Louis do not specify what they mean by "critical." Virginia Richardson (1990), who has also written about how to create cultures of inquiry in schools, argues that critical examination of practice requires dialogue between teachers' theories of action (she calls these knowledge, beliefs, and actions) and external researchers' theoretical frameworks. In such dialogue, practitioners are required to provide and defend their theories of action. They are also required to use published research to heighten their awareness of other perspectives, provide content for reflection, and develop theoretical justifications. She argues that this approach is more likely to foster significant and worthwhile improvements to teacher practice than attempts to disseminate academic research and theory to practitioners without also examining practitioner theory.

Richardson's call to engage practitioners' theories of action is completely consistent with the PBM approach. In order to make such "critical examination" work in schools, however, two things are needed: an evaluative framework for such critique and a social and interpersonal process for overcoming the human tendency to avoid being critical of others' practice. Richardson and other authors who advocate critically collaborative learning communities do not demonstrate how these two conditions can be met. PBM meets the first requirement by providing four standards for evaluating theories of action. It meets the second by providing the principles and skills of a learning conversation. We review each of these in turn.

The first standard for judging theoretical adequacy is accuracy. This evaluates whether factual claims about, for example, what is happening in classrooms, how students learn, and the impact of various teaching strategies, are well founded in evidence. The second standard of effectiveness asks whether current practice meets the requirements of those who are engaged in the practice. For example, does a school's policy on tracking work as the school intended? The third standard goes beyond the question of asking whether or not a theory of action delivers what practitioners themselves see as important. The coherence standard invites outside perspectives that may challenge and change what practitioners take to be important. Finally, the standard of improvability ensures that current theories and solutions can be adapted to meet changing needs, or radically revised to incorporate new goals, values, and contextual constraints. This is crucial to the ideal of sustained, continual improvement. These four standards are applicable to all theories, whether those of external researchers or the theories of action of practitioners.

Once any disagreements about theories of action are framed as theory competition, these standards provide a powerful tool for determining the strengths and weaknesses of the theories about which there is disagreement.

While the research on professional learning communities highlights the tensions inherent in developing a culture of inquiry, it does not resolve them. For example, Toole and Seashore Louis (2002) highlight the tension between being critical of colleagues in order to engage in deep professional learning and the simultaneous need for trust and respect. Too often deep learning is sacrificed in the interest of gaining and maintaining trust (Ball & Cohen, 1999). Since disagreements over practices and problems are inevitable in healthy learning communities, there needs to be a way for practitioners to ensure that their disagreements do not damage the trust needed to establish and sustain a learning community.

In PBM, this tension is dealt with in two ways. First, disagreements are conceptualized as theory competition. Thus the disagreement is depersonalized—it is between theories and not individuals. As described earlier, PBM also provides four standards for determining the relative merits of competing theories. Resolutions are not achieved through the exercise of arbitrary power or with popularity polls. Second, PBM provides a social and interpersonal framework through which to engage in conversations about theoretical differences. This framework, which we call "learning conversations," teaches practitioners how to recognize the theoretical differences that underpin personal disagreements, how to explore those differences and seek common ground, and how to do so in ways that strengthen rather than damage relationships.

Thus the use of PBM builds some of the conditions needed to create a culture of inquiry. It does so by showing how the tension between trust and critical inquiry can be resolved, and through providing an evaluative framework for judging the relative adequacy of competing theories of action. We now illustrate these claims with examples from a New Zealand school improvement initiative.

STRENGTHENING A CULTURE OF INQUIRY THROUGH PBM

The examples are drawn from a government-funded school improvement initiative Mei is involved in. The initiative serves urban schools in a low socioeconomic area comprising minority and indigenous people facing high levels of academic underachievement. The goal of the initiative is to offer high-quality learning environments to raise achievement. This is done by using student achievement information to inquire into the nature of the underachievement, to test competing explanations of its cause, and to monitor the impact of teachers' decisions about how to intervene. In short, the focus is on developing the inquiry skills of teachers to improve school practices and student learning outcomes.

The initiative comprises a number of interventions focusing on improving literacy and numeracy achievement. One of these interventions is a three-year research and development collaboration between schools in the initiative and a university-based research center. The goal of the collaboration is to improve reading comprehension in 9- through 14-year-olds by developing sustainable research-based applications of good practice (McNaughton, Lai, MacDonald, & Farry, 2004). The design of Phase 1 of this intervention is a good illustration of how improving teachers' theories of action through PBM has led to improved teaching and student learning outcomes.

Standardized achievement tests administered by the schools had suggested low levels of comprehension in reading. There were many competing research and practice-based explanations for these results. Rather than privileging any one of these explanations, practitioners and external researchers decided to find out what students really needed by carefully analyzing the results and observing how teachers taught reading.

A professional learning community comprising a representative from each school and external researchers was established to manage aspects of the collaboration and to be the primary forum for critical examination of evidence about the quality of reading instruction and its impact on study comprehension. (Similar communities were formed within each school, comprising groups of teachers and administrators.) In these communities, participants learned aspects of PBM to improve the quality of their inquiry. The three aspects we discuss in more detail are making practitioners' theories of action explicit, developing the idea of theory competition, and using learning conversations to develop trust while maintaining appropriate challenge.

Making Theories of Action Explicit

One role of the professional learning community was to examine baseline student achievement data and identify, through systematic observations, instructional practices that needed to be changed to improve student comprehension. As part of this process, practitioners and external researchers were required to offer explanations for the low achievement levels, search for evidence to support their theories, and check the accuracy of their explanations with others in the learning community. In other words, participants were being asked to go down the ladder of inference (see Chapters 3 and 4) to search for evidence for their theories and to test their accuracy by engaging in learning conversations with other teachers and external researchers. This group testing of competing theories fits the D-E-E-R (Describe, Explain, Evaluate, and Recommend) approach discussed in Chapter 3, because each competing theory was described and evaluated before the group came up with recommendations, based on the most valid theory, about how to improve reading instruction.

One of the initial theories held by most participants was that students would comprehend facts better than inferences, and that teaching practices would have to concentrate more on helping students draw correct inferences from text. In order to gather evidence for that theory, the learning community compared students' capacity for understanding facts and inferences across a number of comprehension passages. They found, much to their surprise, that students performed equally on both facts and inferences. Thus, they modified their teaching practice to focus on both aspects of comprehension.

Karen Mose, a director in the professional learning community, reflected on the value of making theories of action explicit so that they could be evaluated:

> This process challenged us to think about what we kept saying was the problem. We could say the words but we didn't really understand "the problem," nor what was actually causing it. We didn't have sufficient data to accurately pinpoint the aspects of reading where students were strong or weak, nor did we have a robust way of identifying what was causing the problem. We needed these skills of inquiry to enable us to identify the issues and resolve them.

In Karen's view, group members had been making claims at the top of the ladder of inference about the problem of low achievement and what was causing it, and they needed support in moving down the ladder of inference to search for the evidence underlying their claims. As Karen went on to explain, "What was missing was the external research and theoretical frameworks to enable us to generate this kind of inquiry. We couldn't have done it on our own."

Theory Competition

By using the standard of accuracy, the learning community was able to resolve many theoretical disagreements amicably. Everybody's views were evaluated against the same standards. Some teachers in the learning community believed that the low achievement levels were related to students' difficulty in decoding text rather than their capacity to comprehend. Other teachers and external researchers in the initiative disagreed with this theory. They argued that, since the students generally scored very highly on a decoding test but poorly on their comprehension of short passages of text, the low achievement levels in comprehension were not due to poor decoding.

Participants tested these competing theories by comparing the data on students' capacity to decode and their capacity to perform other tasks such as comprehending a paragraph or sentence. They found that students scored significantly higher on decoding than on comprehension. They further found that their decoding scores were similar to the national averages. These data, coupled with other supporting evidence, indicated that widespread decoding problems were unlikely to be the reason for the low achievement levels. As a result, the professional learning community explored ways to improve reading comprehension without a direct focus on decoding. Rather than have ideological arguments about the importance of phonics teaching, the community had set about testing the accuracy of their competing explanations and used the results to guide their intervention.

Aspects of PBM were used to evaluate and improve theories of teaching and learning across multiple levels of the participating schools. The emphasis on making theories of action explicit, testing the adequacy of those theories in on-the-job situations, and using what was learned to improve practice began to build a culture of inquiry in some of the participating schools.

Initially, the challenge to existing practice usually came from the university researchers. The teachers did not take the challenges personally because there had been careful negotiation in setting up the group to minimize risk to teachers and to gain commitment to a collaborative process of learning to teach better. Their professional development on aspects of PBM, such as theories of action, theoretical adequacy, and the ladder of inference, had given them the tools to challenge and check theoretical claims, whether they came from practitioner colleagues or university researchers.

The diffusion of the inquiry process from the professional learning community to participating schools, classrooms, and students is illustrated in the following account of the improvement of the teaching of reading comprehension. One of the external researchers on the intervention, Stuart McNaughton, explained how the inquiry began:

During the observations I noticed that teachers often asked students to predict what happened next in a story. However, teachers seldom asked students to check back in the story to see if their predictions were consistent with the story. My observations showed them doing it nine times in the 16 hours of observations I conducted. Teaching strategies need to be purposeful—the purpose of this prediction strategy is to understand the meanings in a story by activating students' background knowledge about the story and by generating ideas about what might be in it that are grounded in what is already known about the story.

When these findings were fed back to the professional learning community, many teachers recognized this pattern in their own classrooms. Alison Hall, an administrator from Koru School said, "A teacher was reading a story about the beach and asked the students to predict what happened next. One student said, 'They fly to the moon!'" Consequently, teachers began to look for practical ways to implement what they had learned about checking predictions in their classes.

In Koru School, the introduction of checking in classrooms had to meet two important constraints. First, checking had to be introduced as part of teachers' current classroom programs (that is, not an add-on to their existing reading programs) and, second, teachers wanted a practical, structured approach to introducing checking. One teacher adapted a current resource on checking that required students to look at an illustration from a book and make predictions about the story. Students were then asked to read the story and find evidence to support or disconfirm their predictions.

This teaching strategy met both key constraints as it involved a structured approach and improved existing practice rather than added something completely new. Alison sums up the new approach this way:

This approach met our requirement of having something more structured for teachers to use. It also appears to be working. I've noticed that students are starting to check their predictions more, although we need to evaluate this more formally at a later stage. So we've decided to use this approach in all our other classrooms to help our teachers with checking strategies.

The intervention also incorporated the standard of improvability, the fourth standard for evaluating theoretical adequacy. Student learning and teacher practice data were collected from schools at the beginning and end of every year. This information was used to evaluate the changes to teaching practice made throughout the year against the constraint of "Did this raise student achievement?" and to adjust these practices to better meet students' learning needs. For example, the data indicated that some students did not understand the instructions in the assessments, so teachers spent more time explaining the instructions to students. The data collected were also used to inform professional development programs for participating schools. Since checking predictions was a weakness, the learning community developed professional development programs to support teachers in this area. By incorporating the standard of improvability, the research became a cyclical process of continually investigating and revising teaching practices to raise achievement.

Learning Conversations

All these critical discussions took place in an environment of trust in which people could maintain good relationships while being critical about the teaching practices that were being examined. This meant that when data were discussed, there were strict ground rules for their discussion that closely followed the guiding values of learning conversations. For example, one ground rule was that any discussion would be confidential to the group to ensure that all parties (and their data) were treated with respect. Similarly, any disagreements were conceptualized as theory competition so that disagreements were depersonalized and practitioners would not feel as though they were "being personally attacked" when someone was critiquing their practice. In other words, the community used the D–E–E–R approach (Describe, Explain, Evaluate, Recommend) to evaluate each others' theories, and this increased the likelihood that the critical discussions would have the desired effect of improving practice. Perhaps most important, there was a shared understanding that the purpose of the analysis was to learn how to enhance the quality of teaching and learning.

The process, however, was still a scary one for many practitioners. Jason Swann was the first person to volunteer to publicly discuss his school's achievement results with the rest of the learning community.

Personally, I was out of my comfort zone and I was nervous presenting to an areawide forum. But I presented our school's achievement results to the community and invited their feedback and comment. Once the data were presented, the collegial support that was offered was amazing. Everyone in the community had a common goal of raising achievement; everyone recognized the common goal, and my colleagues from other schools offered lots of ideas, possible theories, and constructive support. I felt there was a realization that we were attempting something new and we all wanted to succeed in this. This ensured that while this was a forum of no blame, it was still a critically constructive examination of the data and people's interpretations and analyses. Personally, it was a fulfilling time that produced multiple ideas that were specific to the needs of our school.

The learning community noticed that there was a significant group of students who were just below average. Together, we brainstormed ideas as to why the students were achieving at this level and what the school could change. Several explanations for those results were floated around, such as students' comprehension of the instructions, the fact it was a new test for most students, and so on. A common theory was that the decoding levels of students didn't correspond with their comprehension levels, so there was a significant need to match these up.

When I went back to school, I immediately involved my teachers in investigating the link between decoding and overall comprehension. As we had theorized in the learning community, we found that our students were able to decode much better than they could comprehend. We then looked at possible strategies that the students needed to reach an equivalent level of comprehension. We explored strategies from information that we had compiled from other assessment tools. In short, we acknowledged the gaps in learning and set about addressing these specifically within the teaching program. At the end of the year we found that our students' comprehension results had improved significantly, and this was reinforced by the data collected for areawide comparisons.

Jason's story illustrates how a learning community can be both collegial and critical, and how such a community can improve school practices and student learning outcomes. His story also illustrates the impact of the D-E-E-R approach: Explaining and evaluating different interpretations of the student achievement data in the learning community enabled him and his colleagues to make the necessary improvements in reading instruction to raise student achievement.

The Outcomes of the Collaborative Inquiry

At least four key outcomes emerged from this process of critical collaborative inquiry into practice. First, theories of action were improved. As detailed in each previous example, practitioners and external researchers gained a better understanding of the problem (in this case, the low levels of reading comprehension) and how to resolve it. In particular, these theories of actions were strengthened through the process of theory competition, where all theories were evaluated without privileging any particular participant's views. There were occasions when external researchers' theories provided better explanations of the issue, as in the "checking" example (p. 203), and occasions when teachers' theory provided the better understanding as in the "decoding" example above. The professional learning community adopted the theory that best survived the testing and checking process.

Second, student achievement improved across the year. The learning community collected age-adjusted student achievement information at the end of the year that showed statistically significant improvements in reading achievement in every grade. While these improvements are preliminary and will be followed up throughout the three-year intervention, they suggest that teachers are now using more effective strategies. (The improvements are reported in McNaughton, Lai, MacDonald, & Farry, 2004.)

Third, the trust-critique dilemma posed by Toole and Seashore Louis (2002) appears to be closer to being resolved. In Phase 1, meetings to critically examine practice had virtually full attendance. The group continues to meet regularly in Phase 2 and have continued to build these meetings into their school calendar. This suggests that despite the critique of each other's theories, the relationships between teacher-researchers and external researchers, and between teacher-researchers in different schools, are strong enough to sustain the community.

Finally, by using PBM, the culture of inquiry established in the learning community is closer to the definition given by Toole and Seashore Louis (2002) as "a school-wide culture that makes collaboration expected, inclusive, genuine, ongoing, and focused on critically examining practice to improve student outcomes" (p. 247). The learning community's collaboration is expected, genuine, and ongoing through the regular meetings that are now part of the school's yearly calendar. It is inclusive, as it comprises researchers and practitioners at all levels in the school. It is critical, because its focus is critical examination of practice to improve student learning through describing, evaluating, and improving participants' theories of action.

DEVELOPING A CULTURE OF INQUIRY

In this section we focus on how the initiative is beginning to embed inquiry in schools' regular activities, so that it is not confined to a research project or even a government intervention but becomes an expected part of what teachers do in their daily lives.

The goal of the initiative, as previously mentioned, is to offer high-quality learning environments to raise achievement in the area, with a focus on developing inquiry in schools to improve teaching and student learning. While interventions to improve such things as reading comprehension can develop inquiry skills in practitioners, they can still be seen as isolated research projects. Karen Mose, the chair of the initiative, explained it this way:

> Working on research projects challenged me, but it didn't give me a whole lot of stuff to apply across my school because it was project focused. It wasn't affecting my capacity to think critically. It's actually hard to tie theory and practice together on a day-to-day basis when you're deep in the issues around you.

One of the ways practitioners have started to make inquiry a part of normal school routine is by developing professional learning communities both within and across participating schools. The purpose of these communities is to learn how to inquire into practices to improve them. The relevant PBM concepts were introduced by Mei to school leaders in a series of problem-solving sessions designed to ensure that they would understand what was needed to lead teachers in evidence-based inquiry into teaching practices. These leaders then used these concepts in their schools or in specific interventions, such as the reading comprehension intervention, to examine and modify their practices and improve student learning outcomes. If the modifications were successful, the community discussed how to modify school structures to embed the learning into the appropriate school practices. These modifications differed across schools to fit their different contexts. Two schools in the initiative, Koru School and Jean Batten School, began modifying their school practices to incorporate inquiry into the culture of their schools. Although the ways they have chosen to do so differ, they both focus on developing inquiry through school learning communities and making such inquiry an integral and expected part of the school's routine. We describe next the work of each of these schools.

Koru School

Koru School was involved in the reading comprehension intervention, which, as previously mentioned, focused on improving student achievement by evaluating and improving teachers' theories about reading comprehension. Alison, an administrator at Koru School, wanted to embed what she had learned about making theories of action explicit and checking their adequacy into all aspects of curriculum decision making. This required, first of all, developing the necessary resources to support teachers' focus on these PBM concepts.

In order for teachers to test and check their theories about teaching and learning, Alison needed a system for analyzing student achievement data in a way that would identify student weaknesses and support teachers in identifying what they should teach next. She started by creating a worksheet for each teacher that would enable them to quickly identify the weaknesses of each individual student across key comprehension tasks such as vocabulary and paragraph comprehension. She wanted individuals identified because, as she pointed out:

> Names are more tangible to teachers. For example, if I say six students are scoring below expectations, it means nothing to teachers, but if I say, "Mary, Tom, and so on are below expectations," they can associate the personality with the score. Faces mean much more.

The next step was to change how such data were discussed in the meetings to include making theories of action explicit and evaluating them. She chose to address this by changing the focus of several meetings to examining student learning outcomes and their implications for practice. She identified two regular weekly meetings as the forum in which to introduce such inquiry. Her rationale for choosing already established meetings was to encourage teachers to see this as part of what the school normally does, rather than as an add-on to normal school business.

She then invited Mei to model evaluating theories of action in a series of problem-solving workshops with staff and management. In these workshops, teachers discussed in small groups their analyses of their class data. Mei supported teachers by asking them to make their theories of action explicit and to search for evidence to support their theories. To illustrate, she recounts the following example from that session:

> We were discussing the reasons for the low levels of achievement in a literacy test. Some teachers believed that this was because their students had not eaten breakfast and therefore could not be expected to perform at their best. I asked them for evidence for their theory—did they know of large numbers of students who had not eaten breakfast before the test? How had those who had eaten breakfast performed compared to those who had not eaten breakfast? The teachers did not have any evidence for this initial theory except the general principle that breakfast was an important meal that aided concentration. They decided to start collecting information on who was missing breakfast. A couple of months later, I had the opportunity to listen to some of the original members of that group discuss the reasons for the achievement results. They no longer talked about breakfast as the reason for low achievement but were now focused on other theories for the achievement results that they had found evidence for. I was also pleased to see significant increases in achievement since the first time I talked to these teachers, which suggested that their theories of action have changed in ways that improve student learning.

Over two years, Alison has conducted school meetings where inquiry is a focus. Teachers are now beginning to critique each others' work without input from external researchers or professional developers. She reflects on what the school has achieved, and the challenges ahead:

> I have seen a shift in staff discussions of student learning outcomes. Teachers have stopped saying that patterns of low achievement are what is expected for our students. They now focus on what questions and concepts trip students up and what they need to teach. So inquiry is starting to become part of our school culture. Every week we talk about student learning outcomes. We also have one major session each term monitoring our teaching against student outcomes. But I am concerned about the sustainability of this work. While teachers are now inquiring into their own teaching, they are still only focused on their own class rather than the big picture. If they were more focused on the big picture, they would want to know how the whole school is doing and what they are going to do to support this. I still have to drive the schoolwide learning. We need more teacher leaders and a good succession plan to keep this going. We are not there yet, but we are getting there.

Jean Batten School

Nolarae, an administrator from Jean Batten School, was similarly concerned with improving inquiry amongst her teachers. She said, "You cannot teach if you cannot evaluate your previous teaching. If you don't reflect, how do you know what to teach next?" Although she had strongly held that belief for many years and had often wanted to develop inquiry with teachers, she did not have a process or framework that would support teachers in doing so.

Through the intervention, Mei introduced a practical framework to incorporate PBM into the way schools normally examine evidence so that different theories of action were made explicit and evaluated. This professional development provided Nolarae with the framework to introduce such inquiry to her own staff. She decided to incorporate the methodology into the school's core business by helping teachers develop and implement research projects to investigate and improve an aspect of teacher practice and student learning. These research projects became part of the school's yearly teacher evaluation.

Like Alison, Nolarae had to develop resources for teachers to enable them to focus on these concepts. She developed a template for teachers to follow during the project that included what she had learned about evaluating theories of action. In the template, she specifically required teachers to explain the results (making theories of action explicit). She also required teachers to explain what they learned from examining their theories of action and how they had used these insights to modify their teaching practices. This would allow her to monitor and support the specific aspects of inquiry she wanted to foster in her teachers.

Nolarae also made weekly meetings that the school normally held as the forum in which to introduce these inquiry projects. She discussed the possibilities with teachers, taught them about the PBM framework, and helped them select an area of student learning that needed strengthening. The teachers decided to work in two groups to improve spelling over the school year and evaluate the impact of their changed practices in a jointly written report to school management. They met regularly throughout the year in their normal staff meetings to discuss their progress.

At the end of the year, Nolarae examined the written reports to see if the changed practices had improved achievement and to identify areas that needed further strengthening. The results showed that spelling ages had increased for all students, with 42 percent scoring above their spelling age at the end of the year (compared to only 5 percent at the beginning of the year). An added benefit was the unintended but positive consequence for student motivation. One teacher, when reflecting on the process, wrote, "It is worth noting that the students thoroughly enjoyed their learning and assessment experiences during the program. They have been empowered and their enhanced knowledge of how words work has given them a better tool for written language."

The reports showed that teachers were now making theories of action explicit and evaluating them. When asked to interpret the poor results in spelling at the beginning of the year, the teachers wrote that the problem students had with spelling was that "spelling has not been taught as a specific skill. Although encouraged to spell correctly within the writing program, the emphasis is on writing rather than spelling." They then cited research that showed that children as early as seven were old enough to develop the strategies and concepts of a speller (for example, Calkins, 1994) as supporting evidence for the need to explicitly teach spelling strategies.

Thus, Nolarae has developed teachers' inquiry skills by involving them in teacher-led research projects that are supported by and embedded in ongoing school meetings and evaluation procedures. In fact, the teachers enjoyed the experience so much they are now repeating similar projects in the coming year to improve student learning. Nolarae sums up the benefits of using PBM to develop inquiry in her teachers by comparing the PBM approach with a traditional research approach:

> We currently work with another researcher. She sits in our classrooms, evaluates our students, and has discussions with teachers. She talks with teachers but does not involve teachers in the research. She is purely a researcher rather than a person who improves teaching. The current role adopted by Mei, using PBM methodology to develop inquiry in teachers, is of more value. We find that we can easily adapt the concepts of inquiry in our schools without making huge changes to what we do. These learnings are not an add-on—they are part of our school culture.

CONCLUSION

We began this book with the story of Michelle because the purpose of the book is to show how teachers, through their own collaborative research, can improve the learning and achievement of their students. We proposed problem-based methodology (PBM) as appropriate to achieve this aim, and provided many examples throughout the book to illustrate how this methodology is being used to improve teaching and learning. We also provided practical support by showing how you can plan your own research, collect and analyze your information, and communicate it to a variety of audiences. Throughout, we emphasized the importance of collaboration with those who can help you investigate and improve the practices that interest you.

The four key messages of this book about how you and your collaborators can use PBM to improve teaching and learning in your school can be summarized as follows:

1. You can improve your teaching and contribute to the improvement of your school by integrating research into your everyday practice. This means recognizing the research skills that you already have, expanding those skills and using them in your everyday practice,

and collaborating with others to complete focused research projects on issues you care about and can influence.

2. Improving your school and your teaching requires understanding the theories of action that control the practices you want to improve. Once you understand the relevant theories of action, you can communicate your genuine appreciation of what people are up against and be more insightful in discussions about what and how to improve. In short, improvement starts with describing, explaining, and evaluating the current situation, not with a critique and a set of recommendations.

3. If school and teaching practice is to be improved, the relevant theories of action need to be evaluated, so that people can agree on what is more or less successful. In PBM, theories of action are evaluated against four standards—accuracy, effectiveness, coherence, and improvability. Theories of action can be evaluated in high-quality collegial discussions—PBM does not require resource-intensive evaluations.

4. You need to engage in learning conversations so that the task of improving practice can be achieved without sacrificing the relationships between yourself and others whose practice you wish to influence.

Teacher research is more likely to flourish in schools that already have a culture of inquiry. On the other hand, the reason we introduced the New Zealand school improvement initiative described in this chapter was that it shows how teacher-researchers, in collaboration with professional developers and external researchers, can create a culture of inquiry. The schools in this initiative have used aspects of PBM to improve the quality of inquiry, and this has resulted in better teaching practices and better learning outcomes for students. Teachers have been able to adapt PBM concepts such as theory competition and learning conversations and incorporate them into their normal school practices and routines. These examples demonstrate that what has been proposed in this book is not only desirable but realistic, and that with initial support from a research community, practitioners can integrate inquiry into their work routines.

You are now ready to incorporate these key ideas into your situation. Use all the practical support provided in this book, and surround yourself with colleagues who will engage you in critical discussions on improving practice. For some of you, the goals of contributing to school improvement and building a culture of inquiry will feel far too ambitious for your current situation. If that is true for you, use PBM to tackle the equally challenging task of doing what one teacher-researcher described as "inspecting your own practice." Teachers who can do this rigorously are the building blocks of cultures of inquiry.

References

American Psychological Association. (2001). *Publication manual of the American Psychological Association* (5th ed.). Washington, DC: Author.

Amrein, A. L., & Berliner, D. C. (2002, March 28). High stakes testing, uncertainty, and student learning. *Education Policy Analysis Archives, 10*(18). Retrieved June 13, 2004, from http://epaa.asu.edu.ezproxy.auckland.ac.nz/epaa/v10n18/

Anderson, G. L., Herr, K., & Nihlen, A. S. (1994). *Studying your own school: An educator's guide to qualitative practitioner research.* Thousand Oaks, CA: Corwin.

Annan, B., Lai, M. K., & Robinson, V. (2003). Teacher talk to improve teaching practices. *SET: Research Information for Teachers* (1), 31–35.

Argyris, C. (1982). *Reasoning, learning, and action: Individual and organizational.* San Francisco: Jossey-Bass.

Argyris, C. (1990). *Overcoming organizational defenses.* Needham, MA: Allyn & Bacon.

Argyris, C. (2000). *Flawed advice and the management trap.* Oxford, UK: Oxford University Press.

Argyris, C., Putnam, R., & McLain Smith, D. (1985). *Action science.* San Francisco: Jossey-Bass.

Argyris, C., & Schön, D. A. (1974). *Theory in practice: Increasing professional effectiveness.* San Francisco: Jossey-Bass.

Babbie, E. R. (1990). *Survey research methods* (2nd ed.). Belmont, CA: Wadsworth.

Ball, D. L., & Cohen, D. K. (1999). Developing practice, developing practitioners: Toward a practice-based theory of professional education. In L. Darling-Hammond & G. Sykes (Eds.), *Teaching as the learning profession: Handbook of policy and practice* (pp. 3–32). San Francisco: Jossey-Bass.

Bell, J. (1999). *Doing your research project: A guide for first-time researchers in education and social science* (3rd ed.). Buckingham, UK: Open University Press.

Boyett, J., & Boyett, J. (1998). *The guru guide: The best ideas of top management thinkers.* New York: Wiley.

Bradbury, H., & Reason, P. (2001). Conclusion: Broadening the bandwidth of validity: Issues and choice-points for improving the quality of action research. In P. Reason & H. Bradbury (Eds.), *Handbook of action research: Participative inquiry and practice* (pp. 447–455). London: Sage.

Buch, K., & Wetzel, D. K. (2001). Analyzing and realigning organizational culture. *Leadership and Organization Development Journal, 22,* 40–43.

Burns, R. B. (1994). *Introduction to research methods* (2nd ed.). Melbourne, Australia: Longman Cheshire.

Calkins, L. (1994). *The art of teaching writing.* Portsmouth, NH: Heinemann.

Campbell, D. T., & Stanley, J. C. (1966). *Experimental and quasi-experimental designs for research.* Chicago: Rand-McNally.

Clay, M. M. (2002). *An observation survey of early literacy achievement* (2nd ed.). Auckland, NZ: Heinemann.

Cochran-Smith, M., & Lytle, S. L. (1999a). Relationships of knowledge and practice: Teacher learning in communities. In A. Iran-Nejad & P. D. Pearson (Eds.), *Review of research in education* (Vol. 24, pp. 249–306). Washington, DC: American Educational Research Association.

Cochran-Smith, M., & Lytle, S. L. (1999b). The teacher research movement: A decade later. *Educational Researcher, 28*(7), 15–25.

Cook, T. D., & Campbell, D. T. (1979). *Quasi-experimentation: Design and analysis issues for field settings.* Boston: Houghton Mifflin.

Costa, A. L., & Kallick, B. (1993). Through the lens of a critical friend. *Educational Leadership, 51*(2), 49–51.

Deal, T. E., & Peterson, K. D. (1999). *Shaping school culture: The heart of leadership.* San Francisco: Jossey-Bass.

Denzin, N. K., & Lincoln, Y. S. (Eds.). (2000). *Handbook of qualitative research* (2nd ed.). Thousand Oaks, CA: Sage.

Earl, L., & Katz, S. (2002). Leading schools in a data-rich world. In K. Leithwood & P. Hallinger (Eds.), *Second international handbook of educational leadership and administration* (pp. 1003–1022). Dordrecht, The Netherlands: Kluwer Academic.

Education Review Office. (1998). *Accountability review report: Cockle Bay School.* Wellington, NZ: Author.

Elmore, R. F. (2000). *Building a new structure for school leadership.* Washington, DC: Albert Shanker Institute.

Fay, B. (1996). *Contemporary philosophy of social science: A multicultural approach.* Oxford, UK: Blackwell.

Fichtman Dana, N., & Yendol-Silva, D. (2003). *The reflective educator's guide to classroom research: Learning to teach and teaching to learn through practitioner inquiry.* Thousand Oaks, CA: Corwin.

Fortin, S. (1993). The knowledge base for competent dance teaching. *Journal of Physical Education, Recreation and Dance, 64*(9), 34–38.

Gay, L. R., & Airasian, P. (2003). *Educational research: Competencies for analysis and applications* (7th ed.). Upper Saddle River, NJ: Merrill Prentice Hall.

Haggarty, L., & Postlethwaite, K. (2003). Action research: A strategy for teacher change and school development? *Oxford Review of Education, 29*, 423–448.

Hagood, T. K. (2001). Dance to read or dance to dance? *Arts Education Policy Review, 102*(5), 27–29.

Hammersley, M. (2000). *Taking sides in social research: Essays on partisanship and bias.* London: Routledge.

Hammersley, M., & Atkinson, P. (1995). *Ethnography: Principles in practice* (2nd ed.). London: Routledge.

Hart, C. (1998). *Doing a literature review: Releasing the social science research imagination.* London: Sage.

Hart, C. (2001). *Doing a literature search: A comprehensive guide for the social sciences.* London: Sage.

Hill, L. (2003). *Integrating the theoretical and practical in dance studies: A literature review.* Unpublished manuscript, University of Auckland, New Zealand.

Kahn, R. L., & Cannell, C. F. (1957). *The dynamics of interviewing: Theory, technique, and cases.* New York: Wiley.

Kaplan, A. (1964). *The conduct of inquiry: Methodology for behavioral science.* San Francisco: Chandler.

Labaree, D. F. (2003). The peculiar problems of preparing educational researchers. *Educational Researcher, 32*(4), 13–22.

Lai, M. K., Sinclair, M., Naidoo, P., Naidoo, S., & Robinson, V. (2003). Inclusion: What happened after Special Education 2000? *SET: Research Information for Teachers* (1), 40–44.

Lather, P. (1986). Research as praxis. *Harvard Educational Review, 56*, 257–277.

Lauer, P. (2004, February). *A policymaker's primer on education research: How to understand, evaluate and use it.* Aurora, CO: Mid-continent Research for Education and Learning; Denver, CO: Education Commission of the States. Retrieved

June 28, 2004, from http://www.ecs.org/html/educationIssues/Research/primer/index.asp

Lazaroff, E. M. (2001). Performance and motivation in dance education. *Arts Education Policy Review, 103*(2), 23–29.

Leedy, P. D., & Ormrod, J. E. (2001). *Practical research: Planning and design* (7th ed.). Upper Saddle River, NJ: Merrill Prentice Hall.

Lincoln, Y. S., & Guba, E. G. (1985). *Naturalistic inquiry.* Newbury Park, CA: Sage.

Locke, L. F., Silverman, S. J., & Spirduso, W. W. (2004). *Reading and understanding research* (2nd ed.). London: Sage.

Marino, C., Nicholl, J., Paki-Slater, M., Timperley, H., Lai, M. K., & Hampton, H. (2001). Reporting to parents at Nga Iwi School. *SET: Research Information for Teachers* (2), 31–34.

Maxwell, J. A. (1996). *Qualitative research design: An interactive approach.* Thousand Oaks, CA: Sage.

Maxwell, J. A. (2004). Causal explanation, qualitative research, and scientific inquiry in education. *Educational Researcher, 33*(2), 3–11.

McLaughlin, M. W., & Oberman, I. (Eds.). (1996). *Teacher learning: New policies, new practices.* New York: Teachers College Press.

McNaughton, S., Lai, M. K., MacDonald, S, & Farry, S. (2004). Designing more effective teaching of comprehension in culturally and linguistically diverse classrooms in New Zealand. *Australian Journal of Language and Literacy, 27*(3), 184–197.

Mehrens, W. A. (1998). Consequences of assessment: What is the evidence? *Education Policy Analysis Archives, 6*(13). Retrieved June 28, 2004, from http://epaa.asu.edu.ezproxy.auckland.ac.nz/epaa/v6n13/

Millward, P., Neal, R., Kofoed, W., Parr, J., Lai, M. K., & Robinson, V. (2001). Evaluating a literacy intervention at Dawson Road Primary School. *SET: Research Information for Teachers* (2), 39–42.

Mose, K., & Annan, B. (2003, January). *School managers, student achievement and a problem analyst: Development of a research culture in a schooling improvement initiative, Mangere, New Zealand.* Paper presented at the International Congress for School Effectiveness and Improvement conference, Sydney, Australia.

Nisbett, R., & Ross, L. (1980). *Human inference: Strategies and shortcomings of social judgment.* Englewood Cliffs, NJ: Prentice Hall.

Oakes, J. (1985). *Keeping track: How schools structure inequality.* New Haven, CT: Yale University Press.

Oakes, J. (1987). Tracking in secondary schools: A contextual perspective. *Educational Psychologist, 22*, 129–153.

Oakes, J. (1992). Can tracking research inform practice? Technical, normative, and political considerations. *Educational Researcher, 21*(4), 12–21.

Oppenheim, A. N. (1992). *Questionnaire design, interviewing and attitude measurement.* London: Pinter.

Phillips, D. C. (1987a). *Philosophy, science and social inquiry: Contemporary methodological controversies in social science and related applied fields of research.* Oxford, UK: Pergamon.

Phillips, D. C. (1987b). Validity in qualitative research: Why the worry about warrant will not wane. *Education and Urban Society, 20*, 9–24.

Pring, R. (2000). *Philosophy of educational research.* London: Continuum.

Richardson, V. (1990). Significant and worthwhile change in teaching practice. *Educational Researcher, 19*(7), 10–18.

Robinson, V. (1993). *Problem-based methodology: Research for the improvement of practice.* Oxford, UK: Pergamon.

Robinson, V. M. J. (1998). Methodology and the research-practice gap. *Educational Researcher, 27*(1), 17–26.

Robinson, V. M. J. (2002). Organizational learning, organizational problem solving and models of mind. In K. Leithwood & P. Hallinger (Eds.), *Second international handbook of educational leadership and administration* (pp. 775–812). Dordrecht, The Netherlands: Kluwer Academic.

Robinson, V. M. J., & Lai, M. K. (1999). The explanation of practice: Why Chinese students copy assignments. *International Journal of Qualitative Studies in Education, 12,* 193–210.

Robinson, V., Phillips, G., & Timperley, H. (2002). Using achievement data for school-based curriculum review: A bridge too far? *Leadership and Policy in Schools, 1*(1), 3–29.

Robinson, V., & Timperley, H. (2000). The link between accountability and improvement: The case of reporting to parents. *Peabody Journal of Education, 75*(4), 66–89.

Salkind, N. J. (2004). *Statistics for people who (think they) hate statistics* (2nd ed.). Thousand Oaks, CA: Sage.

Schein, E. H. (1999). *The corporate culture survival guide: Sense and nonsense about culture change.* San Francisco: Jossey-Bass.

Scriven, M. (1991). *Evaluation thesaurus* (4th ed.). Newbury Park, CA: Sage.

Selltiz, C., Jahoda, M., Deutsch, M., & Cook, S. W. (1959). *Research methods in social relations* (rev. ed.). New York: Holt, Rinehart & Winston.

Spillane, J. P., Halverson, R., & Diamond, J. B. (2001). Investigating school leadership practice: A distributed perspective. *Educational Researcher, 30*(3), 23–28.

Sternberg, R. J., & Horvath, J. A. (1995). A prototype view of expert teaching. *Educational Researcher, 24*(6), 9–17.

Stone, D., Patton, B. M., & Heen, S. (1999). *Difficult conversations.* London: Penguin.

Symes, I., Jeffries, L., Timperley, H. S., & Lai, M. K. (2001). Evaluating a new approach to professional development in literacy at Viscount School. *SET: Research Information for Teachers, 2,* 27–30.

Thagard, P. (2000). *Coherence in thought and action.* Cambridge, MA: MIT Press.

Timperley, H. S., & Robinson, V. M. J. (2001). Achieving school improvement through challenging and changing teachers' schema. *Journal of Educational Change, 2,* 281–300.

Timperley, H. S., & Robinson, V. M. J. (2004). O le Tala ia Lita–Lita's story: The challenge of reporting achievement to parents. *New Zealand Journal of Educational Studies, 39,* 91–112.

Toole, J. C., & Seashore Louis, K. (2002). The role of professional learning communities in international education. In K. Leithwood & P. Hallinger (Eds.), *Second international handbook of educational leadership and administration* (pp. 245–279). Dordrecht, The Netherlands: Kluwer Academic.

University of Chicago Press. (2003). *The Chicago manual of style* (15th ed.). Chicago: Author.

Wainer, H. (1992). Understanding graphs and tables. *Educational Researcher, 21*(1), 14–23.

Walker, J. C. (1987). Democracy and pragmatism in curriculum development. *Educational Philosophy and Theory, 19*(2), 1–10.

Walliman, N. (2001). *Your research project: A step-by-step guide for the first-time researcher.* London: Sage.

Weiss, C. (1979). The many meanings of research utilization. *Public Administration Review, 39,* 426–431.

Wolcott, H. F. (2001). *Writing up qualitative research* (2nd ed.). Thousand Oaks, CA: Sage.

Index

**CORWIN
PRESS**

The Corwin Press logo—a raven striding across an open book—represents the union of courage and learning. Corwin Press is committed to improving education for all learners by publishing books and other professional development resources for those serving the field of PreK–12 education. By providing practical, hands-on materials, Corwin Press continues to carry out the promise of its motto: **"Helping Educators Do Their Work Better."**

PRACTITIONER
RESEARCH
FOR EDUCATORS